# IMAGES OF AFRICA IN BLACK AMERICAN LITERATURE

# IMAGES OF AFRICA
# IN BLACK
# AMERICAN LITERATURE

## MARION BERGHAHN

ROWMAN AND LITTLEFIELD

TOTOWA, NEW JERSEY

For my mother
with affection and gratitude

© Marion Berghahn 1977

First published in the United States 1977
by Rowman and Littlefield, Totowa, N.J.


**Library of Congress Cataloging in Publication Data**
Berghahn, Marion, 1941–
  Images of Africa in Black American Literature.
  Includes index.
  1. American literature – Afro-American authors – History and
  criticism. 2. Africa in literature. I. Title.
PS153.N5B46     810'.9'32     77–765

ISBN 0–87471–962–3

PRINTED IN GREAT BRITAIN

# Contents

# Introduction

The 1960s and early 1970s saw the emergence of a lively artistic and cultural movement among blacks in the United States. The intensity and militancy of this movement came as a surprise to many people. It was above all the keen interest in Africa shown by many American blacks which a number of observers found puzzling and completely unexpected. What ties could Black Americans possibly have with Africa, where their forefathers had come from such a long time ago? Could there be, they asked, a greater psychological and cultural gap between an American minority group and their country of origin than between present-day Africans who were just entering the era of industrialisation and the Afro-Americans, who were evidently the children of the technologically most advanced industrial society? But the truth was that in the 1960s Afro-Americans did become fascinated by Africa: they studied its culture, history, arts and languages. Even their life-style became affected by their interest in things African: it influenced their eating habits, the way they dressed, their hairstyle and their art.[1]

The identification with that continent became so close that Africa and not America was often regarded as the real home of the American blacks. There are many examples of this in the black literature of the 1960s, as for instance in Clarence Reed's 'Song from Wasteland': 'Africa, Africa / Wrapped in sorrow / Steeped in Pain / Mother of us all / I must home to the / Warming womb / From whence all sprang . . .';[2] or in Jon Eckel's poem, 'Home is where the Soul is': 'I have never seen Africa / that distant land of mine / but I hear her beauty / sometimes and her colours staring with me through this world / . . . Africa, Africa, / this land of mine / Africa, Africa, Africa / this land of men'.[3] But it was not only Africa which appeared in a new light: the Afro-Americans' image of themselves underwent a considerable change. Indeed, the term 'image' became a key notion in the vocabulary of the 1960s and could frequently be found in black writings. 'We are discovering', said Carolyn Gerald, 'that the image we have of ourselves controls what we are capable of doing.' Hitherto, she continued, the whites had managed to project their image on to the rest of the world. This formed the basis of their claim to superiority. The black man, on the other hand, merely experienced his existence in terms of a 'negative mirror-image' of the white world-view.[4] Or as

Touré put it: 'Reality's blonde / wig smothers the Afros of our souls.'[5] The cultural nationalists regarded it as their most important task to liberate the blacks in America from the 'white' image of themselves. This image, which they had accepted when they had succumbed to Western values and norms in general, had taught them to despise themselves as blacks. And it was this 'slavery . . . in our own minds',[6] the nationalists agreed, which had also prevented the growth of a positive group consciousness, seen as the most important prerequisite of effective political action to counteract discrimination and exploitation of the black minority in the United States.[7] Almost naturally Africa became the decisive point of reference in the search for a new and positive image of the individual Afro-American and the group as a whole, as expressed by Dudley Randall and many other black poets: 'The age / requires this task; / create / a different image; / re-animate / the mask. / Shatter the icons of slavery and fear. / Replace / the leer / of the minstrel's burnt-cork face / with a proud, serene / and classic bronze of Benin.'[8]

However, this process of dissociating themselves from the traditional assimilationist sympathies held by the majority of blacks seemed to have been painful and difficult as numerous exhortations like these imply: 'Check your vision young Africans [Americans]' or Perkins' 'Apology to [his] African Brother' – 'Forgive me! / I have not been a faithful brother. / Memories of my heritage / Have been darkened by cumulus sky. / My mind washed pure / To worship an albino God . . . / O, if I could only build a bridge! / Over the sea which has diluted our blood . . .'[9] The most striking feature of that period, which led to the widely known slogan 'Black is Beautiful', equally seems to indicate that even the most ardent nationalists needed constant reassurance about their 'African' identity: 'Take tools, our strength to break chains / and locks of containment and oppression. / Look – open eyes, / see images. Black images – Beauty images, / cornbread souls and African dust. / Strike blows, death blows. / Be free. / We are beautiful, / Winners.'[10]

To be sure, identification with Africa was not always easy and many Afro-Americans expressed quite ambivalent feelings towards their newly chosen 'home'; but the 'celebration of the African soul' and the intensive preoccupation with Africa seem to indicate that this concern was not just fanciful and unrealistic, as critical commentators often asserted. However, in order to appreciate the significance of that movement, which was largely a reaction against earlier attitudes, one has to go beyond it and look at its roots. One has to try to understand the meaning of Africa for Afro-Americans, the role it has played in their lives and their consciousness in the past. A particularly good reference point for analysing this relationship is provided by Afro-American literature. It is through these personal documents of blacks that one can gain some remarkable insights into the role which Africa assumed in their lives. This book attempts to discuss the manifold aspects of the African image in Afro-American literature and to trace its development from the period of slavery to the present. Yet these subjective views of black authors cannot reveal the whole and very complex significance Africa possesses in the cultural, social and psychological spheres of Afro-American life. It will therefore be necessary to resort to categories of analysis developed by anthropology, sociology and social psychology in order to understand the deeper causes behind the attitudes which Black American writers have, at various times, adopted towards Africa.

This raises also the question of the 'valuation' of the respective images of Africa, of whether the image corresponds to reality or how far it represents an idealised picture, or otherwise, of reality. Here again it will be necessary to draw upon the findings and positions of modern anthropology so that we may move on firmer ground. At the same time it should be emphasised that our discussion will be rather a condensed version of complex historical developments and ideas. Above all the 'evolution of evolutionism' and of anthropology was not as straightforward a process as might appear in some passages. On the contrary, there were repeated overlappings of divergent positions. However, since all we are interested in is to give a general framework in which the relevant intellectual ideas developed, it seems legitimate to provide no more than a broad outline of the main trends.

In order to give a coherent impression of the significance of the 'African background' in the wider sense of the word, we begin with a longer chapter in which various aspects of this 'background' are examined in terms of anthropology and sociology in so far as this appears essential for an understanding of Afro-American literature. For our subsequent analysis a chronological approach was adopted as the basic organising principle, when various authors and their writings are examined. In this way, this book attempts to analyse the continuities and changes in the image of Africa over a longer period.

# Acknowledgements

This book is an abridged version of a PhD thesis presented at Freiburg University and while preparing it I received encouragement and advice from many people among whom I would like to mention in particular the late Janheinz Jahn, Klaus Peter Dressler and Paul Breman. I would also like to thank Professor Jack Goody of Cambridge University who gave me his time to discuss the socio-anthropological aspects of this book, and Donna Lustgarten as well as Barbara Weinberger who read various parts of the manuscript and made useful comments. Warm thanks are also due to Dr Webster Asiedu who throughout a long friendship made me aware of what it means to live in a white world with a black skin. But I owe the greatest debt to my husband who translated the original German version into English and who above all through his untiring interest and understanding was – and continues to be – a constant source of inspiration and encouragement.

I alone, however, bear responsibility for the views expressed in the book – and its shortcomings, some of which may be due to the fact that the German version is more detailed. The original also contains additional chapters on Garveyism and the developments of the 1960s and early 1970s. The manuscript was completed in 1974.

# 1 Historical and Social-psychological Background

The relationship of Afro-Americans with Africa has never been an easy and straightforward one. It comprises a broad spectrum of attitudes which are by no means always consistent with one another. At the one end of the spectrum we find a complete lack of interest in Africa and a strong emphasis on the 'Americanness' of Afro-Americans; at the other extreme there exists a radical identification with Africa, through actual re-migration or at least adherence to a movement propagating ideas of a return to the 'homeland.' However, there is but a small minority of Afro-Americans whose relationship with Africa is so clearcut that they fit into one of those two extremes. As the writings of Black American authors demonstrate, the majority of Afro-Americans take an ambivalent attitude towards the continent, and their attitudes vacillate not merely according to changing historical circumstance, but also according to individual experience within one and the same period.[1]

Despite this variety of attitudes it is none the less possible to discern relatively quickly at least one constant factor in Afro-American writings, namely a preoccupation with the 'white' image of Africa which has exerted a profound influence on the lives and the self-consciousness of Black Americans and thus in turn on their own relationship with Africa. Irrespective of whether they accept or reject this 'white' image, this is where their search for their own position *vis-à-vis* Africa begins and ends.[2] Only a very few Afro-Americans have actually succeeded in emancipating themselves completely from the impact of this 'white' image of Africa. This is why it seems important to introduce this chapter with a discussion of that image.

There is yet another problem which belongs in the context of this chapter. As the literature of Black America will show, Afro-American attitudes towards Africa are not only defined by the dominant ('white') image of the continent, but also by the position which blacks occupy as a minority in white America. In the second half of this chapter we shall therefore have to touch upon certain general aspects of Afro-American reality in the United States, because otherwise some of the individual experiences which black writers incorporate in their works would not become sufficiently clear. Above all, it will be the problem of Afro-American culture and of possible African elements within it upon which we shall have to dwell in that section.

## A: THE 'WHITE' IMAGE OF AFRICA

Whereas the attitude of Afro-Americans towards Africa has not yet been satisfactorily explored, there exist a number of excellent studies on the image of Africa and of blacks as it appears in the world of ideas of the whites. Although we do not possess a comprehensive survey of the problem, such monographs as have been published neatly cover the various epochs which are of relevance here and give a good impression of the continuities and changes in the 'white' image of Africa.[3] As far as the continuity aspect is concerned, all studies emphasise the existence of certain stereotypes. They have persisted over centuries and invariably portray Africans as inferior beings. Basically these stereotypes are rooted in the view that blacks possess something like a 'natural' slave mentality. This has led to the widespread assumption that racism is a product of slavery.[4] Yet intensive research on early American slavery has shown that, although the colonial and slave masters of the more modern period furthered racism, they were not exclusively responsible for generating it.[5] What facilitated the enslavement of Africans and even made it possible with relative ease on a large scale was the prevalence in European culture of certain traditions and habits of thought.[6] The concept of slavery which had been developed long before the establishment of the trans-Atlantic slave trade was one of them. There are many societies which have practiced slavery or serfdom in one form or another. But ethnic criteria were practically insignificant then. People of white or coloured skin were indiscriminately enslaved.[7] The only remarkable fact was that since the slave systems of the ancient period there had existed a tendency to mark slaves with tattoos or other signs in order to differentiate them from free men. Moreover, one tended to justify the total subjugation of a man to the will of another with the slave's 'badness' or 'inferiority', later with his 'sinfulness' or his 'heathendom'. As Jordan has pointed out, 'the slave was treated like a beast. Slavery was inseparable from the evil in men; it was God's punishment upon Ham's prurient disobedience. Enslavement was captivity, the loser's lot in a contest of power.'[8]

This means that even before the colonisation of America a more or less fixed set of assumptions existed about the nature of slavery. The African slave could be fitted into this system of ideas with relative ease. But this is also where the racial dimension, the black-white problem, comes in. By the time slavery was introduced to America, a remarkable differentiation had taken place between the two ethnic groups which also had a bearing on the treatment of black and white serfs. Prior to the codification of the slave laws in the second half of the seventeenth century, both slave groups had the same legal status and were classified as 'bondsmen'. But already in this period there are various indications that 'Negroes were singled out for special treatment in several ways which suggest a generalized debasement of Negroes as a group'.[9] This differentiation between African and European 'servants', as they were called, became most obvious when slavery received legal sanction. By this time a man with a dark skin was identified as being a 'slave' almost as a matter of course. Thus the State of Maryland implemented a law in 1663 which stipulated that 'all negroes or other slaves within the province, and all negroes and other slaves to be hereafter imported into the province, shall serve *durante vita*; and all children born of any negroe or other slave, shall be slaves as their fathers for the term of their lives'.[10] The degradation of the African to an inferior status can thus not simply be seen as a direct consequence of slavery. On the contrary, it appears that the white civilisation had long before developed associations with Africans which made them in every respect more suitable for the status of slaves than whites.

Careful analysis of the causes of this peculiar evolution has shown that the image of Africa which appeared to justify this discriminatory treatment had been shaped in essence during the period of European overseas expansion prior to the eighteenth century. The genesis of this image coincided with an era of revolutionary change which accompanied the dissolution of the feudal structures of European societies.[11] As will be seen, it was to be of great significance that the 'discovery' of Africa and hence the first close contacts with foreign, that is dark-skinned, peoples fell into a period of great psychological and ideological upheaval. In fact, this is where one must search for the roots of all those predominantly negative associations which were, from the very beginning, connected with 'white' ideas about Africa. While this is generally true of all Europeans, this study is concerned with the English-speaking world, and our discussion will concentrate on the Anglo-Saxon image.

# I EARLY ENCOUNTERS OF THE WEST WITH AFRICA

The 'discovery' of Africa, with its societies which were culturally very different from their own, created for the Anglo-Saxons a number of psychological and intellectual problems which are of relevance in our context. They had to develop categories which enabled them somehow to incorporate alien black peoples and their cultures into the existing world-view. But there existed no such instruments with the help of which it might have been possible to grasp the peculiarities of African cultures. There appeared to be only one way of solving the problem and that was to consider African life-styles as representing simply a deviation from Western norms which were held to possess universal and absolute validity.[12]

(a) THE BLACK-WHITE SYMBOLISM

No feature of African reality was seen by the Elizabethans to be more foreign and shocking than the blackness of the skin which they encountered in African peoples. The Spaniards and Portuguese – themselves of darker complexion – were used to the sight of black peoples with whom they were in close contact both during and after the end of Moorish domination. To the English, on the other hand, the encounter with men of very different colour came as rather a surprise and hence made a much more lasting impression on them. They found the contrast of skins all the more fascinating since the polarity of black and white had a firmly established place in the Western system of symbols. Traditionally – and with little change to this day – this polarity is associated with a scale of values on which 'white' evokes predominantly positive responses, such as 'good', 'beautiful', 'pure', etc., whereas 'black' is invariably seen to be connected with 'bad', 'evil', 'night', 'mishap', 'ugliness', 'hell', etc.[13]

This kind of black-white symbolism, it is true, can be found in many cultures including African ones.[14] But nowhere has it become so charged with emotions and experienced such an extension of its associative scope as in the West. It soon included the pigmentation of the skin and lost its purely symbolic character. The colour of a person was believed to be nothing less than the outward expression of his character and 'race'.

The Bible, which for many centuries became the main reading in the Occident and, owing to the general cultural importance of Christianity, made a major contribution to the shaping of basic Western thought patterns, probably gave one of the most important incentives to this development. Because the polarity of black and white is at the centre of the Christian system of symbols, it intensified, if nothing else, the already existing sensibility to colour. 'It has created a "backwash" of fixed impressions and attitudes difficult to efface.'[15] As is well known, the juxtaposition of black and white is used in the Bible in order to relate, on a purely symbolical level, the great conflict which begins with God's separating of light from darkness. It appears constantly in the struggle between God and Satan, between the spiritual and the 'carnal' sphere, between Good and Evil. But also the Bible began to link the negative associations of black with the colour of the skin. A black complexion is seen as a punishment of God or, as the case of Hiob demonstrates, as an expression of sinfulness. From there it was but a small step to connect the 'heathendom' of Africans with the colour of their skin and then to regard them as creatures of Satan.[16]

To this general background must be added another point which is important for an understanding of the specific American context of our topic : the Puritans of New England were particularly prone to accepting the symbolism of the Bible. Like few other Christian sects, they had endowed the Bible with the highest authority and integrated it into their daily lives. They believed God's words to be metaphors for the historical developments in New England and thus used them as keys for an explanation of the world in which they lived. This 'symbolic perception'[17] pervaded the philosophy of the Puritans and subsequently became the cornerstone of the Americans' view of themselves and of the rest of the world. What is particularly significant about this world-view is a thinking in dualities. The world is seen as a 'union of opposites'.[18] The Anglo-Saxons defined themselves as inhabitants of a 'young' continent in search of a national identity clearly delimited from the Old Europe; or they tried to emphasise their separateness from other religious and ethnic groups inside America.[19]

The biblical polarity of black and white now appeared to offer the most plausible confirmation of this thinking in opposites and was applied to people of dark complexion long before the importation of Africans on a massive scale. It was first used to legitimate the struggle against the 'red-skinned' Indians of North America. To white Americans Indian heathendom and unwillingness to become converted to Christianity was proof of their 'diabolical persistence in sin that doomed the Indians to eternal damnation'.[20] In short, quite early on there emerged in New England society the idea that a dark skin was the emanation of a 'black' and hence 'satanic' soul.

American literature contains, perhaps, the most impressive evidence of how the Manichaean tradition which the Puritans did so much to further has left its deep mark on American thinking. While undergoing a process of rich differentiation, the black-white symbolism at one time even developed into a key structural element of American literature.[21] As one might expect, Afro-Americans were particularly affected by this tendency. In fact, black-white symbolism exerted a strong influence on Afro-American literature and we shall have occasion to see below just how powerful it was.

## (b) NOAH'S CURSE

However, it was not merely the Manichaean thinking of the Puritans that led to the predominantly negative connotations of having dark skin. They received further biblical support from the myth of Noah's Curse. The black-white symbolism apart, this myth represents one of the earliest and most widespread attempts to solve the mystery of blackness which so puzzled white men. Although the relevant lines in the Bible are highly problematical and lend themselves to different interpretations, Noah's Curse was likewise used down to the twentieth century to 'prove' the God-given inferiority of blacks. One of the peculiarities of this Curse is that it was first merely used to explain dark complexion. The more extensive interpretation, which adheres actually much more closely to the text, was adopted much later to justify slavery.[22] Still, the fact remains that 'the extraordinary persistence "of the myth" was probably sustained by a feeling that blackness could scarcely be anything *but* a curse and by the common need to confirm the facts of nature by specific reference to the Scripture'.[23]

## (c) THE AFRICAN AS A CREATURE OF NATURE

The Bible provided important models for the 'white' image of Africa, but not the only ones. There are a number of other categories which likewise originated in the period prior to institutionalised slavery and which added further elements to that image. From among the various theories which acquired more general currency, only one important one shall be mentioned here because again it showed considerable persistence and recurs in Afro-American literature. We are thinking of the notion that Africans are closer to the sphere of 'natural' life than white men.

### (i) *The Noble Savage*
This notion acquired a positive meaning in the concept of the Noble Savage who lives, supposedly, in complete harmony with himself and with Nature. Unlike 'degenerate' whites, he lives with his instincts still intact. He has preserved within himself the 'natural' goodness of man because he has not yet been spoilt by civilisation. Thus Montaigne wrote as early as the sixteenth century : 'Ces nations me semble donc . . . estre encore fort voisines de leur naifveté originelle. Les loix naturelles leur commandent encore, fort peu abastardies par les nostres.'[24] In the following centuries this argument was employed primarily by the opponents of slavery who, with their emotional stories of encounters with Noble Savages, tried to generate feelings of sympathy

in their readers and thus to convince them of the injustice of slavery. In particular Aphra Behn's short story of the passions of the heroic Prince Oroonoko, published in 1688, unleashed a flood of similar writings, It can be compared in popularity probably only with Harriet Beecher Stowe's *Uncle Tom's Cabin*.[25]

Africa as the country of origin of the Noble Savage similarly benefited from the corresponding notion. The continent was portrayed as a Garden of Eden or at least as a place which would see the emergence of a truly Christian and peaceful society and culture. The humanitarian impetus of the opponents of slavery notwithstanding, they also adhered to an ethnocentric view in that they 'Europeanised' their African hero by altering, as far as possible, his negroid features. In other words, even they were incapable of emancipating themselves from the racist ideology of their contemporaries and this was a weakness which turned out to be a heavy burden on the anti-slavery movement as a whole.[26]

(ii) *The 'Ape Man'*
The notion of the Noble Savage had a reverse side which was to prove much more damaging to Afro-Americans. Given the climate of suspicion and hostility, Africans could equally quickly be likened to animals. It was but a small step from there to regard them as 'beastly' and non-human and to treat them accordingly. Again the notion can be traced back well into antiquity. For there has existed a widespread conviction since Aristotle that Africa was a continent full of monsters conceived of as a union of men and wild beasts. Although Africans were rarely identified with these monsters, the myths survived in modified form down to the twentieth century. Quite frequently Africans were placed at least in association with animals.[27]

Such comparisons, it must be added, also appear in other cultures and were not confined to Africans.[28] But what caused this image to show such great persistence in the case of blacks was that it was allegedly supported by 'scientific' evidence, as we shall see below. The likening of blacks to beasts was, as Jordan points out, considerably reinforced by the fact that man-apes and Africans were discovered by Europeans in about the same place at about the same time. They were struck by the similarity between chimpanzees and humans in general and by the black skin which Africans and apes had in common. Reports even appeared of alleged sexual intercourse between African women and monkeys. All this seemed to support the argument that Africans, though not directly of the same species, were at least akin to apes.[29]

This argument must be seen in connection with another stereotype which has survived to this day – namely the myth of the extraordinary sexual prowess of blacks. Apes were traditionally regarded as particularly lascivious and were widely associated in European culture with the devil and with sexual sin; and since a close contact was alleged to exist between Africans and apes, the former were believed to be endowed with similar qualities. The idea of the sexual lewdness of black people received further support from British Puritanical ethnocentrism, although this notion is to some extent already contained in the above-mentioned religious association of black with satanic sinfulness. The important point is again that the Anglo-Saxons measured African customs with the norms of their own puritanism. Consequently polygamy, nakedness and the apparently less restrictive sexual life were mistaken for promiscuity, 'sinfulness' and obscenity.[30]

## II   THE 'WHITE' IMAGE OF AFRICA DURING THE PERIOD OF SLAVERY

The previous discussion ought to have shown that relations between blacks and whites were influenced, long before the introduction of slavery, by the negative image which whites had of Africa. In subsequent centuries, which were characterised so much by scientific and technical progress, this negative image remained essentially the same, especially in the United States. In fact, with the emergence of legalised slavery those who benefited from it had every interest in perpetuating existing arguments about the inferiority of Africans. Their arguments were now expanded into systematic theories to justify slavery.[31]

*(a)* EVOLUTIONISM

The spectacular advances of the sciences provided a major boost to the spreading and growing popularity of racist doctrines. After all, if they could be supported scientifically, what more did one want in an age which fervently believed in science? Starting from traditional notions such as that of the 'Great Chain of Being' or from the assumption that the Europeans occupied a central, norm-creating position among the races of the world, the desire of eighteenth-century science to classify and order all creation resulted in the construction of strictly hierarchical systems. Mankind was divided into ethnic groups, with the Europeans supposedly standing at the top of the racial hierarchy. The Africans, on the other hand, were placed at the lower end of the scale near the man-apes. Some scientists even considered them the 'missing link' which they were looking for. There is no need to go into these scholarly debates about the evolution of the races which began to replace earlier theological explanations. It suffices to say that they centred above all around such issues as the controversy over mono-versus polygenesis and 'nature' versus 'nurture'. The crucial point is that these debates did nothing to change the traditional negative image of the black races. On the contrary, the scientific enquiries of the eighteenth and nineteenth centuries aimed, almost without exception, to confirm the existing image.[32] Thus, when evolutionary theory had finally become the all-pervasive creed of the nineteenth century, earlier speculations about the character of Africans, above all the idea of the Noble Savage, petered out – at least for the time being. The traditional image of blacks, once systematised, was merely expanded to the extent that further negative elements were added to the prevailing stereotypes. Racism had received the blessing of the sciences and became generally accepted.

The relatively great unity as well as persistence of this 'scientific' image of Africa and the black races make it legitimate to speak of *the* 'white' image of Africa without risking the charge of oversimplification. Moreover, it allows us to confine ourselves to a discussion of the most important aspects of nineteenth- and twentieth-century racism on which there exist many reliable studies.[33] While the systematising of cultures was going on, biologists began to develop the idea that all organisms and species evolve progressively from a lower to a higher form of life. This principle of constant change, which was assumed to be 'progress' *per se*, was now transposed to different social systems by the proponents of a theory of cultural evolution. Of course, what facilitated the application of categories of the natural sciences to the human sphere was that man was no longer seen as a species above and apart from the animal world, but as an integral part of a biological universe. The conviction that man was determined solely by his biological existence was so deep that not only man's physical characteristics were said to be inherited and hereditary, but also his culture. Culture was supposedly 'an accumulated mass of memories in the race, transmitted through the genes'.[34]

This led to the practice of seeing societies as living biological organisms and of classifying different societies as one classified the species. They were placed somewhere along a linear development from simple to complex cultures. To quote Edmund Leach :

> . . . all human societies must necessarily evolve through the same sequence of stages – technological, political, moral and intellectual. In the outcome, monogamous, individualistic, capitalist, 'democratic' Western industrial man emerged as the culminating product of a natural law of inevitable progress. The manners and customs of non-European peoples were then type-cast as belonging to 'earlier' stages of social evolution and were thus 'primitive' and inferior by definition.[35]

And in order to make absolutely certain that Western civilisation appeared at the top of the scale, technological progress was turned into the decisive criterion of ethnic superiority. Although technology was a factor which had come to play a primary role only quite recently in Western history, it was declared the binding norm for measuring the degree of cultural advancement. Moreover, according to these theories, the ability to develop was practically reserved for the 'Caucasian' races. Other races were allegedly so far behind that they hardly had a hope of ever reaching the final goal of 'civilisation'. As to the black races, it was denied that they were at all capable of even surviving in the struggle for existence. They would, it was argued, soon degenerate and probably even die out altogether.[36]

Since culture and race were constantly used interchangeably, the 'proof' of this argument was seen to be in physiological differences. Pigmentation of the skin, shape of the skull, face and nose, size of the brain, in short the entire physique of the African were cited to deduce the cultural and intellectual inferiority of the black races, again showing them not to be too different from man-apes. To support the thesis that their backwardness was hopeless, reference was made to Africa and its cultures which, if they were actually accepted as such, were considered 'stagnant', 'barbaric', 'wild', 'cannibalistic' – to mention but the most common attributes.[37]

Those scholars – the anthropologists – whom one might expect to have been in the best position to examine and correct these notions largely shared them.[38] Without ever having lived in the country to which they devoted their lifework, many relied exclusively on the innumerable, though for scholarly purposes not always useful, accounts of travellers, missionaries and businessmen. All these sources were accepted uncritically; myths were taken for facts; factual information torn from its context and used at random.[39] In this fashion anthropologists formed their opinions about Africa from contemporary reports, overlooking the fact that nineteenth-century African societies represented even less than before 'pure' cultures; rather they were largely influenced by the slave trade – possibly the greatest single disturbing factor in African history because it led to very serious internal conflicts and social convulsions. A number of powerful West African states in fact owed their emergence to the slave trade, and they survived only by means of lucrative wars and slave-hunts. Nineteenth-century Africa, in short, was in many ways closer to modern Europe than the anthropologists and their contemporaries imagined.[40]

This, of course, did not prevent them from measuring everything with an idealised European yardstick. Without an understanding of the intrinsic laws of African cultures, many anthropologists thought that there was nothing to understand. What they saw appeared chaotic and irrational to them. Not surprisingly they merely found the *a priori* expectations with which they approached non-European societies confirmed. Adhering to the theory of evolution, they were convinced that African cultures represented anachronisms which were as such without any significance. They viewed them as relics of cultural developments comparable to the 'primitive' early phases of European culture.[41] Ignorance and a tendency to consider only those cultures as 'dynamic' which underwent a development analogous to their own – 'dont le developpement serait doté pour nous de *signification*'[42] – gave rise to the widespread notion of the 'static' character of African cultures. Since they lacked an adequate frame of reference, divergent cultural patterns were not even perceived. All they concluded was that such patterns were manifestations of the 'infantility' and 'primitiveness' of the African world of ideas – 'pre-logical', 'irrational', 'mythical' and 'incoherent'.[43]

The case of Leo Frobenius, one of the most famous ethnologists of his age, may illustrate how deep-rooted these views were. Frobenius, it is true, did much to question some of the established European assumptions about African societies. By actually studying them on the spot, he contributed to a new wave of interest in Africa which seized Europe at the turn of the century. Nevertheless, he wrote the following commentary on discoveries which he made in a tomb in West Africa :

> Strange instruments were placed along the walls, on a simple structure the above-mentioned sacred objects [consisting of] masks, about two metres high, wooden sticks, clothes etc., some of them well preserved, others fallen to dust and destroyed; all in all [it was] a delicious ethnological find for me. But even though [the find] was strange and mysterious, it was, if one took style and contents, the same weak carving and ornamental work which so often stares at us in the shape of typically African trash, no matter how stylised it may be. I felt very satisfied – as an ethnologist.[44]

'Logical' thinking and rationality, on the other hand, were believed to be inseparably connected with technological progress and hence seen as proof of a general intellectual superiority. Even today there exists a widespread notion 'that people who get through life with a primitive technical outfit have minds in which the irrational elements predominate'.[45] Elements that pointed to 'higher' forms of culture and were too obvious to be overlooked were, as a rule, traced back to 'Aryan' or European rather than African roots. Monotheism, certain moral norms, and forms of art are cases in point. Attitudes towards African intellectuals were based on similar assumptions : they were not 'genuine' Africans, but people who had become alienated from their original 'primitive' cultural background.[46]

This picture of a barbaric continent inhabited by spiritually, morally and intellectually backward and inferior peoples met with little opposition until the end of the nineteenth century. It was only from the 1880s onwards that the research methods of anthropology became more refined and, above all, that rigorous standards of source selection and interpretation were employed, leading to a far-reaching revision of evolutionary theory and to a rejection of the ethnocentrism on which previous research had been based. But before dealing with this revision, we shall have to turn to the practical uses to which evolutionary theory was put.

## (b) EVOLUTIONARY THEORY AS A JUSTIFICATORY IDEOLOGY

The extraordinary popularity of evolutionary theory both before and after Darwin cannot be explained without reference to a growing need to justify certain political developments. On the one hand, the European Powers set out in this period to gain complete domination of Africa; on the other, the slave system, while being tightened up, came under increasing pressure from the abolitionists in the early nineteenth century. Imperialists and slave-masters felt an obvious desire to justify their policies. The end of slavery after the American Civil War saw the growth of an extreme conservatism, and evolutionary theory in the shape of Social Darwinism now offered a welcome lever against the radical change that appeared to be in the offing. Especially in the American South, it was used to defend the existing social and political status quo which the formal abolition of slavery threatened to upset. Science and politics converged to create a powerful ideology without which the lasting popularity of racial theories which pervaded most social groups cannot be understood.[47]

Prior to emancipation, these theories were compressed into the simple formula that Africans were 'natural' slaves. Although, as has been mentioned, this view was held even before the introduction of slave laws in the United States, evolutionary theory now gave it the appearance of an immutable law of nature. The arguments which had been developed by anthropologists and other scientists re-emerged in non-scientific literature in the shape of two stereotypes, 'Sambo' and 'The Brute'. Both these stereotypes, it is true, had a long-standing tradition going back some 300 years. But it is interesting that they achieved real prominence only after about 1830, the period when the need to justify racism became more and more urgent.[48]

## (i) 'Sambo'

This word was widely applied both in the American South and in the North to describe blacks.[49] There are many examples in contemporary literature testifying to the general popularity of this notion.[50] At the same time the stereotype has shown a remarkable persistence far beyond the Civil War. Over the years it even assumed a more vivid connotation which Elkins described as follows :

> Sambo, the typical plantation slave, was docile but irresponsible, loyal but lazy, humble but chronically given to lying and stealing; his behavior was full of infantile silliness and his talk inflated with childish exaggeration. His relationship with his masters was one of utter dependence and childlike attachment : it was indeed this child-like quality that was the very key to his being. Although the merest hint of Sambo's "manhood" might fill Southern breasts with scorn, the child, "in his place", could be both exasperating and lovable.[51]

This was the image of the black as a member of an 'inferior' infantile race, who, lacking a sense of responsibility and character, was totally unsuited to a free existence. He actually preferred to be 'guided' and 'protected' by his white slave-master. To the protagonists of slavery this was therefore an ideal institution. Even after abolition they argued that there was no better way of educating Afro-Americans and of turning them into 'civilised' human beings.[52] Warning of the emancipation of the slaves, John Calhoun said : '. . . the African, instead of being improved, has become worse. They have been invariably sunk into vice and pauperism, accompanied by bodily and mental afflictions incident thereto – deafness, insanity and idiocy – to a degree without example . . .'[53]

But the advocates of slavery and dyed-in-the-wool racists were not the only ones who were convinced of the natural childishness of Africans. The great majority of abolitionists similarly found it impossible to escape the impact of racial theories. At times they would even admit quite openly that they harboured prejudices against blacks. More often, however, they were naïve enough to write, hoping that this would defeat the more radical racist arguments : 'The African is so affection-ate, imitative and docile that in favourable circumstances he catches much that is good; and accordingly the influence of a wise and kind master will be seen in the very countenance of his slaves.'[54] If Africans were described as 'natural Christians' or as sensitive and 'feminine', it was done to emphasise how immoral and irresponsible it was for the 'stronger' race to exploit them so crudely. Clearly, the abolitionists did not doubt the intellectual and general cultural superiority of the whites.[55]

'Sambo' did not die with the abolition of the slave system. The protagonists of slavery used this stereotype to warn against further change and to prove how happy the blacks had been under the old

order. The 'liberals' of the Progressive Era and the paternalistic abolitionists, on the other hand, cited the image of the infantile, peaceful
and harmless Negro in support of his further integration and in order
to counteract the fear of 'The Brute' which spread after the Civil War.
Black abolitionists, in turn, found the paternalism of the white abolitionists repulsive and split off to establish their own movements. But,
as subsequent chapters will demonstrate, the belief that Africans were,
by their very nature, innocent, emotional and sensitive proved very
attractive to them – so much so in fact that the notion of the 'Negro
Genius' can be found throughout Afro-American literature. And at
times this concept even assumed a central place.[56]

## (ii) *'The Brute'*

Whereas 'Sambo' represents in many respects a 'late edition' of the
Noble Savage (with whom he shares many characteristics), 'The Brute'
quite evidently continues the tradition of the ape-man argument.[57]
The Brute is equal to the 'Savage African', supposedly 'a primitive
creature given to fits of violence and powerful sexual impulses'.[58]
Anatomy and mentality show him to be a kind of 'superior' ape, a
bloodthirsty being driven by unpredictable and primitive instincts.
These qualities were again linked to his origin in Africa – the continent
of war, cannibalism, murder, promiscuity and superstition. In these
circumstances slavery was argued to have been an act of mercy, liberating the Africans from barbarism and 'domesticating' them. Only the
firm hand of the slave-master was said to guarantee that the slave
developed into a happy, pacific and docile being. Any attempt, on
the other hand to withdraw this supervision would set free 'the brutish
properties of the Negro' and lead to a terrible end, i.e. 'the slaughter
of his white master, and through the slaughter, he strides (unless he
himself is exterminated) to the full exercise of his native barbarity and
savageness'.[59]

We have seen before that emancipation did not significantly change
the white image of the black race. In particular, the American South
vigorously resisted the attempt to integrate the Afro-Americans into
the social and political system. As W. F. Cash concludes in his well-
known study of the South : 'If the war had smashed the Southern
world it had left the Southern mind and will arising from, corresponding to, and requiring this world – entirely unshaken.'[60] But the North
also witnessed an intensification of racism and between 1880 and 1930 :
it reached dimensions which were hitherto unknown in American
history. In fact, 'racism became virtually an official national ideology'.[61]
One result of this was the introduction of segregation which, for all
practical purposes, threw the Afro-Americans back into their former
slave status. Moreover, there appeared a flood of racist justificatory

literature which was responsible for the continued survival of the nine-teenth-century stereotypes well into the twentieth century. As before, blacks were considered capable of at best partial development. They were likened to apes and called a 'lazy, lying, lustful animal which no conceivable amount of training can transform into a tolerable citizen'.[62] This soulless 'beast', as described in Lewis Carroll's [in]famous book *The Negro – A Beast*, published in 1900 by the American Book and Bible House, could only be tamed by force and had to be kept in his tradi-tional place. Now the stereotype of the lewd Brute served to justify violence and lynchings which rose at a rapid pace after about 1880.[63]

Later the tide of racist literature receded. But 'Sambo' and 'The Brute' lived on in the mind of the whites, and this fact alone time and again forced Afro-Americans to confront these stereotypes as well as the argument about the alleged inferiority of the African race on which such images were based. As Myrdal and Dollard, above all, have shown, evolutionary theory and racism as its vulgarised and crude derivative proved amazingly persistent, even when they gradually lost their scien-tific foundation. The discriminations against Afro-Americans which racism invented have, it is true, frequently been turned into a self-fulfilling prophecy. Scientific anthropology, however, meanwhile developed fundamental doubts about the validity of this theory or at least of the racism and ethnocentrism associated with it.[64]

## III  AFRICA IN MODERN ANTHROPOLOGY

While most anthropologists of the nineteenth century spent their time at their desks speculating about non-European societies, a few among them – later to become leading authorities in their field – began to go out to distant continents to conduct field studies. They learned to speak foreign languages and dialects and observed those societies on the spot. It was due to their activities that a fundamental revision of the evolu-tionary idea of race and culture was initiated. Above all, they abandoned the concept of 'universal culture' which had dominated the nineteenth century and thus succeeded in escaping 'from the straitjacket of thought imposed by the axiom of unilinear social evolution'.[65] By the same token, anthropologists moved away from the notion that culture and intelligence were genetically conditioned. An 'educated' African, Philip V. Tobias argued, was just as much a 'genuine' African as all other blacks. There was, he added, no reason to believe 'that a particu-lar culture, language or outlook on life is inseparably bound up with particular physical features . . . The whole of history and prehistory consists in the adoption by some peoples of the ideas and inventions of other peoples.'[66]

Anthropologists began to reject the idea of selecting merely one among many elements of culture – technological progress – and of measuring the degree of sophistication of other societies with this yardstick. The new emphasis was on the 'plurality of local cultures as functioning and organized wholes'.[67] It was hence impossible to judge individual cultural components except within their respective cultural totality. Cultures were now seen as comprehensive systems in their own right. Consequently, there could also be no larger or smaller measure of culture, no juxtaposition of 'uncivilised' and 'cultured', but only a side-by-side development of various forms. These may not be identical, but are of equal value. This pluralist argument became the dominant theory of American and European anthropology from about 1910 onwards.[68]

Up to the 1950s its leading representatives adhered to its most radical form, namely a complete cultural relativism. It was based on the axiom that 'the conceptual world of each people is unique and can only be understood in its own terms'.[69] There appeared to be no plausible reason why 'all societies should reach certain stages of differentiation or . . . should necessarily develop the same types of institutional contours once they attain such stages'.[70] It was, it seemed, not even possible to discover a linear development within a particular society. After all, progress in one sphere had all too often been paid for with losses in another. The cultural relativists hence flatly rejected any attempt to pass value judgements on other cultures. Such judgements, they maintained, were merely based on criteria 'derived from the categories, limited by space and time, of a particular culture, usually that of the observer'. In other words, the categories were 'ethnocentric (or culturocentric) and hence cannot claim universal or even absolute validity'.[71]

This was a most important point. Since technology was now no longer the yardstick with which non-European cultures were measured, it became easier to appreciate that societies with a primitive technology frequently evolve highly complex social and cultural institutions. Consequently it was difficult to call such cultures 'primitive', unless the term was used without its pejorative connotation in the sense of 'simple'.[72] Similarly it emerged from the study of languages and philosophies of other societies 'that many of these languages had more precise and more subtle systems of reference than our own'.[73] 'Primitive thought' was discovered to be no less 'rational' than Western thought, whose irrationalism had long been underestimated and was exposed only with the advent of twentieth-century psychology. Having studied the cultures of the South American Indians, Claude Lévi-Strauss came to the following conclusion : 'The logic of mythical thought appeared to us to be as sophisticated as that on which positivist thought is based, in fact at heart almost the same. The difference lies not so much in the quality of the intellectual operations as in the nature of those objects toward which these operations are directed.'[74] It is this appreciation of the differences of non-European cultures which led the cultural relativists not only to reject comparisons with Western civilisation, but also to abandon the search for all-embracing criteria of judgement which might have facilitated such comparisons.

This clear-cut position must, of course, also be seen against the background of anthropology's confrontation with racism, which gained a good deal of doubtful popularity, especially in the inter-war period. Since then radical cultural relativism has become more moderate and the interest in universalist theories has increased. What has not been affected by this recent development, however, is the theory of pluralism. Moreover, modern anthropologists would uphold a central element of cultural relativism, i.e. 'moral and ethical relativism'.[75] In the meantime it had been recognised that all cultures have certain basic elements in common, which are due not to their own particular development, but to the fact that all cultures are part of an 'eco-system' which forces them into making adaptations to this system. 'If Social Anthropology shows how human cultures differ, it also shows that the people who have these cultures are fundamentally alike.'[76] All of them, confronted with similar problems, developed similar structures which – like, e.g. social and family structures – can be analysed with the help of universal categories. 'However, the variety of possible "functional equivalents" of institutionalized solutions to such problems, as well as the possibilities of "regression", stress the fact that the paths of development of different societies are neither necessarily common nor given.'[77]

This means that the emphasis lies no longer on the *content* of cultures which preoccupied and worried the 'pure' cultural relativists so much, but rather on the *structures* of the various institutions which divergent cultures have developed. Linguistics has greatly helped anthropology in arriving at this most recent position. For it was linguistics which discovered that languages are not, as the cultural relativists believed, completely self-contained unique systems. On the contrary, the differences between various linguistic systems are relatively insignificant. They are differences of 'content but not structure, of details but not general principles'.[78] And the structures are thus comparable. But this is not to imply that anthropology is now more prepared to make value judgements on entire cultures. They are considered far too complex as to permit classifications of this kind. To understand other societies, one must study their world-view, i.e. their systems of thought, their norms and symbols. Cultures are seen by modern anthropology as systems of communication, analogous to languages, which decipher the universe each in its own peculiar way. However, men who speak a different 'language' in the wider sense of the word are not, for this reason, unintelligible as a matter of principle. The problem, as Leach has pointed out, is 'to reach down into the "grammar" of the other culture, so as to establish a translation, not just of the words, but of the poetic meaning'.[79]

It is important to realise that the metamorphosis of anthropology from ethnocentric race theories based on evolutionism to a pluralistic approach of cultural relativism barely touched the views of the general public. Most people continued to adhere to the ideas of the nineteenth century, and only very recently has a change of attitude set in. Among those who adopted the modern position of anthropology were the Afro-Americans. As will be seen below, their search for a positive image of themselves received a fresh boost from the revised theories of culture. All in all, however, it is no more than a drop in the ocean. The evolutionary theories were, after all, rooted in traditions which had been prevalent in the Western world for centuries. To this day the images created by these theories largely define the attitude of American whites towards blacks. The great persistence of evolutionism must in the final analysis be seen within the context of the psychologically and politically stabilising function which racism possesses for the American socio-economic order. We have seen repeatedly how racism was expanded into a theory to justify what were ultimately hard-and-fast economic interests. This is true above all of the plantation owners of the South who relied on cheap slave labour. It is also true of the so-called 'poor whites' whose social and economic position would have been threatened had the Afro-Americans been given equal status. Not surprisingly therefore these groups were susceptible to even the most fantastic racist arguments.

At the same time, the above-mentioned racial theories developed a dynamic of their own and thus contributed to so distorting the white image of the Afro-American that he was seen and treated as a wild animal. The process of dehumanising the Afro-Americans and Africans by the white majority, including those whose economic interests were not directly involved, erected almost insuperable psychological barriers. It was these barriers which made it so difficult for whites of whatever background to establish a 'reciprocal emotional interaction . . . on the basis of equality'.[80] The example of the abolitionists and later of the 'Liberals' — supposedly the friends of the blacks — illustrates just how strong the dynamic of this process was to be. In fact, it was so strong that even the Afro-Americans themselves could not escape its influence. Faced with the widespread view that they did not possess any human dignity, blacks frequently found it impossible to convince themselves of the notion that this was totally wrong. The weight of the white image of Africa proved to be overwhelming, as we shall see later.

## B : THE AFRICAN ELEMENT IN AFRO-AMERICAN CULTURE

It is the purpose of this section to analyse the importance of Africa to Afro-Americans in a more general sense, so as to be able to arrive at a more accurate estimate of the specific attitudes of Afro-American writers towards that continent. For it is only in the broader framework of African–Afro-American relations that we can assess the significance of the intellectual struggles of a particular writer with his African origin. There are, in this context, two major aspects which are relevant to an understanding of the literature which will be discussed below. To begin with, we must examine the role which Africa plays in the self-image and the group consciousness of Afro-Americans. The second point, which is becoming increasingly important, relates to the question of how 'African' Afro-Americans really are and whether Afro-American culture actually contains, and offers, an alternative value system which would make it possible for them to emancipate themselves from the dominant – Anglo-Saxon – culture.

## I THE ROLE OF AFRICA IN THE SELF-IMAGE OF AFRO-AMERICANS

As has been seen in the previous section, racial theories invariably defined Afro-Americans as Africans. Although, from a biological point of view, a growing number of Afro-Americans could no longer be placed in this category, the 'white' element in Afro-Americans was totally ignored. As a well-known black sociologist, Adelaide Cromwell Hill, put it : 'Since Africa was indeed the basis of our non-white status, it provided from the beginning a fragile source for our identity.' And she adds : 'Africa was never absent from our self-image.'[81] To many individual Afro-Americans this was clearly a most unwelcome fact which they tried to remove from their consciousness. Nevertheless, there can be little doubt that, as Isaacs discovered in over 100 interviews with Afro-Americans, 'in nearly every instance the early discovery of the African background was in fact a prime element in the shaping of each individual's knowledge of himself and his world and his attitude towards both'.[82]

Knowledge about Africa was, as a rule, not acquired by direct experience, but was transmitted via the dominant white culture. And, as we have shown above, the 'white' image of Africa abounded with horror stories. Afro-Americans were confronted with this negative image in reports by travellers and missionaries, in the mass media, in theatre, literature and school text-books. History books especially tended to portray whites as eminent personalities. The 'typical' African, on the other hand, was usually depicted as a simple man, with the accompanying texts removing whatever doubt may have remained in the reader's mind as to the 'primitiveness' of blacks. Only very rarely did Afro-Americans succeed in escaping the powerful grip of this 'white' image. There existed, after all, a general belief that their dark skin, their curly hair, their physiognomy were direct manifestations of their 'backwardness' and of the 'wildness' of their African ancestors. The pictures and texts which Afro-Americans encountered everywhere could not but have an overwhelming effect on them. With a few exceptions, they had no other information at their disposal which might have acted as a corrective to the 'white' image of Africa.[83]

However, it was not only their 'barbaric' origins, but also their ignominious enslavement which appeared to lend credibility to the notion that the black races were permanently inferior. This view was seemingly further supported by the general social and economic predicament in which coloured people found themselves. In the United States most of them lived in appalling conditions; in the Third World, most of them existed on a starvation diet. Thus W. E. B. DuBois, to whose attitude towards Africa we shall devote a longer chapter, admitted in *Dusk of Dawn* :

> What every colored man living today knows is that by practical present measurement Negroes today are inferior to whites. The white folks of the world are richer and more intelligent; they live better; have better government; have better legal systems; have built more impressive cities, larger systems of communication and they control a larger part of the earth than all the colored peoples together.

Was it surprising that, faced with these circumstances, Afro-Americans would ask themselves : 'Suppose, after all, the World is right and we are less than men? Suppose this mad impulse [of striving for freedom and equality] is all wrong, some mock mirage from the untrue?'[84]

Judging from Isaacs's interviews and other studies on the subject, practically all Afro-Americans were torn by such self-doubts.[85] At the same time it is probably too early to know reliably how the first contacts of Afro-Americans with the textbook-Africa influenced their attitudes towards that continent. Detailed studies on the subject are still lacking. Nevertheless, the present state of research does permit the general conclusion that the role of Africa in Afro-American thinking was predominantly a negative one. Many of them adopted the above-mentioned white attitudes towards their country of origin from early childhood onwards. They believed, as Isaacs has found, 'that blackness was ugly, that blackness was evil. And this blackness was African.' In the Afro-American universe, 'black' became

a key word of rejection, an insult, a fighting word. Prefixed to any name of obscenity, it multiplied the assault many times . . . Every time black was used or perceived in this way, the word *African* came after it, whether it was actually spoken or not, whether it was there or remained an echo in the mind. For the Africans were the blacks, the source of all the blackness, the depths from which all had come and from which all wanted to rise.[86]

In short, the acceptance of the white image of Africa led to a rejection of the 'wild' and 'barbaric' continent. Yet for Afro-Americans to do this was tantamount to rejecting their own 'African' ego.

(*a*) THE REPERCUSSIONS OF THE REJECTION OF THE 'AFRICAN' EGO

Psychological studies of Afro-American children have shown that they identified strongly with the value system of white culture. This included the adoption of the black-white polarity as developed by Western civilisation. What is more, Afro-Americans, like white Americans, saw this polarity as a direct expression of their own self. From childhood on they associated black with evil and white with positive characteristics. At the same time they projected these symbolic values onto human beings so that 'Negro' was synomymous with 'dirt'. Whites, on the other hand, invariably appeared in a friendlier, brighter and in all respects more positive light. The Afro-American psychologist Poussaint saw the consequences of this as follows :

From that point in early life when the Negro child learns self-hatred, it molds and shapes his entire personality and interaction with his environment. In the earliest drawings, stories, and dreams of Negro children there appear many wishes to be white and a rejection of their own color. They usually prefer white dolls and white friends, frequently identify themselves as white, and show a reluctance to admit that they are Negro. Studies have shown that Negro youngsters assign less desirable roles and human traits to Negro dolls. One study reported that Negro children in their drawings tend to show Negroes as small, incomplete people and whites as strong and powerful.[87]

Most Afro-Americans therefore conceived of their skin as being a mark of their repulsive character, as was made cruelly clear by the advertising slogan : 'Are you too dark to be loved?'[88] Lincoln relates a case which appears to be no less absurd : 'In a well-known southern city a leading

Negro church for years discouraged the attendance of would-be worshippers who were darker than a *café au lait* stripe painted conveniently on the doorjamb of the sanctuary.' The colour of the skin had thus become a sort of cultural norm, in fact 'so much so that a complex of rewards, punishments and the strictest taboos have grown up around it'.[89] Just as an African physiognomy, curly hair and a dark skin were regarded as 'evil' and ugly; the highest value was attached to a white skin and North European features. Many Afro-Americans did everything to come as close as possible to this ideal type and thus to widen the gulf between themselves and the evil colour of black. They would straighten their hair and use bleaching creams. But all these aids were of no avail : in the economic and social sphere the position of the whites remained even more unreachable. As a result, the Afro-American held an almost ineradicable conviction that he was inferior. A black skin became indeed a curse which, in its turn, was seen to confirm traditional prejudices – a vicious circle. The inferiority complexes which result from such impressions can lead to severe psychic disturbances. There are, of course, a number of defence mechanisms by which the individual will try to preserve his inner balance and to protect himself against the self-destructive influence of self-hatred. But, in order to avoid being eaten up by self-hatred, valuable psychic energies must be spent which could otherwise have been invested in other activities. In short, Afro-Americans suffered from handicaps which came on top of the economic and social discriminations to which they were constantly exposed.[90]

The difficult process of adaptation did not, of course, affect all Afro-Americans in the same way. There were considerable individual differences which, at least according to Frazier's famous study on the *Black Bourgeoisie*, appeared to be connected with social stratification. For it was the black middle classes which were exposed to more powerful frustrations than the lower strata of black America. The black bourgeoisie had closer contact with the white majority and hence experienced discrimination more directly while having become rather alienated from its ethnic roots. On the other hand, recent research has shown that the whole of Afro-American behaviour cannot be interpreted as being a pathological reaction to the blacks' position as a discriminated minority.[91] Still, the psychologically destructive repercussions of racism which, to this day, plays a central role in Afro–American life are undeniable; and we shall have ample opportunity of studying them in the literature of Afro-America. At the same time it is safe to say that the effects can be counterbalanced most easily by those who have not 'turned their backs on Africa', that is by those who have least made the racist stereotypes about their African heritage part of their own selves.[92]

## (b) THE SIGNIFICANCE OF GROUP CONSCIOUSNESS

Afro-American group consciousness is closely connected with the self-image of the individual. If an Afro-American despises his 'black ego' or is ashamed of it, the resulting self-hatred is, as a rule, not restricted to his individuality. It is also transferred to other blacks in whom he encounters his own 'despicable ego'. This projected self-hatred can express itself in aggressive behaviour towards other blacks; or it can lead to a 'bitter inner criticism of Negroes directed in upon themselves, which is widespread. It tends often to fierce, angry, contemptuous judgment of nearly all that Negroes do, say, and believe.'[93] It is this tendency which drives the Afro-American into isolation and prevents the emergence of a group consciousness. He thus ends up in a vicious circle. For it is only where there exists a developed group consciousness that collective action and social and political advancement of the group becomes possible; and this, in turn, is an important prerequisite of a non-pathological self-image. In view of this, it is vital for Afro-Americans that they solve the problem of their ethnic identity, of the African 'link', as Hill has called it. J. Mercer Langston remarked as early as 1849 : 'We must find a nationality before we can become any-body.'[94] And Harold Cruse has been even more explicit on this question :

> As long as the Negro's cultural identity is in question, or open to self-doubts, then there can be no positive identification with the real demands of his political and economic existence. Further than that, without a cultural identity that adequately defines *himself*, the Negro cannot even identify with the American nation as a whole. He is left in the limbo of social marginality, alienated and directionless on the landscape of America.[95]

In other words, if integration into the larger body of American society is to succeed, there is no alternative to creating a consciousness of one's own identity first.[96]

Today this view is held not merely by Afro-Americans. Research which has been done into the problem of acculturation has led to the conclusion that ethnic origin fulfils a much larger function among immigrant groups in the United States than had been suspected. This integration of immigrants into American society is no longer seen as a 'triumph of assimilation'.[97] Against the backdrop of this change in our perspective with regard to ethnic group consciousness, the position of the Afro-American minority appears in a different light from only a few years ago when the civil rights movement and its liberal integrationism dominated the scene.

B

To begin with, it became clear that the notion of the 'melting-pot', which had been so central to the American self-image in the past, could not really circumscribe what had been happening in the United States for quite some time. The process of 'melting' did, after all, imply that the immigrant groups which had followed the first Anglo-Saxon settlers had become integrated into the existing political and social structures in such a way that new institutions and a new – American – identity-consciousness had emerged, combining divergent elements of the various ethnic groups. Unfortunately, there is no sign of this having taken place. Both the norms and the institutions of 'American' culture have retained their essentially Anglo–Saxon mould.[98] This was, of course, precisely what the Anglo-Saxon immigrants and their heirs had always favoured. As late as 1800, they were numerically the strongest group and considered the continuation of English culture, even if slightly modified, as axiomatic.[99] It is no accident that the most ardent advocates of the melting-pot idea came from non-Anglo-Saxon groups, among them the Frenchman Crèvecoeur in the eighteenth century or the Zionist Zang-will at the beginning of the twentieth.[100] The Anglo-Saxons, on the other hand, rejected the notion of a racial and cultural mixing and, as far as the Afro-Americans are concerned, repeatedly planned to send them back to Africa.[101] What is more : they erected one barrier after another to stop the stream of non-Anglo-Saxon immigrants 'until, by the National Origins Act of 1924, the nation formally adopted the policy of using immigration to reinforce, rather than further to dilute, the racial stock of the early America'.[102]

If the 'melting-pot' has therefore turned out to be a mere fiction, it is not implied that the minorities have been assimilated completely into the dominant Anglo-Saxon culture. Though assimilation has taken place in many spheres of life, there are still considerable differences between the various minorities and the dominant Anglo-Saxon group with regard to family life, education, religion, voting behaviour, etc. These differences are so marked that it is possible to this day to discern a specific ethnic pattern. American society has retained a cultural pluralism which is regarded by many as an asset rather than a liability today. The social sciences have meanwhile come to recognise the great socio-psychological importance of group consciousness for the economic and social integration of new immigrants :

> When immigrants were faced with discrimination, exploitation and abuse, they turned in on themselves. Sustained psychologically by the bonds of their cultural heritage, they maintained family, religious and social institutions that had great stabilizing force. The institutions in turn fostered group unity. Family stability and group unity – plus access to political machinery jobs in industry and opportunities on

the frontier – led to group power . . . Group power and influence expanded individual opportunities and facilitated individual achievement, and within one or two generations most immigrants enjoyed the benefits of first-class American citizenship.[103]

However, the decisive point is that this worked only in the case of those immigrant groups which had sufficient scope for their economic advancement and which possessed political rights to assert themselves. African 'immigrants' did not, of course, fall into this category. Although, as will be seen later, they preserved many of their ethnic, i.e. non-Anglo-Saxon characteristics, they were as slaves deprived of their most important weapon for gaining 'group power', namely 'economic and political opportunities'.[104] Nor could 'black power' develop after the abolition of slavery because continuous discrimination stood in the way of economic and social advancement. These and other factors, above all psychological ones, compounded to form the so-called 'ghetto syndrome' which isolated the black minority more than any other group from the rest of American society. Afro-Americans found it impossible to rid themselves of their status as a 'subordinate caste'.[105]

There is yet another aspect to this problem which may be even more important and which differentiates Afro-Americans from other ethnic minorities. There exists, as the above quotation from Comer has shown, a close connection between group power and group consciousness. To put it differently : in order to wield group power a minority's group consciousness must be intact. But a healthy group consciousness is in turn only guaranteed when the individual members of that group feel a certain pride in their cultural heritage. They must be prepared to identify strongly with their own group. This is generally true of white and other coloured immigrant groups, such as the Chinese and Japanese. In fact, Asian immigrants would even consider themselves culturally superior to the rest of American society and reject total 'Americanisation'.[106] The Afro-Americans, on the other hand, present a different case. Since their original group consciousness was badly damaged and since the 'white' image of Africa made a revival of their own cultural traditions very difficult, they were particularly prone to adopting an 'American' identity. As a [black] apologist of assimilation put it, they should 'avoid being stigmatized as a uniquely different and unassimilable race of African ancestry [and] should at all times emphasize their essential Americanism'.[107]

Yet this 'American identity' is largely defined by the white majority. It is this majority which not only opposes the assimilation of the blacks but also, by virtue of its cultural and social norms, reinforces the frustrations and the self-hatred of those Afro-Americans who try to conform to these norms. The result was paradoxical : the ethnic group which was most eager to join the mythical melting-pot was not only the least welcome, but also, in striving for assimilation, acted against its own interests. For it was not assimilation but the development of an ethnic group consciousness which was required. There was no other way of overcoming the difficulties which stood in the way of an integration of the Afro-Americans into American society – integration, of course, in the sense of an equal co-existence with other ethnic groups.[108]

While the great majority of Afro-Americans found it impossible to identify with Africa, there always existed a small, but active minority whose adherents were more or less aware of the mechanisms which we have discussed so far and therefore attempted to create a 'racial solidarity' in order to activate a group consciousness which had been so badly mauled. They belonged to various nationalist movements which can be traced throughout the history of Black America. At times their existence was not directly noticeable.[109] During these periods, their activities were confined to a group consciousness geared to pragmatic co-operation. It did not take the form of a 'full-blown nationalist ideology'.[110] The consciousness of their African descent found expression in the names which they gave to their organisations, such as Free African Society, African Methodist Episcopal Church, African Benevolent Society, African Nationalist Pioneer Movement, African Orthodox Church, The [American] Republic of New Africa, and Sons of Africa.[111]

The separatist tendencies inherent in nationalism received a considerable boost, however, whenever the situation of the Afro-Americans worsened after a period of high, but unfulfilled expectations. An upsurge of nationalist feeling took place around 1800 when the first abolitionist movement failed to prevent a strengthening of slavery, which was now explicitly incorporated into the American Constitution; in the middle of the nineteenth century, when the position of the slaves again worsened; towards the end of that century, when the Reconstruction Era resulted in the introduction of semi-slavery. The latest wave of nationalism finally arose in the 1960s when the failure of the integration movement of the previous decades became obvious.[112]

If one compares these different stages of Black Nationalism, it is clear that each time it became more intense. The wave of the sixties represented a fresh leap forward which surpassed all previous movements with regard to the popular support it gained. Today Afro-Americans identify strongly with their African past to an extent which has not been observed before. There are many signs that the acceptance of their ethnic identity has resulted in a group cohesion and a strengthening of their political position to an extent which earlier nationalists had merely been dreaming of.[113]

# II ASPECTS OF THE PROCESS OF AFRO–AMERICAN ACCULTURATION

In the previous section we have emphasised the importance of ethnic group consciousness. This leaves one last aspect to be dealt with, namely whether and how far one can speak of African–Afro-American elements of culture without which an ethnic identity would, after all, be unthinkable. We must, in other words, ask what 'makes black culture a real sociological phenomenon rather than a group myth'.[114]

## (a) PROBLEMS OF AFRO-AMERICAN CULTURE

Blauner's question actually implies that there exists something like a black culture in its own right or at least that it is conceivable that it exists. For a long time such a possibility was of course never even contemplated by social scientists. Yet, just as anthropology has undergone a considerable metamorphosis which has been analysed above, a similar change of perspective has taken place with regard to black culture. Until recently Anglo-Saxon middle-class culture was seen to represent the norm for American culture, as Western culture had been used as a yardstick for measuring all other cultures on a more general level. Both assumptions have meanwhile encountered serious objections from modern anthropology. As far as the relationship of Afro-American culture to Anglo-Saxon culture is concerned, a number of black scholars and writers have first pointed to the methodological fallacies to which white sociologists and psychologists had succumbed. As early as 1944 Ralph Ellison, in a review of *An American Dilemma*, produced by a team of researchers under Gunnar Myrdal, raised his voice against the underlying assumption that Afro-Americans had no culture of their own and were nothing but passive products of a 'social pathology' reduced to living a secondary existence : '. . . can a people', Ellison replied to Myrdal's argument, 'live and develop for over three hundred years simply by *reacting*? Are American Negroes simply the creation of white men, or have they at least helped to create themselves out of what they found around them?' He then provided a partial answer :

> Men, as Dostoievsky observed, cannot live in revolt. Nor can they live in a state of 'reacting'. . . Much of Negro culture might be negative, but there is also much of great value, of richness which, because it has been secreted by living and has made their lives more meaningful, Negroes will not willingly disregard.[115]

Ellison had pinpointed the core of a problem which was to occupy scholars of various disciplines some twenty years later.[116] Although

there are many questions still left to be answered, few experts would
doubt today that their predecessors have made rather too rash deduc-
tions from Afro-American behaviour when they saw it one-sidedly as an
expression of a 'poverty culture'.[117] It became also clear that many
methodological problems which are of importance to the analysis of
race relations, and in particular of the minority position of black
Americans, had not been sufficiently developed.[118] Hitherto all cultural
forms which did not conform to what was defined as 'normal' were
regarded as 'disorganization, disorientation, retention, deviance'. Moreover, one selected merely the negative aspects of Afro-American life
and took them to be typical of this life as a whole. What was overlooked
was that 'every person's psychosocial identity contains a hierarchy
of positive *and* negative elements'.[119] After all, white middle-class
culture also contains a considerable number of elements and forms of
'cultural deprivation' and 'spiritual impoverishment'.[120] But no one
except some cultural pessimists and present-day Black Nationalists
would dream of deducing from this that 'white' culture as a whole is
pathological.

However, it was not simply a problem of the uncritical adoption of
accepted frames of reference by the earlier students of Afro-American
culture. There was also the problem of perception which has been
alluded to in connection with our discussion of European attitude
towards non-European societies. Some cultural elements were either
considered unimportant or were not even recognised, merely because
they had little or no significance in the observer's value system.
The same can be said of older attitudes towards Afro-American culture.
Thus one failed to understand the significance of the lively oral tradition
in Afro-American culture. A good many misunderstandings also arose
because of a lack of comprehension of a specific Afro-American linguistic
style, not to mention the divergent 'body languages' of blacks and
whites.[121] Finally, the former tendency to mistake Afro-American culture
for a plain 'poverty culture' and thus to deny the existence of any
ethnic elements persisted for so long because little was known about
the African background of Afro-Americans. This is not to say that the
issues are now clear-cut. On the contrary, the analysis of this back
ground and its function in Afro-American culture raises a number of
problems which are quite difficult to solve.

(*b*) THE SIGNIFICANCE OF AFRICANISMS

As long as Europeans and Americans were convinced of the lack of
culture and of the African's 'racial impotence' to develop a culture
the answer as to whether there existed Africanisms in Afro-American
culture was very simple. Culturally speaking, African slaves were

thought to have come to the United States as 'blanks'. At best one was prepared to acknowledge the existence of certain racial characteristics which were taken to symbolise the slave's 'culturelessness'. 'The Negro', wrote Weatherly in 1923, 'belongs perhaps to the most docile and modifiable of all races. He readily takes the tone and the color of his social environment, assimilating to the dominant culture with little resistance.'[122]

Following the revision of such theories, another argument was brought up to explain the lack of Afro-American culture. The shock of enslavement, of the terrifying conditions during the transport across the Atlantic and of the dehumanising impact of slavery in America, it was argued, had been so profound as to wipe out all memories of African cultural traditions. Alternatively, it was said that, since the slaves had been brought in from different parts of Africa, they belonged to widely divergent cultures and hence were unable to communicate with each other. Consequently they were supposed to lack a common basis for the development of an Afro-American culture.[123] In the final analysis, all these arguments were based on the conviction that 'the Negro is . . . a man without a past'.[124]

Meanwhile serious objections have been voiced against this view on all counts. As we have seen above, evolutionary cultural and racial theories have lost the battle more or less completely. Similarly one was forced to revise the notion that the area from which slaves were taken was too large to permit cultural integration. We now know that slaves came almost exclusively from West Africa.[125] This area, it is true, did not possess a uniform culture. But there existed nevertheless many points of contact, not the least among them being the similar structure of West African languages. In short, the slaves possessed important prerequisites for the preservation of African cultural elements.[126] But the question of how far this was actually the case has not yet been fully answered. Although we cannot here go into the complex problem of Africanisms in detail, we shall try to summarise at least its most important features. What, in other words, are the central issues of the so-called Survival Debate?

To begin with, it must be made clear that we are not dealing with comprehensive and intact structures, but with *elements* of African culture. This is as such nothing unusual in the American context. Other minorities have also been forced to abandon many of their own cultural institutions. The specific ethnic character of these minorities consists mainly 'in a certain number of distinctive values, orientations to life and experience and shared memories that co-exist within the framework of the general American life-style and allegiances'.[127] Although slaves had been denied conscious observance of many of their cultural traditions, this does not, of necessity, mean that they lost these traditions altogether and hence existed in a cultural vacuum. 'Culture and personality', says Rawick, 'are not like old clothes that can be taken off and thrown away. The ability of anyone to learn even the simplest thing is dependent upon utilizing the existing cultural apparatus.'[128]

It is fairly safe to assume that African slaves did not simply discard their culture when they arrived in the United States. There are even indications that a number of them resisted forced 'Americanisation' as far as possible. Thus many of them opposed baptism or refused to assume a new name and to adopt English in the place of their African language.[129] Although it was impossible to arrest the process of de-Africanisation which had set in under the pressure of the slave system, the acceptance of American cultural elements still did not lead to a complete loss of the slave's African heritage. As has been seen repeatedly in the course of this chapter, the transmission of culture is tied to a 'particular civilisatory equipment' only at a secondary level. At the primary level it expresses itself 'in the standardisation of behaviour, of thought and emotions, of attitudes and value judgments, of action and reaction by men in a particular community'.[130] This means, in the case of the African slaves, that they too found ways and means of building 'their own community out of materials taken from the African past and the American present, with the values and memories of Africa giving meaning and direction to the new creation'.[131]

Unlike other minority cultures which were able to preserve their language, religion, family structure, etc., African traditions in black culture have seldom assumed shapes which make the African elements visible at a glance. Rather they are preserved in a sublimated form and hence elude easy discovery. A further complicating factor is that African and European elements are frequently tightly interlocked and that Afro-American culture is at least to some extent also a 'poverty culture'. Nevertheless, we do possess a number of firm pointers to the existence of African 'survivals'.

There was relatively little interference with those Africanisms which continued more subconscious traditions of what has been called expressive culture. Examples that come to mind are speech style, music, dancing, folklore, with their inherent aesthetic and creative possibilities. But even in the religious and social sphere one can discover certain continuities and Africanisms.[132] Yet, given the present state of our knowledge, it remains a difficult task to arrive at a reliable estimate of the place which the African heritage occupies in Afro-American culture. What is certain, however, is that Africa represented a primary frame of reference for the slaves and gave a special ethnic flavour to their acculturation in the New World. This heritage must therefore be regarded as a relevant culture-shaping element. Subsequently, of course, other factors, such as slavery, urbanisation and the constant exposure to racism made their own contribution to the formation of an Afro-American style of behaviour.[133] But although the pressure of a racist social system forced the Afro-Americans to develop pathological attitudes of adaptation, most experts would now no longer see them flatly as psychically mutilated, passive victims of oppression and destitution. The literature which has been mentioned in this section shows, on the contrary, that Afro-Americans have, in spite of the difficulties they encountered, succeeded in making *creative* use of their African traditions and their subsequent experiences. They have been, it is argued, quite capable of developing an autonomous and lively culture of their own with many valuable elements. This culture would have been capable of offering them a positive image of themselves and of giving them some protection against the soul-destroying impact of racism, had the black Americans themselves been aware of the value of their own traditions and customs.[134] Unfortunately, this was not always the case and the literature of Afro-America, which will be analysed in later chapters, will provide a number of good illustrations of this.

## III SUMMARY

We have so far given an outline of the social and psychological framework in which the Afro-American image of Africa must be viewed. When discussing the emergence of racial theories, it became clear that their African origin plays a very important role in the life of Afro-Americans. It provides the basis for their status as a discriminated minority. Afro-Americans are therefore more seriously and more directly affected by their origin than any other minority in the United States. Since slavery tried systematically to eradicate and denigrate African cultural traditions, Afro-Americans have very often found it impossible to use Africa consciously as a reference point. Instead they adopted Anglo-Saxon values, thereby implicitly rejecting Africa and accepting their own supposed inferiority. This resulted in profound psychological disturbances with demoralising effects not only on the individual, but also on the group as a whole. Recent critical research on the reality of the American 'melting-pot' myth has demonstrated how important it is for the economic and political ascendancy of immigrant groups to possess a healthy group consciousness. On the other hand, such a consciousness will be generated only if the individual members of the group have a feeling of solidarity and profess their adherence to common values which can act as a focus of group consciousness.

The great importance of ethnicity was recognised by a number of

Afro-Americans quite early on. They tried to bring about a reorientation of their group and to give Africa a positive meaning in Afro-American consciousness. These 'nationalists' never attracted more than a few followers in the past, although it is difficult to obtain a representative picture. Today, however, a great many more Afro-Americans are prepared to develop a sense of solidarity and to include Africa as a conscious element into their culture. The reason for this shift must be seen to lie primarily in the revision of accepted notions of 'culture' which also affected our image of Africa and led to a reassessment of the character and value of Afro-American culture. Today Africans are no longer regarded as 'primitive' and 'barbaric', or Afro-Americans as having no culture of their own. Special historical conditions as well as the discovery of the African heritage have, it is argued, resulted in an Afro-American culture which is not merely a pathological phenomenon. And this time the task of discovering the positive aspects of black culture did not remain confined to a small circle of social scientists. It is now the Afro-Americans themselves who try to clarify their attitudes towards this culture and its African elements.

By using selected literary sources, we shall try to show in subsequent chapters how this growth of consciousness evolved and what kind of personal struggles individual writers in different periods had to go through when they set out in search of their African origin.

# 2 The Early Image of Africa

## I THE FIRST AFRO-AMERICAN POETS AND AFRICA

The earliest writings documenting an interest in Africa can be traced back to the second half of the eighteenth century and originate from the best-known among the Afro-American poets of that period, i.e. Jupiter Hammon, Phillis Wheatley and George Moses Horton. All three of them were slaves and had been able to publish their poetry only because they lived in particularly fortunate circumstances.

### (a) JUPITER HAMMON

The eldest of these poets was Hammon (1720?–1806?), whose master came to like his poems and hence did not interfere with his writing.[1] However, it was presumably the content rather than the quality of Hammon's poetry which found favour with his master and other readers. Hammon conformed exactly to 'Sambo', the obedient type of slave, which was so dear to the hearts of many slave-masters. This emerges from his well-known dialogue between 'The Kind Master and the Dutiful Servant' which ran as follows:

> Master
> Come, my servant, follow me,
> According to thy place;
> And surely God will be with thee
> And send thee heavenly grace.
> . . .

> Servant
> Dear Master, that's my whole delight,
> Thy pleasure for to do;[2]
> . . .

Hammon's was no doubt an extreme case. His preparedness to conform went so far as to make him prefer slavery to freedom – except for certain reservations which he had with regard to the younger generation of Negroes:

Now I acknowledge that liberty is a great thing, and worth seeking for, if we can get it honestly; and by our good conduct prevail on our masters to set us free : though for my own part I do not wish to be free; . . . for many of us who are grown-up slaves, and have always had masters to take care of us, should hardly know to take care of themselves; and it may be for our own comfort to remain as we are.

Hammon has completely accepted the biblical arguments of the pro-tagonists of slavery and admonishes the Afro-Americans to accept their fate as God-given and hence without reproach. For

who of us dare dispute with God! He has commanded us to obey, and we ought to do it cheerfully, and freely. This should be done by us, not only because God commands, but because our own peace and comfort depend on it. As we depend upon our masters for what we eat and drink and wear, and for all our comfortable things in this world, we cannot be happy unless we please them. This we cannot do without obeying them freely . . .[3]

In view of this it is not surprising that his attitude towards Africa is identical to that of the slave-masters. Slavery is seen by him as the alleged liberation from barbarism and as a sign of divine grace :

## Address to Phillis Wheatley

### I

O come you pious youth ! Adore
    The wisdom of thy God,
In bringing thee from distant shore
    To learn his holy word.

### II

Thou mightst been left behind,
    Amidst a dark abode;
God's tender mercy still combin'd,
    Thou hast the holy word.

### IV

God's tender mercy brought thee here;
    Tost o'er the raging main;
In Christian faith thou hast a share,
    Worth all the gold of Spain.

IX
> Come you, Phillis, now aspire,
> And seek the living God,
> So step by step thou mayest go higher,
> Till perfect in the word.[4]

## (*b*) PHILLIS WHEATLEY

Hammon dedicated this poem of 1778 to Phillis Wheatley (*c.* 1753–84). But it appears that he also considered it a rejoinder to Wheatley's poem 'To the University of Cambridge', written in 1767. At least both poems are remarkably similar, partly even identical, in attitude and style :

> 'T was not long since I left my native shore,
> The land of errors and Egyptian gloom :
> Father of mercy ! 't was thy gracious hand
> Brought me in safety from those dark abodes.[5]

There is nothing unusual about Hammon's Christian piety. He had been active as a preacher. But the deep religiosity which exudes through every line, the evenly balanced rhythm and the sophisticated language of Wheatley's poetry come as a surprise. After all, she was probably no older than fourteen at this time, and it was only six years since she had been brought as a slave from Senegal.

To account for her free acceptance of Christianity, one must know something about her peculiar experiences : with the traumatic crossing on the slave ship behind her, she was lucky enough to be bought by a well-to-do and honest Methodist, John Wheatley, on the Boston slave market. He freed her after twelve years of service, but during those twelve years in Wheatley's very religious house Phillis received every possible support and encouragement. The kind of Christian love as practised and taught by John Wheatley was bound to convince her of the constructive power of Christianity and to turn her into a willing and grateful pupil.[6]

On the other hand, she had still vivid memories of Africa, although she did not voice a desire to return to the homeland anywhere in her writings. Rather she felt a profound gratitude for her conversion to Christianity which offered her a hope of redemption. In fact, to her Christianity signified something like a revelation :

> 'Twas mercy brought me from my PAGAN land,
> Taught my benighted soul to understand
> That there's a God, that there's a Saviour too;
> Once I redemption neither sought nor knew.[7]

In a later poem she wrote about her African childhood spent in free-dom, and it may be this memory which prevented her from falling victim to a 'servilité simpliste' like Hammon's.[8] As the last four verses of the above poem demonstrate, she does not deny her African-ness by any means. On the contrary, she courageously counters the arguments of those Christians who, in referring to the Bible, try to imprint the mark of permanent inferiority on the black race :

> Some view our sable race with scornful eye,
> 'Their color is a diabolic die.'
> Remember, 'Christians', 'Negroes', black as 'Cain',
> May be refined, and join th' angelic train.[9]

It was precisely the Christian idea of the basic equality of all men and hence of all races, to be achieved by conversion to the faith, which formed the bedrock of Phillis Wheatley's religiosity. This was what she hoped to bring to Africa so that its inhabitants, too, would find shelter and consolation in Christianity :

> Take him, my dear Americans, he said,
> Be your complaints on this kind bosom laid :
> Take him, ye Africans, he longs for you;
> Impartial Saviour is his title due;
> Washed in the fountain of redeeming blood,
> You shall be sons, and kings, and priests to God.

In other words, the humanitarian, non-racialist element of Christianity exerted a great attraction on her. Only against the background of her fortunate personal position, and the religiosity which stemmed from it, can we understand her best-known, but also most controversial lines :

> Should you, my lord, while you peruse my song,
> Wonder from whence my love of *Freedom* sprung,
> Whence flow these wishes for the common good,
> By feeling hearts alone best understood,
> I, young in my life, by seeming cruel fate
> Was snatch'd from *Afric's* fancy'd happy seat :
> What pangs excruciating must molest,
> What sorrows labor in my parent's breast?
> Steel'd was the soul and by no misery mov'd
> That from a father seiz'd his babe belov'd
> Such, such my case. And can I then but pray
> Others may never feel tyrannic sway?[10]

Afro-Americans have objected above all to the words 'seeming cruel fate' and 'Afric's fancy'd happy seat'. They argue with Redding that ' "seeming cruel" and "fancied [*sic*] happy" give her away as not believing either in the cruelty of the fate that had dragged thousands of her race into bondage in America nor in the happiness of their former freedom in Africa.'[11] Yet these critics overlook the special significance which Christianity assumed for Phillis Wheatley; nor do they take account of the context in which these lines must be seen. Certainly the other verses and especially the words 'My love of *Freedom*' which she calls a 'common good', as well as her 'I then but pray' undermine this criticism. Moreover, there exudes through the above extract in which she talks about her childhood a surprisingly strong tie with Africa. She speaks with a warmth here which cannot be found elsewhere in her language. Today it is above all her neo-classicist 'bloodless and un-racial' technique which is being criticised and which Henderson takes as proof of her inability 'to come to grips honestly with her blackness'.[12] Sterling Brown, on the other hand, while deploring her technique, comes to her defence by emphasising that 'these limitations are not solely hers but of the period itself'.[13]

If, in addition, one takes into consideration the Methodist education which she received in a loving and caring family, it appears rather nonsensical to expect her to have emancipated herself during her short life from the influence of the Wheatley family and professed her 'Blackness'. Nevertheless, the above lines in which she proudly proclaimed her African-ness are indicative of an incipient 'racial consciousness' and invalidate the criticism against her at least to some degree.

(*c*) GEORGE MOSES HORTON

Horton (1797–*c*. 1883) lived on a plantation in the Deep South. But his master gave him permission to hire himself out to the Rector of the University of North Carolina at Chapel Hill. There he learned to read and write and attained such literary skills that he served the students as a sort of 'poet on campus' who, for a moderate fee, would provide them with love poems. He also published his own poetry which has given him the reputation of being the first Afro-American 'protest writer'.[14] Unlike Hammon and Wheatley, he rebelled against slavery, writing angrily :

> Alas ! and I am born for this,
>     To wear this slavish chain ?
> Deprived of all created bliss,
>     Through hardship, toil and pain !

> How long have I in bondage lain,
>   And languished to be free !
> Alas ! and I must still complain –
>   Deprived of liberty.

> Oh, Heaven ! and is there no relief
>   This side the silent grave –
> To soothe the pain – to quell the grief
>   And anguish of a slave?

And then he asks for 'Liberty' :

> Soar on the pinion of that dove
>   Which long has cooed for thee,
> And breathed her notes from Afric's grove,
>   The sound of Liberty.[15]

In other words, Africa is the place of freedom for Horton, a freedom for which he longs so much. This is why he idealises Africa as a Garden of Eden. By using words like 'dove', 'cooed', 'breathed her notes' and 'grove', he generates associations with the *locus amoenus*. The above poem first appeared in 1828 in a volume entitled *The Hope of Liberty*. With the royalties of this volume he hoped to buy his freedom and to emigrate to Liberia. But the publisher kept the royalties for himself and Horton had to wait for his freedom, which he expected to find in Africa, until the abolition of slavery.[16] Nevertheless, his desire to go to Liberia reflects a general and vivid interest in emigration which set in during the nineteenth century. It is by analysing the literature on this emigration movement that we can gain an insight into the ambivalent attitude of Afro-Americans towards Africa in this period. The following section will therefore examine a few representative concepts with special reference to prominent individuals of the emigration movement.


## II   THE SIGNIFICANCE OF AFRICA FOR THE
##      EMIGRATION MOVEMENT OF THE NINETEENTH
##      CENTURY

Even before the nineteenth century there had been a certain amount of support among Afro-Americans for a return to Africa.[17] Evidently this support reflected in a very fundamental way the manifold connections of black Americans with Africa. The earliest resettlement plans which have survived date back to the eighteenth century. Thus, in 1773, a group of slaves submitted a petition asking to be given permission to return to their homeland. Similar efforts were made in subsequent years by other slaves who described Africa as 'a Populous, Pleasant and Plentiful country'.[18] The idea of emigration was finally taken up in 1789 by a number of members of the 'Free African Society'. But interest was lacking among the free blacks of Philadelphia, where the Society had its headquarters, and the idea was dropped again.[19] Yet, three years later, in 1792, there were over 1000 Afro-Americans who emigrated to Sierra Leone, a country which had been founded in 1787 as a colony by ex-slaves returning from Britain. The next successful resettlement programme was initiated by P. Cuffe, a wealthy black ship's master, who together with 38 settlers sailed to Freetown, the capital of Sierra Leone, in 1815. By this time interest was clearly rising. Cuffe, at any rate, received so many applications that he thought 'he might have colonized the greater part of Boston and vicinity'.[20] With the exception of brief interruptions, Afro-American interest in emigration continued to grow throughout the nineteenth century. But none of the movements initiated by blacks became a resounding success because few slaves were freed after the end of the eighteenth century and free blacks were in no position financially to pay for the liberty and journey across the Atlantic of fellow-blacks. That the potential of blacks who were keen to emigrate was none the less considerable is demonstrated by the example of the American Colonization Society (ACS) which, founded primarily by whites, was wealthy enough to finance the trip to Liberia for between 12,000 and 15,000 Afro-Americans. The actual interest in emigration was even greater as is evidenced by the fact that the number of applicants was much larger. In fact, more Afro-Americans than ever before became involved in the emigration movement through the ACS. For the first time Africa became a clear alternative to living in the United States and challenged Afro-Americans to take a stand on the issue of Africa.[21]

Most documents which have survived are of black middle-class origin. These blacks had been able, increasingly, to get an education. Some of them had even as slaves enjoyed the privilege of a training in reading and writing; for it was largely from the mulattoes that the black middle-class originated who had been employed as house slaves and had frequently been set free by their masters. Their closer relationship with the whites generally enabled them to acquire a higher educational standard than the field slaves. Above all, they learned how to write, which was otherwise strictly prohibited. They became 'a sort of black aristocracy',[22] a status which was fostered by the abolition of slavery. This fact must be borne in mind when one analyses statements concerning the emigration movement from these strata of black society. Their privileged position had alienated them from the mass of Afro-Americans. At the same time they were more open to the idea of assimilation into white culture and to adopting white life-styles and values. These attitudes were reinforced among the 'freedmen'. Their growing prosperity and the puritanical education which they received in schools founded and run by whites further widened the gap between them and Africa and the black majority.[23]

## (a) AFRICA — THE STRANGE COUNTRY

As a consequence of their special position, there existed a considerable number of Afro-Americans who felt rooted in the United States. 'This is our country, and we have no claim on any other', wrote a 'colored American' in a letter to a journal called *Liberator* in 1859 : '. . . we are not going to Africa. We have no more claim on Africa than has [the white American]; that country belongs to the Africans and not to us. We are Americans.' America was said to be the 'native land'; Africa, on the other hand, was a 'strange land'. This, at any rate, is how another black letter-writer expressed his feelings about the subject. But at the same time, and interestingly enough, this writer speaks of Afro-Americans as 'Africans'.[24] Many middle-class blacks based their rejection of Africa on more precise notions of Africa, however. As was common in the nineteenth century, they looked at Africa through the eyes of Western civilisation by which they had been so profoundly influenced. They called it 'barbaric' and 'primitive' and considered a return to it unthinkable. This emerges very clearly from a resolution which was adopted by a number of free blacks from Philadelphia : 'Resolved that, without art, without science, without a proper knowledge of government, to cast into the savage wilds of Africa the free people of color seems to us the circuitous route through which they must return to perpetual bondage.'[25] Similar statements were made by Frederick Douglass, probably the most famous Afro-American 'leader' of the nineteenth century prior to Booker T. Washington. As late as 1872 when the position of Afro-Americans in the United States was already beginning to deteriorate Douglass still adhered to the view that there existed no reason 'why anyone should leave this land of progress and enlightenment and seek a home amid the death-dealing malaria of a barbarous continent'.[26]

What contributed to hampering the development of a more positive attitude of the black population towards Africa was that most white founders and supporters of the ACS made it perfectly clear why they had joined the Society : it was not in order to help the blacks, but in order to get rid of unwelcome free Afro-Americans.[27] Obviously, those who considered themselves the most advanced of the black race were very offended that the whites held them to be 'useless'. They found this policy all the more irritating since they believed few whites could deny 'that the descendants of Africa, when transplanted in a country favorable to their improvement, and when their advantages are equal to others, seldom fail to answer all of the ends suited to their capacity, and in some instances rise to many of the virtues, to the learning and piety of the most favored nation'.[28] To emigrate in these circumstances would have been tantamount to admitting that they were as incapable of development as the whites maintained.

Another declared goal of the ACS likewise encountered much criticism, namely that by exporting the free blacks and other undesirable black elements, one would be in a better position to control the remaining slave population. This was why the above-mentioned Philadelphia resolution continued : 'that we never will separate ourselves voluntarily from the slave population in this country; they are our brethren by the ties of consanguinity, of suffering and of wrong; and we feel that there is more virtue in suffering deprivations with them than fancied advantages for a season.'[29] Douglass, who was one of the most outspoken opponents of emigration was guided by similar considerations. He criticised the 'African dream' as being a dangerous squandering of energies which would be far better used in the struggle for the emancipation of the slaves as well as for civil rights inside the United States.[30] The following comment on this problem is particularly interesting :

Depend upon it, the savage chiefs of the western coasts of Africa, who for ages have been accustomed to selling their captives into bondage, and pocketing the ready cash for them will not more readily accept our moral and economical ideas than the slave traders of Maryland and Virginia. We are, therefore, less inclined to go to Africa to work against the slave-trade than to stay here to work against it.[31]

Douglass touches upon a sore point of African–Afro-American relations here, i.e. the fact that they had been sold into slavery by their own ancestors. It was this point which did so much to alienate Afro-Americans from Africa.[32] Others not only reproached their ancestors for their deeds but were also ashamed of the fact of slavery as such :

I have no pride of ancestry to point back to. Our forefathers did not come here as did the Pilgrim fathers in search of a place where they could enjoy civil and religious liberty. No – , they were cowardly enough to allow themselves to be brought manacled and fettered as slaves, rather than die on their native shores resisting their oppressors.[33]

(b) AFRICA – THE LAND OF HOPE

Yet if there was a group of Afro-Americans who rejected emigration or showed no interest in Africa because they thought they could achieve their political, economic and 'cultural' ascendancy only inside North America, there were others who supported colonisation ventures. Their spokesmen were convinced that any solution of the problems with which the blacks were confronted in the United States would have to include the question of Africa. But this did not result in a uniformly and unequivocally positive image of Africa in their minds. On the contrary, it is precisely by referring to this group, whose members must be considered the precursors of Pan-Africanism, that we can study the ambivalence in the relationship of Afro-Americans towards Africa.

To begin with, they were all convinced that the blacks would 'never become a people until thy com [sic] out from amongst the white people'. Hence they set all their hopes on Africa, above all on Liberia where they expected to find the freedom of which they had been deprived for so long. Typical of this attitude is a declaration by the 'Movement Among the Colored People of Cincinnati – OHIO IN AFRICA' which read as follows : '*Resolved*, That we believe that Liberia offers to the oppressed children of Africa a home where we can establish a nationality and be acknowledged as men by the nations of the earth.' Afro-Americans, in other words, regarded themselves as settlers who wanted to emigrate with the intention of 'regenerating' their 'fatherland', i.e. to build a 'civilised' nation which the West would recognise.[34]

One of the most important representatives of the black colonisation movement of the nineteenth century was Martin Delany. Although Delany, like other black supporters of the emigration movement, sharply condemned the racism of the ACS, he was nevertheless convinced that 'a new country, and a new beginning is the only true, rational, political remedy for our disadvantageous position'.[35] His original plan had been to establish settlements in other parts of America. Later, however, and stimulated by the books of explorers like Livingstone and Bowen, he developed great enthusiasm for West Africa. He undertook exploratory journeys well beyond Liberia and was instrumental in developing a settlement project in the Niger valley.[36] Delany, whom his contemporaries described as 'unadulterated in race, proud of his complexion, and devotedly attached to his fatherland [Africa]',[37] must be regarded as the first genuine Pan-Africanist.[38] He called Africa the 'fatherland' of all Afro-Americans and explicitly asserted the joint responsibility of blacks on both sides of the Atlantic for Africa's future. A feeling of solidarity or even identity with Africa could, according to Delany, be generated only if the Afro-Americans were taught to be proud of their African ancestors and of their colour. Delany clearly recognised that a positive self-image was an important prerequisite of an independent mind and energetic political action. Feelings of inferiority would not merely result in the blacks resigning themselves to a life as '*a whole race of servants*'; rather they would also be full of distrust against fellow-blacks and lean on the whites instead of their own group. Delany now tried to offer them an alternative positive image and to foster their self-confidence by describing Africa with its wealth and highly cultured inhabitants. The development and prosperity of the United States, he argued, had been possible only because of the outstanding abilities of the Afro-American population. In his words : 'Farmers, herdsmen, and laborers in their own country, they required not to be taught to work and how to do it – but it was only necessary to tell them to go to work and they at once knew what to do and how it should be done.' This view of the Africans as a capable and 'civilised' people displays an impressive detachment from the dominant notions of the time. The following statement is even downright revolutionary considering the age in which it was written : 'Heathenism and Liberty, before Christianity and Slavery.' It was only towards the end of the century that a similarly critical attitude towards Christianity was gaining ground.[39]

This traditionalism is not surprising in view of the fact that the 'regeneration' movement was borne primarily by the leading black churches which left its mark on the emigration movement as a whole. Although the churches were opposed to colonisation on a large scale, they approved of an ethnic identification with Africa and supported limited emigration 'as a means of Christianising Africa'.[40] These tendencies arose, above all, from two of the leading black churches in the United States, the African Methodist Episcopal Church and the African Methodist Episcopal Zion Church. Both of them had played an important part in the struggle for black emancipation in the United States. Consequently they felt predestined to 'save' the Africans. However problematical this aim may have been, it is certain that it gave a sense of purpose to the course of Afro-American history and thus offered a genuine consolation : the expulsion from the homeland and the period of slavery could be interpreted as having been guided by God. As Turner, the famous bishop of the African Methodist Episcopal Church put it, the Afro-American was destined 'to learn obedience, to work, to sing, to pray, to preach, acquire education, deal with mathematical abstractions and imbibe the principles of civilization as a whole, and then to return to Africa, the land of his fathers, and bring her his millions'.[41] Thus those Afro-Americans who were motivated by a missionary zeal believed that they had, as the most civilised element of the blacks of the world, a special obligation towards their 'African brothers' to 'regenerate' the continent.

At the same time they expected that their policy would lead to a solution of the racial problem in the United States. Christianising and 'civilising' Africa and a general improvement of the living conditions in the land of their ancestors were supposed to prove to the world the real 'capacity of the Negro race'. This, they thought, would gain them the respect of the whites who would then at last grant them civil rights in the United States as well.[42] The missionary activities of Afro-Americans, to be sure, were marginal if compared with those of the white churches, but they were significant in so far as through them contact was maintained with Africa and existing ties even considerably strengthened. The missions provided important channels of communication which were kept open throughout the decades and contributed much to fostering a feeling of 'racial solidarity' between Afro-Americans and Africans. On the other hand, the missionaries must bear considerable responsibility for the difficulties of communication which continued to exist. Since they were convinced that Christianity was the highest stage in the intellectual and moral development of mankind, they had no understanding for African mores and customs. They condemned them as being 'immoral' and 'uncivilised' and thought the Africans to be 'superstitious' people. In view of the great influence which the Afro-American churches wielded among blacks in the United States, the reports and views of the missionaries had a profound effect which lasted well into the twentieth century.[43] Thus it was almost a commonplace among black emigrants that their task was one 'of accomplishing the great design, of causing the glorious light of the gospel to shine upon Africa's benighted tribes'. In another letter to the ACS this point was made even more bluntly : 'We too have a great work to perform. To the Anglo and Africa–American is committed the redemption and salvation of numerous people, for ages sunk in the lowest depth of superstition and barbarism.'[44]

The missionary movement therefore put great store by the Liberian experiment which was to prove to the Western world that 'the descendants of Africa, when placed in a fair position, are not inferior in civilisation, religion and morality to those nations amongst whom it was their lot to be cast for a given time'.[45] In a curiously literal sense, this experiment may be taken to have been a success. At least the Western image of Africa which the Afro-Americans had adopted never led them to consider their own integration into the indigenous African societies. Many of them even refused to have social intercourse with the native populations. As a free 'Man of Color' reported, many of them had objections 'to emigrating to a country whose inhabitants are shrouded in deep ignorance – whom long and deep-rooted custom forbids us to have real social intercourse with in the various relations of civilised life upon fair and equal terms of husband and wife, and whose complexion is darker than many of ours'.[46] Not surprisingly Afro-American immigrants to Liberia soon reproduced not only 'the American pattern of stratification based on color',[47] but also the ideas of imperial domination as developed by the colonial powers. For a good number of Afro-Americans, 'moral and political liberty'[48] which many black Americans had held up as an ideal became reduced to the simple formula : 'Here you can rule instead of being ruled.'[49]

Of course, not all Afro-Americans who showed an interest in Africa subscribed to this view. Although their ideas about Africa reflect the generally accepted notions about the continent, thus supporting our introductory argument concerning the inescapable force of the 'white' image of Africa, they refused to believe in the alleged inferiority of the black race. On the contrary, they were convinced of the great value of this race. As a result, nineteenth-century black nationalism became an odd mixture of Pan-Africanist, missionary-colonialist and evolutionist concepts. The ideas of the two most influential representatives of the missionary emigration movement, Crummell and Blyden, provide ample evidence to demonstrate how complex the attitude of the black nationalists was towards Africa. It is to these two leading intellectuals that we shall now have to turn.

Alexander Crummell was one of the most ardent advocates of the 'Regeneration of Africa'. There was, in his view, no hope for the blacks in the United States. 'Race prejudice and divinely ordained race distinctions made the hope of a great future for the Negroes in the United States nothing but a silly dream.'[50] He therefore left the United States for Britain to study at Cambridge University. He took his degree in 1853 and went to Liberia where he worked as a minister and teacher for the following twenty years. He returned to the United States in 1873 to take up a position as a parson in Washington. His congregation grew rapidly in size and Crummell became a well-known figure and 'tireless commentator on Negro affairs both in Africa and America'.[51] Full of pride in his purely African background[52] and of impressive stature, he embodied the ideal type of the self-confident Pan-African. He was an Afro-American in the genuine sense of the word 'who stood for Negro accomplishment in education, science and the arts'.[53] And yet his attitude towards Africa was not without that measure of ambivalence which was widespread among Afro-Americans. On the one hand, it is true, he firmly believed in the glorious future of the black race; its valuable and unique qualities, he argued, gave it an important place in the community of nations. On the other hand, however, his ideas and moral positions remained deeply rooted in, and shaped by, his Western education and his profession as a Christian minister. He unreservedly praised Western civilisation as the highest stage of cultural development. From this perspective Africa, not surprisingly, looked to him like a barbaric wilderness, a place 'of ancient despotism'. Africans, in his eyes, were heathens, a 'rude people, incapable of perceiving their own place in the moral scale, nor of understanding the social and political obligations which belong to responsible humanity'. Yet they were not, Crummell believed, inherently vicious or hopelessly backward. On the contrary, he had lived in Africa long enough to have learned to value certain qualities of the African very highly : 'In his character you see nothing stolid, repulsive, indomitable. On the contrary, he is curious, mobile, imaginative.' This, he thought, was clear enough evidence to prove 'that he has the needed qualities to make a proper man. Everywhere, where the trial has been made, he has passed out of his primitive rudeness, and made a step in advance of his former state.' It was thus certain that one would have to reckon with the Africans as 'a future element of society'.[54]

Crummell was confirmed in this view by the theory of evolution whose axiom of a linear cultural evolution was supposed to be equally applicable to all races. He believed that, if only they tried hard enough, Africans could develop culturally, just as the Anglo-Saxon had been able to change 'from the rudeness of his brutalized forefathers into an enlightened and civilized human being'.[55] To be sure, he could not achieve this without outside assistance. In order to liberate the Africans from ignorance and backwardness, Western support was required, i.e. Western knowledge, Western technology, but above all the help from Christian missionaries. Conversion to Christianity was imperative partly because of what Crummell called its 'controlling influences', but partly also because all Christian nations lived under the commandment of 'Prepare ye the way of the Lord'. Firmly under the spell of colonialism in a Christian guise, Crummell went so far as to hold that the resistance of natives had to be crushed by force. After all

> both our position and our circumstances make us the guardians, the protectors, and the teachers of our heathen tribes. And, hence, follows that all the legitimate means which may tend to preserve them, which anticipate bloody antagonisms and which tend to their mental, moral, and social advancements determine themselves as just and proper.[56]

If it was for the West to initiate the 'Regeneration of Africa', this did not imply that the whites were capable of it. According to Crummell, they had – all their achievements notwithstanding – frequently failed in the past. Above all they had been culpable of establishing a slave system. Moreover, physical handicaps prevented them from engaging in their missionary work in Africa for any length of time. In short, 'the children of Africa scattered abroad in distant lands, are the indigenous agency – the men . . . who are yet to accomplish the large and noble work of uplifting Africa from degradation.'[57]

To Crummell, Liberia was the ideal base for a regeneration movement. This state possessed 'the first free, civilized, and Christian Negro government that Africa had ever known from the dawn of history'. What was more, Liberia's natural resources seemed to guarantee a future of greatness. In this fashion, Crummell's expectations concerning Liberia became closely linked with his belief in the rise of the 'children of Africa' which only Liberia would assure.[58] For this reason he supported the resettlement of Afro-Americans in that country. But he was realistic enough to see that, in view of the sheer number of blacks in the United States, emigration was hardly an adequate solution to the American racial problem. The 'regeneration of Africa' was an important step, however, for creating a black group consciousness the lack of which he deplored many times and which he regarded as essential if the poor social and economic conditions of the blacks were ever to be improved. And this, in turn, would be possible only if the Afro-Americans succeeded in overcoming their feelings of inferiority. Crummell urged them no longer to ignore the 'fact of race', to develop racial pride and 'black' institutions. What he advocated was, in other words, an early version of the Black Power Movement of the 1960s.[59]

However, in his view there were also reasons of 'race history' which made assimilation an absurdity. He believed that each race possessed a specific character of its own and 'that individuality is subject at all times to all the laws of race-life. That race-life, all over the globe, shows an invariable proclivity, and in every instance, to integration of blood and permanence of essence.' All races therefore 'instinctively' tried to survive and – following a law of nature – to preserve their own specific characteristics. Still – and this is typical of Crummell's ambivalence towards Africa – his attitude is marked by a number of illogicalities. One of these is his demand that the specific characteristics of the 'Negro race', such as its spontaneity, its aesthetic sense and its sensibility, be backed up by elements of Western culture :

Spontaneity, valuable as it is, requires the restraints and limitations which come from judgment and which can only be furnished by imperial faculties of moral and mental nature, the conscience and Reason. . . No people can be fed on flowers. Aesthetics, while indeed they give outward adornment, and inward delicate sensibility, tend but little to furnish that hardy muscle and grim fibre which men need in the stern battle of life.[60]

The characteristics with which he endows the Africans sound familiar to us today. For in some respects, though by no means all, Crummell anticipated with his 'racial theories' the *négritude* philosophies of Senghor and Césaire.[61]

In this respect, Crummell was surpassed only by Edward Wilmot Blyden whose 'racial consciousness' was even more strongly developed. Like the former, Blyden was a deeply religious man who worked in Liberia as a minister and teacher for some twenty years. During the fifty years of his life in which he was most active, he repeatedly travelled between the United States and Africa and emerged as the best-known and most influential Pan-African of his time. A number of organisations and institutions, such as the Blyden Club of New York and the Edward Wilmot Blyden Library at Norfolk, Va., were named after him.[62] He coined the controversial and widely used term of 'African Personality' of which he might be said to have been an early embodiment.[63] His 'philosophy of Africanness' possessed a magnetic attraction for his contemporaries as well as for later generations and eventually established him 'as a spokesman for all members of the Negro race'. Blyden's work is hence of considerable importance in our context, both as a reflection of the 'regeneration of Africa' and of his position as an influential forefather of the African and Afro-American *négritude*.

His entire background predestined him to become a mediator between the various regions of the Afro-American world. He was born in 1832 into a family of pure African stock. An American Presbyterian minister who quickly recognised Blyden's unusual intelligence and his linguistic talent sent him to the United States at the age of eighteen so that he could get a college education. His stay there was brief and disappointing, however, because the system of discrimination barred him from entering a suitable educational establishment. With the help of the New York Colonization Society, he left for Liberia where he resumed his studies. He advanced rapidly and, as early as 1858, was promoted to the position of headmaster at his school in Monrovia at which he had been teaching before. Also during that year he became minister of the Presbyterian Church of West Africa. Three years later, he was given a professorship of Greek and Latin at the newly-founded Liberia College. Crummell was one of his colleagues there. It is interesting how Western education and protest against the discriminating elements of Western culture merged in both men to form a strongly race-conscious nationalism. This nationalism was Blyden's reaction to the subjugation by the European powers of Africa and the racism that followed in its wake. The racist doctrines became so all-pervasive that even their victims could not escape their influence.

It is certainly not surprising therefore that he should have adopted this particular framework and that it should never have occurred to him 'to scrap the whole structure with its network of unconscious assumptions which so completely prejudiced the case'.[65] On the contrary, he wholeheartedly agreed with those contemporary anthropological theories which have been discussed in an earlier chapter and which classified races according to cultural and physiological criteria, although he did object to some of their arguments. Thus he felt that there indeed existed differences between the races, but rejected as totally unjustified the Social Darwinist inferences which were drawn from them : 'There will never be of the original races any "survival of the fittest". All are fit, equally fit, for the work they have to do, and all will continue. They are co-operating forces or forces that must co-operate in order to the progress and perfection of Humanity as a whole [*sic*].'[66] This was in his view the task with which they had been charged by God. Races were not superior or inferior, but simply different. These differences endowed each with a special value and made it an integral part of Divine Nature. What determines man's individuality is his belonging to a particular race. According to Blyden it is the task of every human being to develop his race and thereby his personality. His argument is an implicit attack on those Western-educated Africans who tried to imitate the whites and were ashamed of their own culture; against those who, upon returning to Africa, hired an interpreter in order to avoid having to speak a 'primitive' language. 'Your place', he said,

has been assigned you in the universe as Africans, and there is no room for you as anything else. Christianity pointed out the importance and purpose of race preservation and development and provided for it. Science has recognized and accepted this truth, both as regards individuals and Races. But the world is far behind Christianity, and still in the rear of science.

The religious element which transpires through this statement runs like a red thread throughout Blyden's work. His aim was to teach the blacks to love and to respect themselves. He frequently invoked the Second Commandment in support of his theory. But there is also a slight and significant shift of emphasis in his argument : the imperative 'Thou shalt love thy neighbour as thyself' denoted in his view that the blacks, lacking self-esteem, should love and respect their racial specificity. Only when this had been achieved could they, Blyden argued, also respect their (other) neighbours. Blyden untiringly reminded all blacks :

Honour and love your Race. Be yourselves, as God intended you to be or he would not have made you thus. We cannot improve upon his plan. If you are not yourself, if you surrender your personality, you have nothing left to give the world. You have no pleasure, no use, nothing which will attract and charm men, for by suppression of your individuality you lose your distinctive character.[67]

In order to develop one's personality, Blyden continued, 'the preservation of race integrity' was axiomatic. But this could only be achieved if the Europeans were kept at a distance. Racial mixing would merely 'expose our institutions to the dangers and decay of mongrelism, confuse our instincts, and postpone the assertion of our individuality as a distinct group in the family of nations – called by our traditions, our peculiar instinct, and our geographical position to fulfil a special function in the great work of the world's civilization.'[68]

This statement touches upon three aspects of Blyden's notion of 'racial integrity', a notion which is central to his entire theory. 'Racial integrity' assumes a cultural as well as biological and geographical significance for him. In order to fulfil the God-given task of self-realisation, Africans are expected to uphold their own culture and to protect it against foreign influences. But this kind of 'cultural integrity' can only become a reality if it coincides with certain geographical conditions, i.e. territorial seclusion. This Fate had supposedly provided for Africa whose climate was unsuitable for Europeans and which therefore 'must ever prevent any considerable number of them being resident in Africa'.

It was but a small step from there to demanding 'Africa for the Africans'. Blyden took this step intellectually, but he did not turn into a political agitator against white penetration. He stopped short of this, seeing that the powerful drive of the West into Africa destroyed all hope of an early evacuation of the colonial territories. Instead he took refuge in his racial theories, and it is here that the third, biologistic, aspect of these theories emerged to the surface : the slogan 'Africa for the Africans' now appeared to be a biologically conditioned necessity. Blyden was so convinced of this that it was merely a matter of time for him 'until the laws of Nature made the whites painfully aware that West Africa could be developed only by African agency'.[69]

He thus was completely under the spell of the nationalist notions of his age, in so far as they propagated the homogeneity of a 'race' as being an integral feature of nationhood. The successes of Garibaldi in Italy and of Bismarck in Germany were, according to Blyden, proof of 'the indestructible vitality and tenacity of race'. With the example of the European 'races' in front of him, he always extolled Africa as 'the negro's home'. Without agitating against the colonial masters, Blyden became the untiring promoter of Afro-American re-migration. He kept in close touch with the Colonization Society which had paid for his own migration to Africa. In the course of many lecture tours, he reminded the Afro-Americans that the United States was no more than an exile for them. The true home of the blacks, he said, was Africa. For

> Africa is his, if he will. He may ignore it. He may consider that he is divested of any right to it; but this will not alter his relations to that country, or impair the integrity of his title. He may be content to fight against the fearful odds in this country; but he is the proprietor of a vast domain. He is entitled to a whole continent by his constitution and antecedents.

'Blood ties' gave him the right to settle in Africa.

Blyden felt confirmed in his views by the fact that the emigration movement received its main impulse from the blacks of the American South. 'Their instincts', he believed, 'are less impaired by the infusion of alien blood and by hostile climatic influences. There we find the Negro in the almost unimpaired integrity of his race susceptibility, and he is by an uncontrollable impulse feeling after a congenial atmosphere which his nature tells him he can find only in Africa.' Also the Afro-Americans returning to the homeland would 'find rich and stimulating blood in the Mandingoes and Jalofs and Foulahs; in the Veys, Kroomen, and Greboes. Let him hasten home and mingle his blood with the blood of these tribes, and the fusion will be wholesome . . . [He will] be strengthened and improved by blending with the native tribes.'[70] The ominous notion of race which was so widely held in the nineteenth century found an ardent adherent in Blyden. To him only blacks 'of pure race-stock' were acceptable and he urged the Colonization Society to give priority to their emigration. He abhorred mulattoes, whom he proposed to bar from Africa and whom he called 'a nest of vipers who hate the country and the race'. There can be little doubt that his violent reaction against fair-skinned Afro-Americans stemmed from his own experiences with them. Blyden himself had a very dark skin and he was therefore particularly indignant at the social hierarchy in the United States which was largely based on colour differentiations. He despised mulattoes even more than whites who at least likewise adhered to the idea of racial purity and hence with whom there existed a common meeting ground. Mulattoes, on the other hand, with the 'blood of their oppressors' in their veins, violated Blyden's principles and thus endangered his 'regeneration of Africa', i.e. the racial and hence cultural renaissance of the continent.[71] As was usual in the nineteenth and twentieth centuries, he saw the culture of a particular 'race' as being bound to its genetic structure. As far as environmental factors were concerned, he felt that they could merely influence specific features of culture.

The unique value of African culture now lay in the fact that it was capable of forming a vital counterweight to European culture. He regarded the latter as individualistic and materialistic. He acknowledged that the West had provided the world with great technological innovations, but only at the price of justice in the sense that but a few benefited from the newly created riches. Further corollaries of Western civilisation were mental illnesses, atheism and a rise in the crime rate.[72] The communal organisation of African societies, on the other hand, had provided a fairer distribution of wealth; the close family network had taken better care of the individual. In short, conditions were more favourable from the individual's point of view. In Blyden's view this harmonious order of things also explained certain specific features of the Africans, namely their 'cheerfulness, sympathy, willingness to serve';[73] here Africa's willingness to serve the rest of the world was particularly noteworthy. Africa had been a source of raw materials for Europe and a purveyor of slaves who had helped to develop the United States economically. Since these missions had been imposed by God, there was nothing degrading about them. On the contrary, 'if service rendered to humanity is service rendered to God, then the Negro and his country have been, during the ages, in spite of untoward influences, tending upward to the Divine'. But the most important mission of the Africans was, Blyden argued, to humanise Western materialism. Moreover, black religiosity, friendliness and hospitality predestined them to keep alive the love for the neighbour which was practised by them much more regularly than by 'many a civilized and Christian community'.

Thus Blyden finally came to the conclusion that

Africa may yet prove to be the spiritual conservatory of the world. Just as in past times, Egypt proved the stronghold of Christianity after Jerusalem fell, and just as the noblest and the greatest of the Fathers of the Christian Church came out of Egypt, so it may be, when the civilized nations, in consequence of their wonderful material development, shall have had their spiritual perceptions darkened and their spiritual susceptibilities blunted through the agency of a captivating and absorbing materialism, it may be that they may have to resort to Africa to recover some of the simple elements of faith . . .[74]

Although he continued to hope for the salutary effects of the Christian faith, Blyden nevertheless became increasingly critical of the activities of the missionaries. He even reproached institutionalised Christianity of having aided and abetted racism and imperialism. On the other hand, he was extremely impressed by Islam. He studied the Islamic faith and concluded that it offered a more appropriate form of religion to the Africans because the Muslims practised 'Christian' virtues more frequently in daily life than the Christians. The interest in Islam is thus another area in which Blyden became a forerunner of twentieth-century black nationalism. As with the twentieth-century variety, he turned his back on Christianity in its existing form. For basically he wanted nothing more than a return to a 'purified' Christianity – a Christianity of humility and love. It is typical that he should see Christianity as being 'the ultimate and final religion of humanity. Indeed, I believe that it has always been and always will be the system which raises mankind to the highest level.' Islam, on the other hand, was no more than a transitional form of religion to him. In this sense he therefore did not contradict himself, as one might think at first glance, when he wrote the following : 'These are the views I am now teaching, that Mohammedanism is the form of Christianity best adapted to the Negro race.'[75]

Just like some of his intellectual heirs Blyden clearly idealised Islam and the 'natural communism' of African societies. Nevertheless, and unlike his colleague and contemporary Crummell, he must be credited with having freed African cultures from the stigma of barbarism. He was among the first to open the eyes of blacks on both sides of the Atlantic to the importance of the pre-colonial civilisations of Africa. But in the process, Blyden became more and more alienated from his original profession, Afro-American missionary work. Ultimately he completely identified with Africa and made his name as a leading black nationalist and scholar. He considered it his task to restore the dignity of the black race 'by his insistence on a long and distinguished history of the people of Africa'.[76]

In this respect, Blyden acted as a bridge for the next generation, which developed a new consciousness of Africa. Crummell, on the other hand, remained a true representative of the missionary colonialism of the Afro-American middle classes in the nineteenth century. As we have seen, there existed no marked difference in the image of Africa between the integrationists and those blacks who joined the emigration movement. They merely drew opposite conclusions from their attitude towards Africa. There was a large group which rejected all links with Africa and tried to find salvation in assimilation. The nationalists, on the other hand, regarded separation as the only solution and felt called upon to transform Africa from its state of barbarism into a bridgehead of 'black power'.[77]

(*c*) AFRICA – THE LAND OF PROMISE

The aspirations of free Afro-Americans and of the black middle classes may be said to be well documented and it is thus possible to gain a fairly good view of their attitudes towards Africa. But it is considerably more difficult to reconstruct the ideas of the slaves and the lower strata of black society. As mentioned in the previous chapter, it was only in very recent years that attempts have been made to open up this *terra incognita*. One major obstacle is, of course, that most slaves were illiterate. Even after the abolition of slavery, illiteracy remained a serious problem to which there was only a gradual solution.[78] Moreover, the strict control mechanisms of the slave system militated against the slaves expressing their views. Apart from various rebellions which can be taken to have been very general protests against slavery,[79] primary sources are largely missing which might give an insight into the daily life and thought of slaves. What has survived are semi-literary and oral sources such as folklore and music. However, these sources require particularly sensitive and occasionally even new tools of analysis. For it is important not only to remember the special character of such documents, but also the specific cultural environment in which they originated. According to Patterson, 'the historian relying on non-written sources must discard, to a certain extent, the highly specific and instrumental use of sources and the speedy and mechanical manner in which literary sources are consumed and discarded'.[80] In view of these methodological problems which only specialised studies will be able to unravel, our analysis must confine itself to touching upon certain aspects which may offer some clues as to how the mass of the slaves in the United States looked upon Africa.

The spirituals have traditionally been seen as an important source for an understanding of the slave mentality. As early as 1862 one of the first collectors of slave songs said : 'I dwell on these songs not as a matter of entertainment but of instruction. They tell the whole story of these people's life and character. There is no need, after hearing them, to inquire into the history of the slave's treatment.'[81] And yet most studies have concentrated on the purely musical aspects of the spirituals and investigated their origin. Research is less advanced as far as the texts of spirituals are concerned. Interpreting them poses greater problems and two divergent views have developed, with the controversy going on to this day. For many years a purely religious and Christian interpretation of the spirituals predominated. What gave it plausibility was the assumed 'natural' religiosity of the blacks.[82] But what was conveniently forgotten by its protagonists was that spirituals were not primarily sung in church, but on many other non-religious occasions.

Equally, there existed quite a number of songs which had no religious content at all and which, because some of them even parodied spirituals, became known as 'devil tunes'.[83] It is safe to assume that the majority of these songs have been lost. Spirituals with a religious content are therefore over-represented and this has misled later scholars. One reason for the present imbalance is that the first transcripts of spirituals were made by whites and more particularly by white ministers 'who had little understanding of the culture from which they [the spirituals] sprang, and little scruple about altering or suppressing, undesirable texts. Some of them even admitted 'that many of the songs they collected were "unprintable" by the moral standards which guided them.' To this must be added the fact that even well-meaning whites found it difficult to overcome black distrust. More than once a collector therefore merely heard those songs which 'the black man wanted him to hear'.[84]

In view of the considerable distortions which many spirituals experienced and of the undiluted 'realism' of some of them, other experts came to doubt the purely religious interpretation of the texts. Miles M. Fisher in his well-known study finally arrived at the opposite conclusion and argued that spirituals contained no religious elements whatsoever. He saw them as mirrors of the social reality in which the slaves were forced to live. Although Fisher's book offers many invaluable insights into the character of the spirituals, his analysis was, it appears, just as one-sided as the earlier hypothesis. He was no doubt on the right track in feeling that a religious interpretation in the traditional sense failed to do justice to the problem. But to reject it completely did not imply that he had successfully 'transcended' it. In the final analysis, neither Fisher nor his opponents provided a satisfactory approach to the subject because they never tried to define their central concept, i.e. religiosity, or if they did, they interpreted it in the Christian-occidental tradition as being a purely transcendental phenomenon.

Yet spirituals, as we now know, cannot be approached in the same way as we approach 'white' hymns. This is true at least of all those songs which originated from a slave population which, for all practical purposes, remained largely unassimilated. Large-scale Christianisation started relatively late, i.e. not before the nineteenth century. There was hence a considerable period in which religions brought across the Atlantic were adapted to the changed conditions in the United States and transformed into a specifically Afro-American brand of religion with clearly discernible African features.[85]

Whereas Christianity makes a sharp distinction between the day-to-day social and religious spheres and, in fact, sees them as antitheses, African religions include the transcendental world of God very directly

C

in the human world. For the slaves, religion similarly 'never constituted a simple escape from this world, because their conception of the world was more expansive than modern man's . . . Their religious songs, like their religion itself, was of this world as well as the next.' This meant that stories from the Bible were taken by the slaves as reflecting their own immediate predicament. Events and personalities from the Old Testament, 'all of whom were delivered in *this* world and were delivered in ways which struck the imagination of the slaves', were frequently used as examples.[86] Since the slaves did not pray for deliverance from sin, we rarely find a consciousness of sin – a central concept of Christianity – in spirituals. What the slaves were hoping for was in fact liberation from slavery. They wanted a life in freedom in this world.[87] It was because they believed God and the personages of the Bible to be so near to them that they found this hope. The spirituals therefore offered to many Afro-Americans a sort of emotional safety valve. They permitted the individual slave 'to express deeply held feelings which he ordinarily was not allowed to verbalize'.[88] The ambivalence of the Biblical language enabled him to articulate his protest and his desire to be free with impunity. Ex-slaves have frequently pointed to the ambiguous language of spirituals. Booker T. Washington, for example, wrote in his autobiography :

Most of the verses of the plantation songs had some reference to freedom. True, they had sung those same verses before, but they had been careful to explain that the 'freedom' in these songs referred to the next world, and had no connection with life in this world. Now they gradually threw off the mask ; and were not afraid to let it be known that freedom in their songs meant freedom of the body in this world.[89]

A similar statement has survived from Harriet Tubman who helped many slaves to escape to the North :

Slaves must not be seen talking together, and so it came about that their communication was often made by singing, and the words of their familiar hymns, telling of the heavenly journey, and land of Canaan, while they did not attract the attention of the masters, conveyed to their brethren and sisters in bondage something more than met the ear.[90]

But the secret messages did not only refer to a general desire to be free, but also to countries like Canada for which Canaan was merely a code. Similarly, as ex-slaves have confirmed, the 'Yankee' in the North was translated into the 'Lord' whom one asked to bring liberty.[91] Since the slaves could not dare to say that they wished to return to Africa, they also had to use code-words to express a desire for emigration. In fact the spirituals contain only few direct references to Africa. But a number of texts permit the conclusion that Africa was at times included in the list of deliberate linguistic ambiguities.

This point, which will be illustrated below, must be seen against the following background. First of all we must remember that there existed a lively interest in emigration among the slaves and the lower strata of Afro-American society. It led to thousands of blacks applying either to the ACS or other organisations in order to return to Africa. They represented those who were 'the most alienated from society and therefore the group most likely to identify with Africa'.[92] This is why we must also add a rider to the ACS statistics mentioned above.[93] The Society insisted that only such people be given support who had a basic education, belonged to a Christian church and, if possible, had learned some craft. Yet most of those who wanted to emigrate were 'barely literate, poverty-stricken individuals'. They failed to obtain ACS support and very few of them had saved enough money to pay for their liberation, not to speak of the passage across the Atlantic. In view of this, the figures which we have are very unlikely to be an 'index to the sentiment for colonization, as most of those who expressed a desire to go were never able to do so'.[94]

Letters to the ACS provide ample evidence of this. In these documents, slaves time and again asked the Society to pay for their liberation and to send them to Africa. The letters also show that Africa was an important topic of conversation in many parts of the American South. The pros and cons of emigration were discussed with considerable passion.[95] Moreover, there were many slaves who were actually born in Africa and who by reporting on their background kept the memory of Africa alive. Imports of slaves continued up to the middle of the nineteenth century and the newcomers guaranteed that contact was never lost.[96] Former slaves have added their own testimony and confirmed the existence of uninterrupted contacts. They reported that there were some slaves 'who were born in Africa [and who] would sing some of their songs or tell different stories of the customs in Africa'.[97] The following report by an ex-slave is interesting because it relates how a spiritual was created in the course of a church service :

And, honey, de Lord would come a-shinin' thoo dem pages and revive dis ole nigger's heart, and I'd jump up dar and den and holler and shout and sing and pat, and dey would all cotch the words and I'd sing it to some ole shout song I'd heard 'em sing from Africa, and dey'd all take it up and keep at it, and keep a-addin' to it, and den it would be a spiritual.[98]

In short, Africa never fell into oblivion among the slave population. The following spirituals may serve as further illustrations of how strongly the blacks identified with the continent beyond the Atlantic :

> See these poor souls from Africa
> Transported to America;
> We are stolen, and sold in Georgia.

> Working all day
> And part of the night,
> And up before the morning light.
> When will Jehovah hear our cry
> And free the sons of Africa ?[99]

Freehling, in his study on slavery, mentions a revealing episode. In 1833 a missionary lectured in front of a mixed audience on 'the degradation, physical, intellectual, moral and religious, of the African tribes he had visited' and argued that life as a slave was much better if compared with life in Africa. His white listeners nodded approvingly, as might be expected. But 'in the gallery, "many of the slaves, offended at the accounts Mr. P. gave of their countrymen in Africa . . . rose and left the house in disgust".'[100]

So far we have concentrated on the notion of Africa as the 'homeland' of the slaves, and in fact this was the notion which traditionally had been most widespread. Both black nationalist leaders and members of the lower strata of black society talked in this vein. One such ordinary Afro-American put it rather touchingly like this : 'I am bin Looking in my mind for a home and I find that Liberia the onley place of injoyment for the Culerd man and their fore I wish to in form you that I the Said Peter Butler wish to be and Emigrant for that Land of my auntsestors as I wish to do them all the Good in this World.'[101]

It has already been mentioned that most slaves were illiterate. However, a few of them came from the Islamic parts of Africa and wrote their autobiographies in the Arab language. Here, too, Africa appears as the true homeland of the blacks and as the 'promised land of freedom from slavery'.[102] The spirituals contain many allusions to this :

> I am huntin' for a home, to stay awhile,
> O Believer / Po' sinner / got a home at las'.

> Sometimes I feel like a motherless child,
> A long ways from home.[103]

The following might be taken as a song by an emigrant cheerfully bidding farewell :

> Good-bye, my brudder, good-bye, / Hallelujah !
> Good-bye, sister Sally, good-bye, / Hallelujah !
> Going home / Hallelujah !
> Jesus call me / Hallelujah !
> Linger no longer / Hallelujah !
> Tarry no longer / Hallelujah !

Another emigrant announces his journey across the Atlantic by singing :

> Old Satan told me to my face / O yes, Lord,
> De God I seek I never find / O yes, Lord,
> True believer, I know when I gwine home.

These and other spirituals seem to justify the conclusion that the term 'home' was not merely used in its transcendental meaning, but referred specifically to Africa. 'Heaven' may be regarded as another synonym for Africa. The following spiritual implores Jesus to lead the slaves on to the road which they know so well. It then continues :

> Heaven bell a-ring, I know de road,
> Jesus sittin' on de waterside.
> Do come along, do let us go,
> Jesus sittin' on de waterside.

Another example is this spiritual which objects to the whites' excluding black Christians from the Service on grounds that they were too noisy :

> When I get to Heaven goin' to sing and shout,
> Nobody there for turn me out.

Or take the following lines :

> Dere's room enough, room enough in de heaven, my Lord,
> Room enough, room enough, I can't stay behind.

These lines might also be interpreted in the sense that Africa is being praised here as a country which offered sufficient space and freedom for the Afro-Americans to do what they felt like doing.

As the letters to the ACS demonstrate, emigrants regularly corresponded from Liberia with their friends and relatives back in the United States : 'Dear Sir, I had the plesur of receving a letter from my wife in Liberia informing me of hur good healt and hur injoying of hur freedom in a land which afords me much plesur.' Or : 'I have Recd leters from my Relation in Lince Greanvill all well and Ear much please with thear a dopted country & Ear doing well.'[104] The argument that 'heaven' or 'home' were synonymous for Africa receives further support through the notion, widespread among Afro-Americans, that their soul would travel 'home to Africa' after their death.[105]

It has already been mentioned that blacks who called themselves 'Sons of Africa' regarded themselves as direct descendants of the Children of Israel. Obviously, the sufferings of the Jews, who like the Africans lived in captivity and wanted to be led back to their homeland, provided a perfect allegory for the blacks in the United States. By going to Liberia they expected 'delivernce fr the present Bondege an degredation they ear labering ounder'.[106] In view of such exaggerated expectations with which the emigrants went to Liberia, it is all too understandable that Africa assumed a mythical importance in their mind. In the end, religious and worldly elements became inseparably intertwined. Africa as the 'land of Promis to the collord men' was therefore a widely used expression among emigrants.[107] And it recurs with similar frequency in spirituals :

> Don't you see that ship a-sailin'
> Gwine over to the Promised Land?
> I asked my Lord, shall I ever be the one,
> to go sailin', sailin', sailin',
> Gwine over to the Promised Land?

Thus Canaan does not only appear to stand for Canada or the North of the United States, as has been mentioned above, but also for Africa. Here are two examples : the title of an article talks about an 'African Canaan for American Negro',[108] and a spiritual runs as follows :

> O brothers, don't get weary,
> We're waiting for the Lord.
> We'll land on Canaan's shore,
> We'll meet forever more.

Water plays a literally crucial part in the spirituals, usually recurring as 'River Jordan'. Evidently this can be regarded as a code-word for the Atlantic Ocean which represents the greatest obstacle between the Afro-American world and the 'Land of Promise' :

> Deep river, my home is over Jordan, Deep river,
> Lord, I want to cross over into campground;

Lord, I want to cross over into campground;
Oh, chillun, Oh don't you want to go to that gospel feast,
That promised land, that land where all is peace?
Walk into heaven and take my seat,
And cast my crown at Jeses feet.
Lord, I want to cross over into campground.
Deep river, my home is over Jordan, Deep river.

'Campground' is a reference to the cult sites of the slaves where they met at night to carry on their own rituals. Significantly enough the whites called these activities 'the African cult'. It was also on these occasions that contact was made between the slaves who had lived in this area for a long time and those who had just arrived from Africa.[109] If seen in this context, even the term 'campground' in the above spiritual could be interpreted as signifying Africa – Africa as the homeland not merely of the slaves but also of their God.

Finally, it emerges from the letters to the ACS that people took a lively interest in the sailings of ships to Liberia. Time and again the Society was asked to furnish copies of its newspaper, *The African Repository*, so that emigrants and their relatives could inform themselves about times of departure. Redkey tells us about a farewell ceremony, celebrated with considerable pomp at the turn of the century, at which some 300 emigrants were seen off by some 5000 people, gathered along the quay of Savannah. Not all sailings, to be sure, turned into such an impressive spectacle and certainly not before the abolition of slavery. But the ritual itself does not seem to be untypical of what happened on these occasions : the glory of Africa and the great future of Liberia were praised in a long speech, interrupted by the audience's shouting of 'Amen', 'Hallelujah' and 'God bless Liberia'. The meeting ended with the crowd on the quay and on board ship singing : 'I am going home to part no more.'[110] This event in the harbour of Savannah provides another good illustration of the interesting link between the religious and social spheres in Afro-American life or, as Levine puts it, of the 'process of incorporating within this world all the elements of the Divine'.[111] It was a merger of the two spheres which finds its reflection also in the spirituals. Against this background, one can also see the frequent mention of 'Ship of Zion' or, simply, of sailing to assume a very direct significance :

Dis de good ole ship o' Zion :
And she's makin' for de Promis Land.

Just as 'Lord' had been serving as a code-word for both God and the Northerner, many spirituals show that Jesus is frequently transformed into a figure of the Old Testament, a martial saviour. He is portrayed as a 'conquering king', a 'man of war', a commander of an army.[112] It is not even impossible to picture him as the master of a ship on its way to Africa.

There are other spirituals in which visions of a life in freedom are blended with images of an idealised Africa. It is a continent without slave work which one is forced to perform in rain and snow :

> No more rain fall for wet you,
> No more sun shine for burn you,
> No more parting in den kingdom,
> No more backbiting in den kingdom,
> Every day shall be sunday.

There are other references which correspond to the lines quoted so far. Liberia (or Africa in general) is described as the land of sun, as in 'suny shores of Liberia' and 'Africa's suny clime'. Another letter to the ACS gives an impression of the fantastic notions which circulated about Liberia (and of which the above-mentioned poem by Horton may serve as another illustration) : 'My Thoughts Ran with lightning Speed across the Great Atlantic to the future home [of my friends] and contemplating them under their own vine and figg tree in full Enjoyment of all the Blessings of True Freedom and Equality.'[113]

The evidence presented in this chapter ought to have shown that there exists a remarkable correlation in the use of images in the sources which can hardly be regarded as accidental. Everything rather seems to point to the existence of a specific attitude towards Africa among the lower strata of the black population. In it memories of Africa merge with the desire to return to the 'homeland'. It is a feeling which, if compared with that of the black middle classes, is fairly unbroken and alive. Since the blacks desired nothing more urgently than their liberation from the chains of slavery and economic misery, Africa regularly appears as a place of freedom. It is idealised as a sort of El Dorado and this occasionally led to serious disappointments when the emigrants came face to face with the hardships and deprivations of their new life as settlers in West Africa. But if Africa was idealised, then the same did not necessarily apply to her inhabitants. As the letters to the ACS show, the influence of the regeneration movement, as transmitted by the missionaries, can also be discovered in places. Thus wrote a slave : 'I Beleav [it] is from god that I should go to Liberia and Spend and Be Spent in that field to Preaching the gospel to those milans who are in heathon Darkness thearfore I was ConStrand to ask my master the Liberty to Try purchase myself . . .'[114]

## III ON THE THRESHOLD OF THE TWENTIETH CENTURY – THE GENESIS OF THE 'NEW NEGRO'

The interest of the lower strata of Black American society in Africa which has just been examined went through a period of decline during and after the Civil War, only to experience a revival from about 1880 onwards. The ACS for instance reported in 1891 that never during its whole history had applications been so 'numerous and urgent'. Among the black middle classes the majority still rejected emigration; but many members 'did maintain an ethnic identification with Africa'[115] which developed into a distinct nationalism towards the end of the century. It manifested itself above all in a growing interest in the history of Africa and in an effort to correct the traditional and negative, 'white' image by promoting a better understanding of Africa's civilisations and history. They were concerned to 'vindicate the race' by 'setting the record straight', by defending themselves against the charge of 'a people without a past' and of being the descendants of 'savage and uncivilized people'.[116] This trend to 'rehabilitate Africa' had first set in around the middle of the century. But the emphasis had then been put on ancient Ethiopia or Egypt and on the negroid elements in these civilisations since people were clearly less certain about the value of the West African cultures.[117] It must also be remembered that educational facilities at schools and universities improved only towards the end of the century; early authors thus often proceeded in rather an amateurish fashion.[118] None the less – together with authors like Delany, Crummell and Blyden who directed public interest towards West Africa – they provided a basis for a more profound consciousness of Africa and for a more thorough examination of the subject. The same trend is reflected also in the founding of a number of historical societies which took place around the turn of the century. They aimed at collecting facts and documents concerning the history of the Afro-Americans. The most important of these societies were the Negro Society for Historical Research, founded in 1912, and more particularly the Association for the Study of Negro Life and History (ASNLH), founded in 1915. Significantly enough the first encouraged Afro-Americans to learn Arabic, arguing that many aspects of their lives were interwoven with Islamic-African traditions and with the history of that part of the world. The second society was founded by Carter G. Woodson who, after DuBois, was the most important black historian in the first half of this century. In his works Woodson emphasised the value of Africa for an understanding of Afro-American culture. He believed that 'the contemporary school of thought which taught that the American Negro had been torn completely from his African roots in the process of enslavement had done incalculable harm, especially in the education and training of younger Negro scholars'.[119] He therefore gave much space to articles about Africa in the journal of the ASNLH, the *Journal of Negro History*, which he founded and edited, and which remains an important periodical today.

Parallel with this more or less scholarly interest in Africa there developed an interest in the history and culture of the Negroes in America. The rehabilitation of Africa also caused black popular culture, much denigrated hitherto, to be seen in a different light. This process resulted in the founding of associations such as the 'Society for the Collection of Negro Folk Lore' in Boston. Crummell took an important part in these developments and was elected one of the presidents of the 'American Negro Academy', founded in 1897. Its main aim was to further scientific, literary and other artistic activities of the Afro-Americans.[120] For the new positive attitude towards their own culture stimulated Afro-American creativity and led to first cautious attempts to express their newly-found consciousness – it would be too early to speak of self-confidence – in prose or lyric poetry. Black authors were even advised to look for material on the islands off Georgia and South Carolina, 'where they could study the Negro in his original purity', and as part of an almost untouched African culture.[121]

This awakening cultural nationalism cannot be separated from a growing feeling of a 'racial' solidarity, of 'Negro Nationality', which must be seen as a reaction against the rising hostility of the white population. This solidarity manifested itself in various organisations, such as those for the defence of civil rights which DuBois above all had initiated, the 'Niagara-Movement', and its successor, the National Organisation for the Advancement of Colored People (NAACP). It also found expression in an 'economic nationalism' which Booker T. Washington, the most famous Negro leader of that time, proclaimed with great vigour as well as in the founding of numerous 'Liberia Emigration Clubs', and in the migrations within the United States which aimed at establishing purely black parishes. A similar feeling of solidarity, and one which was possibly even more important for the future, was touched off by the urbanisation of Afro-Americans which started around 1915 and which originated in the great shortage of labour in the towns of the north with their war industries and their new prosperity. This development was accompanied by the formation of ghettos, by a slowly growing 'black' economy, but also by economic discrimination and violent racial disturbances. Throughout the country the numbers of violent crimes committed by whites, particularly lynch-murders, reached new heights. This was a reaction against the growing determination to resist on the part of the blacks. They wanted to see democracy – which was after all being defended in the war in Europe

— realised in their own country. The wave of white hostility in turn intensified the consciousness of 'racial' solidarity and strengthened existing nationalist tendencies further.[122] These eventually led to profound changes in the consciousness of the Afro-Americans and were instrumental in creating a New Negro whose ideal type has been described by Meier as being

> resourceful, independent, raceproud, economically advancing, and ready to tackle political and cultural ambitions. He believed in collective economic effort, for the most part denied any interest in social equality, and at the same time denounced the inequities of American racism and insisted upon his citizenship right. He was interested in the race and its past; he was becoming more conscious of his relationship with other colored peoples and with Africa – an identification which the lower classes perhaps never really lost.[123]

But a closer look at the image which this New Negro had of Africa, shows that his relationship to his country of origin and to other black peoples was much more complex and ambivalent than Meier makes out. This is shown particularly clearly in the case of one of the fathers of the concept of the New Negro who was at the same time an early representative of this type : W. E. B. DuBois. He was one of the most important and controversial personalities in the whole of Afro-American history. His image of Africa – as it emerges from his literary work – will be analysed in greater detail in the following chapter.

# 3 Pan-Africa as a Myth in the Literary Work of DuBois

DuBois's meandering career, his long life (1868–1963), and his lively temperament which may well be responsible for a number of ambiguities in his world of ideas have stood in the way of an unequivocal critical assessment of him.[1] The often conflicting means and devices which he used to pursue his aims are confusing, unless one simply sees him as an 'opportunist'.[2] But the 'Paradox of W. E. B. DuBois'[3] can perhaps be solved by attempting to discover the underlying impulse on which his restless search for new ways is based. Such an approach shows that there *is* continuity in DuBois's life, namely in his faithful adherence to ideas which he formed in his youth back in the nineteenth century. These ideas and concepts revolve around his interest in the cultural progress of the 'black race' and in Africa : 'On it he centred some of his most personal and some of his largest dreams.'[4] His greatness, but ultimately his failure as well, are based on his strongly emotional attachment to these two concepts. There can be no doubt that his achievement is imposing; through his writings and his actions he was an indefatigable defender of the emancipation of Black Americans and Africans. He influenced black attitudes more than any other Afro-American leader and contributed to the formation of a 'black consciousness'. His historical representations and poetical descriptions of Africa inspired many Afro-Americans with enthusiasm and helped them to overcome their shame at their 'primitive' origin.[5] His rhetorically brilliant analyses of the reality of Afro-American life and Africa's role among the shifting forces of the European powers were also very influential.[6] He possessed the perspective of the Afro-American and the sensibility of the oppressed, and this enabled him to recognise a large number of problems and to articulate them persuasively, thereby helping other Afro-Americans to acquire a better understanding of their own predicament. His achievement, directly and indirectly, as a 'motor' of black history is not belittled by errors he made or by his sometimes grotesque vanity and egocentricity.

Nonetheless his untiring political and journalistic activity may easily give the misleading impression that his relation to men of dark skin generally and to the 'dark' continent in particular was wholly positive.

This was not so; his attitude was much more ambivalent than is implied by his reputation as one of the greatest 'black leaders' in the history of America and as the supposed author of the 'whole concept of what is today known as black consciousness'.[7]

The best insight into his attitude to Africa is gained through his 'personal' – or better, 'literary' – writings, i.e. his essays, novels and poems, where his lively imagination is freely displayed. The present chapter examines these writings in order to clarify his relationship with Africa and black people generally – two subjects which cannot be separated when one talks of DuBois. These writings have generally been neglected hitherto or have been looked upon as divorced from DuBois's political and sociological thinking. Certainly, they offer a particularly important key to an understanding of DuBois's ideas about Africa and the role of blacks, as well as of the hopes and dreams which 'spilled over' into his political thinking and actions. While his sociological studies, articles, commentaries, 'Editorials', programmes and pamphlets show up individual aspects of his overall system of ideas, the closed form of his literary works provides a more complex insight. His literary production enables us to trace many of his ideas about Africa and blacks back to their roots, and to reinterpret his ideas with the help of the newly-found perspective.

Even a superficial reading will refute Broderick's assumption that DuBois was bound to the 'dark' continent by a 'deep racial kinship'.[8] On the contrary, DuBois turned to Africa consciously and at a relatively late date. He had little contact with other blacks during his childhood and youth, and Africa meant nothing to him. There was only one single cultural link between his family and Africa of which he was conscious, and DuBois takes pains to give a lovingly embroidered description of this detail in all his autobiographical writings :

My grandfather's grandmother was seized by an evil Dutch trader two centuries ago; and coming to the valleys of the Hudson and Housatonic, black, little, and lithe, she shivered and shrank in the harsh north winds, looked longingly at the hills, and often crooned a heathen melody to the children between her knees, thus :

Do bana coba, gene me, gene me ! Do bana coba, gene me, gene me !
Ben d'nuli, nuli, nuli, ben d'le.

The child sang it to his children and they to their children's children, and so two hundred years it has travelled down to us and we sing it to our children, knowing as little as our fathers what its words may mean, but knowing well the meaning of its music.[9]

This little song, of which he did not even know the meaning, could hardly serve as the basis of an 'African' identity. His decision none the less to adopt Africa, which was completely unknown to him, as his 'motherland', as a 'homeland' to which one is bound by personal and emotional bonds, and to think of himself simply as an 'African', is doubtless a problematical one. He himself seems to have become conscious of this later when he strove for a more discriminating attitude towards Africa :

> . . . neither my father nor my father's father ever saw Africa or knew its meaning or cared overmuch for it. My mother's folk were closer and yet their direct connection, in culture and race, became tenuous; still, my tie to Africa is strong. On this vast continent were born and lived a large portion of my ancestors going back a thousand years or more. The mark of their heritage is upon me in color and hair. These are obvious things, but of little meaning in themselves; only important as they stand for real and more subtle differences from other men. Whether they do or not, I do not know nor does science know today.[10]

These lines correctly characterise the attitudes of many Afro-Americans to Africa – except his own. For there is hardly another American black who thought the 'physical bond' and the 'badge of color' to be as important as DuBois did. He himself complains in another passage that 'every ideal and habit of my life was cruelly misjudged . . . white people said I was ashamed of my race and wanted to be white! And this of me, whose one life fanaticism had been belief in my Negro blood!'[11] These two apparently contradictory statements represent the two poles between which DuBois moved. But the contradiction disappears when one looks in detail at his attitude towards Africa.

Like many Afro-Americans DuBois conceived his ideas about Africa and the mission of the 'black race' in hostile reaction against the white majority. These ideas can therefore only be understood if they are seen in connection with their causes, that is DuBois's subjective and objective predicament. To put it differently : the key to DuBois's ideas and dreams lies in his individual experiences, his personal contact with the racism of his time of which he gives many examples in his autobiographical writings. Moreover, DuBois, more than any other black 'leader', equated his own world-view, which was the view of a black bourgeois intellectual, with that of all blacks. This means that his concept of Negro liberation and the Pan-Africanism which he developed in the course of his life must be seen largely as an abstraction from his own experiences, as a transposition of his personal formula for success and, equally of his group interest. Thus we must first of all examine those factors in DuBois's life which clearly exerted a major influence on his attitude towards Africa and the blacks. It suffices at this point to hint at the roots of his ideas, since the ideas themselves are analysed later in greater detail on the basis of his novels and essays.

## I  BLACK AND WHITE IN DUBOIS'S WORLD OF IDEAS

DuBois was born in Great Barrington, a small town in Massachusetts, in 1868, where he spent the years of his childhood and early youth. His New England origin was to be quite important, as he himself confessed : 'In general thought and conduct I became quite thoroughly New England.'[12] None the less, he tried to deny that the hated Anglo-Saxons had had any influence on him by emphasising that his parish belonged to the Dutch rather than the Anglo-Saxon valley of the Hudson and by boasting that he had no Anglo-Saxon blood in his veins; and yet the culture of New England left its indelible stamp on him to the end of his life. His attitude towards people was to be determined above all by the puritanical moral values of a small town : 'The marriage laws and family relations were fairly firm. The chief delinquency was drunkenness and the major social problem of the better classes was the status of women who had little or no opportunity to marry.' But the 'essence' of his life was, as he thought,

> race – not so much scientific race, as that deep conviction of myriads of men that congenital differences among the main masses of human beings absolutely condition the individual destiny of every member of a group. Into the spiritual provincialism of this belief I have been born and this fact has guided, embittered, illuminated and enshrouded my life.

It is not unimportant that DuBois's painful experience of the racism in his country came relatively late when his self-confidence had become sufficiently consolidated and could no longer be profoundly shaken. As he himself reports, he experienced hardly any racial problems at school. There were few Afro-Americans in Great Barrington, and it was therefore not necessary to draw a clear line separating blacks from whites, even though such a line existed unofficially. The general contempt for the 'poor, drunken and sloven' Irish and South Germans living in the slums – which the black population shared – helped to obscure the 'color line'. DuBois's schoolmates were often the sons of affluent whites whom he outstripped in intelligence and performance at school and who frequently chose him to be their leader at play. Because of this he thought of himself as belonging to the 'rich and well-to-do', although his own family lived in modest circumstances. Isaacs thinks that 'his natural impulse was to gravitate to the top'.[13] The older DuBois grew, however, the clearer it became that this 'impulse' was not quite so 'natural'; rather it seems to have originated in a psychological compensating mechanism. For gradually DuBois did grow conscious of the fact that his darker skin and his slightly negroid physiognomy were regarded as a blemish by a number of whites and that 'some human beings even thought it a crime'. But he refused to be disconcerted by this attitude, '. . . although, of course, there were some days of secret tears; rather I was spurred to tireless effort. If they beat me at anything, I was grimly determined to make them sweat for it!' And indeed he succeeded, through diligence and energy, in turning his negroid appearance into an advantage; it set him visibly apart from his peers and helped to emphasise his above-average intelligence all the more clearly. He won the respect of his schoolmates, and this led him to assume that 'the secret of life and the losing of the color bar, then, lay in excellence, in accomplishment . . . There was no real discrimination on account of color – it was all a matter of ability and hard work.' This ethic of work and accomplishment governed his whole life : 'God is Work', one of his fictional characters says. Nor did he ever abandon his childhood belief in the power and superiority of knowledge above all other human activities.

DuBois developed yet another, very characteristic, attitude during his early youth : in order to avoid being humiliated he never sought contact with whites himself. This meant that his schoolmates were never given an opportunity 'to refuse me invitations; they must seek me out and urge me to come, as indeed they often did. When my presence was not wanted they had only to refrain from asking.' Even when, later, after some initial difficulties, he had won a place at Harvard, he was too proud to seek associations with white students. He even boasted of not having known most of his contemporaries, some of whom became very well known later. Yet he is frank enough to admit that

> something of a certain inferiority complex was possibly a cause of this. I was desperately afraid of intruding where I was not wanted; . . . I should in fact have been pleased if most of my fellow students had wanted to associate with me; if I had been popular and envied. But the absence of this made me neither unhappy nor morose. I had my 'island within' and it was a fair country.

Above all he avoided white or very light-skinned 'black' women and for the same reason rejected any thought of racial mixing : 'I resented the assumption that we desired it.' These and similar statements show how deeply DuBois's pride was hurt by any actual or potential threat of being rejected by the whites. 'He wanted recognition, acceptance, eminence, a life among peers. When he was denied, he cut himself off.'[14] Thus DuBois – who had spent his early youth primarily in the company of whites – developed into a passionate black nationalist; it was among blacks that he would find the satisfaction of his pride which the whites had denied him. This need 'to show it to the whites', to prove to them that blacks are equal or even superior to them which grew out of humiliations is one – maybe even the most important – root of his later cultural nationalism, and it explains as well as any other reason his fixation with white culture.

But before we move on to this point, an important intermediate stage on this journey into the cultural ghetto must be considered : the time he spent at Fisk, the black University in Tennessee where he had been sent after leaving school. It is true that, having seen himself as part of the élite of his school, he had unwarily chosen Harvard for his further education; but this first attempt failed, as was to be expected. This rejection was an important turning-point in his life. It completed his deliberate isolation from the world of the whites and his conscious identification with the Afro-Americans whom he met in large numbers for the first time at Fisk University : 'Into this world I leapt with enthusiasm. A new loyalty and allegiance replaced my Americanism : henceforward I was a Negro.' But as the world of the blacks was his second home, the country of his choice, he could not fail to idealise his *Ersatz* group to compensate for the loss of that group of which he had originally felt himself to be a member. This idealisation was all the easier for him as he had lived largely isolated from the rest of the black community at Great Barrington and had acquired little knowledge of their way of life. Thus his descriptions of his first contact with the South and with his 'brothers' not only reflect the charm of novelty, but also clearly betray an attempt at idealisation :

Consider, for a moment, how miraculous it all was to a boy of seventeen, just escaped from a narrow valley : I willed and lo ! my people came dancing about me, – riotous in color, gay in laughter, full of sympathy, need, and pleading; darkly delicious girls – 'colored' girls – sat beside me and actually talked to me while I gazed in tongue-tied silence or babbled in boastful dreams. Boys with my own experience and out of my own world, who knew and understood, wrought out with me great remedies . . . I was thrilled to be for the first time among so many people of my own color or rather of such various and such extraordinary colors, which I had only glimpsed before, but who it seemed were bound to me by new and exciting and eternal ties . . . at Fisk the never-to-be-forgotten marvel of that first supper came with me opposite two of the most beautiful beings God ever revealed to the eyes of 17. I promptly lost my appetite, but I was deliriously happy !

At Fisk he came into contact with all the problems which confronted the blacks in the South : racial hatred, lynch murders, ignorance and poverty of the blacks as a result of ubiquitous discriminations. DuBois, full of energy and with his self-confidence relatively unharmed, was far from being discouraged by the depressing situation of the 1880s. In his eyes the group which had to bear all that misery was no 'lost group', but 'a microcosm of a world and a civilization in potentiality'. For at Fisk he had not only discovered the existence of an independent black culture, 'a closed racial group with rites and loyalties, with a history and a corporate future, with an art and philosophy', but also became convinced of the great potential for development inherent in this black group : 'There was not the slightest idea of the permanent subordination and inequality of my world.' And it was this belief in 'the ability and future of black folk', which, when he went to Harvard, caused him to continue voluntarily the segregation which he knew from his stay in the South. However, he did not strive for definitive separation. He emphasised repeatedly that this 'black nationalism', as it would be called today, should only be seen as a necessary stage of transition on the way to a society in which 'full human intercourse without reservations and annoying distinctions' would be achieved. This hope or even conviction, he went on, 'made me all too willing to consort now with my own and to disdain and forget as far as was possible that outer, whiter world'. His aim was thus to integrate the blacks into a free 'truly democratic' society, and he did not doubt that it would come. As he himself says, his criticism was not directed against 'the world movement in itself. What the white world was doing, its goals and ideals, I had not doubted were quite right. What was wrong was that I and people like me and thousands of others who might have my ability and aspiration, were refused permission to be part of this world.'

The blacks had to be prepared for this future world; and this was to be done through education, disseminated by an élite – yet to be created – of Afro-Americans trained at black universities. This educated class, the 'Talented Tenth', would ascetically renounce all self-interest and like DuBois guide the black masses solely by means of their knowledge and experience, so that eventually, with the help of this élite and 'in mass assault, led by culture, we Negroes were going to break down the boundaries of race; but at present we were banded together in a great crusade and happily so'. This was the foundation on which most of DuBois's later ideas and theories were built : his belief in the power of knowledge, in the 'educative' force of culture, capable of bringing about changes, and in the establishment of an intellectual élite in possession of this culture and able to lead the masses; and even DuBois's anti-materialism emerges in these early statements.

Full of these budding ideas he set out in 1892 on his great journey to Europe; his energy and his excellent academic record had got him a grant. In accordance with his maxim that the black élite should receive the best possible education he had decided 'that what I needed was further training in Europe'. It was not by chance that he chose Germany and Berlin as his place of study. German universities had an excellent reputation at that time, so that 'any American scholar who wanted preferment went to Germany for study'; also, while at Fisk, he had first become interested in the aspirations of the German *Reich*. In complete ignorance of the real circumstances – as he himself was to realise later – he had chosen 'Bismarck' as the topic of his final examination. For

> Bismarck was my hero. He had made a nation out of a mass of bickering peoples. He had dominated the whole development with his strength until he crowned an emperor at Versailles. This foreshadowed in my mind the kind of thing that American Negroes must do marching forth with strength and determination under trained leadership.

Thus he went to Europe, thirsting for knowledge, keen to learn and to receive new impulses for his life's work, the unification and liberation of the black people under the leadership of an élite. As was to be expected, the contact with the Old World became a key experience for him. On a superficial level this can be seen from the fact that thenceforth his writings are embellished with quotations from German classical authors, particularly Goethe, that he openly displayed his intimate knowledge of European, and particularly German, music, and that – out of admiration for the Crown Prince – he 'even trimmed [his] beard and moustache to a fashion like his and still follow[s] it'. But the influence was much more profound than this; DuBois states that Europe

> modified profoundly my outlook on life and my thought and feeling toward it, even though I was there but two short years with my contacts limited and my friends few. But something of the possible beauty and elegance of life permeated my soul; I gained a respect for manners. I had been before, above all, in a hurry. I wanted a world, hard, smooth and swift, and had no time for rounded corners and ornament, for unhurried thought and slow contemplation. Now at times I sat still, I came to know Beethoven's Symphonies and Wagner's *Ring*. I looked long at the colors of Rembrandt and Titian, I saw in arch and stone and steeple the history and striving of men and also their taste and expression. Form, color and words took new combinations and meanings.

Yet the fascination which the old bourgeois world of Europe and particularly of Germany had for him is not so much explained by the fact that, as DuBois thought, its culture revealed to him entirely new habits of thought and life, but rather by a kind of spiritual affinity. His own personal leanings which have been outlined above were almost identical with very similar tendencies in the Wilhelmine Germany before the turn of the century. Even if it seems surprising at first glance, this affinity was not accidental.

The black middle class grew in strength towards the end of the nineteenth century and began to look for means to overcome the suppression and obstruction of their economic progress by the dominant white society.[15] This quickly led to a polarisation : one group, usually the largest by far and headed by Booker T. Washington, renounced political influence from the beginning in favour of economic development and sought compensation in a rigorous social hierarchy chiefly based on education and gradations of skin colour.[16] Another, much smaller, group sought compensation for their lack of power through the ideal of an educated élite, an ideal which DuBois, the self-proclaimed spokesman of this group, defined in 1903 as the 'Talented Tenth' theory.[17] Both groups shared the optimistic liberal belief in progress typical of the nineteenth century. DuBois himself was not fundamentally opposed to economic development, at certain times he even emphasised its desirability; still, his whole life was governed by the ethic of achievement and education which had already characterised his youth and with the help of which he – who had been refused entry into the white élite – wanted to create a black élite.

The situation of the middle classes in Germany was almost identical with that of black America : here too the 'propertied bourgeoisie' on the one hand had largely renounced participation in the political power structure 'to advance the economic development with the help of the state'; on the other hand the non-propertied 'educated bourgeoisie had found in their mostly a-political cultural ideals and educational aspirations compensation for their lack of political influence.'[18] As a consequence of the 'glorification of culture and the high esteem and the perfection of science' with its roots in German Idealism, the 'ethical necessity of education' had become a dogma; the 'self-realization of the individual' was seen to be possible only through an 'education of the spirit and intellect'.[19] The free 'development of personality through strict confinement to the private sphere, through spiritual but not through active self-realization' had become the 'highest accomplishment'. This had led to a 'gradual secularization of religion' on the one hand, and to a 'growing importance of the spiritual and aesthetic aspects of culture' on the other; 'philosophy, literature and art were seen as the greatest revelations of the human spirit'; they became an *Ersatz* religion. Towards the end of the century this idealism degenerated more and more into a 'belief in the nation's mission and worth'.[20] Ostensibly a-political, this belief was to be used in a very political way not only to strengthen the exclusive claim to culture by an élite and to widen the 'social gap' between the bourgeoisie and the masses,[21] but also to justify the desire for world domination by 'an exceptional cultural mission of Germany'.[22]

As her attempts at colonial expansion brought Germany into confrontation with the other colonial powers of the West, the Wilhelmine bourgeoisie drew a sharp line between German culture and 'western civilization'. In the name of a superior German culture it censured the brutalizing influences' of the West, which were also spoken of as the threat of Americanization', such as democracy and liberalism; the same applied to 'British materialism and utilitarianism'.[23] This intense Anglophobia which was particularly widespread in Germany after 1890 prepared the ground for various Pan-German ideas which eventually led to the foundation of the *Alldeutscher Verband* in 1894 in Berlin, DuBois's place of study. The main aims of this association are important in this context, as they are similar to DuBois's own, yet to be defined, Pan-Africanism. In a nutshell, Pan-German aims were the creation of a German national consciousness and the promotion of a radical' feeling of cultural solidarity among all people of German origin in Europe and abroad.[24]

These were in rough outline some of the most important tendencies among the German bourgeoisie, which DuBois began to warm up to quite willingly and without difficulty. As a member of the American middle class he was to some extent predisposed to such a development.[25] What is more, these ideals were presented to him in a venerable and imposing form, ennobled through tradition and world-wide admiration, so that they were almost bound to make an overpowering impression on the young student from Great Barrington. Nor is it unimportant that DuBois happened to be in Germany at a time when those tendencies were particularly flourishing, and lived in Berlin, then the cultural and political centre of Germany. He came into direct, personal contact with some of the eminent protagonists of the notion of the educated bourgeoisie such as Gustav Schmoller, Adolph Wagner, Max Sering, Max Weber and Heinrich von Treitschke, who were his university teachers. Treitschke, whom DuBois called a 'fire-eating Pan-German',[26] had been particularly prominent in castigating Anglo-Saxon materialism. DuBois was very impressed by Treitschke's anglophobia and his vehement anti-Americanism. It gave him much satisfaction, he wrote,

that they, with me, did not regard America as the last word in civilization. Indeed, I derived a certain satisfaction in learning that the

University of Berlin did not recognize a degree even from Harvard University, no more than Harvard did from Fisk . . . All agreed that Americans could make money and did not care how they made it. And the like. Sometimes their criticism got under even my anti-American skin, but it was refreshing on the whole to hear voiced my own attitude toward so much that America had meant to me.

On the other hand, for the first time in his life he himself was treated not as a Negro, as 'something sub-human', but as a human being, even as 'a man of the somewhat privileged student rank, with whom they were glad to meet and talk over the world; particularly, the part of the world whence I came'. Thus it was only natural that he came to the conclusion that 'German university training . . . left no room for American color prejudice', while connecting America's racial discrimination with her lack of 'civilization', against which the humanitarian and educational ideals of a better world, Europe, had to be defended : 'I felt myself standing, not against the world, but simply against American narrowness and color prejudice, with the greater, finer world at my back.'[27] The ugly corollaries of the bourgeois society of Europe, such as its marked anti-Semitism, seems to have remained hidden from him, although as a black he ought to have had a particularly sensitive feeling for any kind of racism. At least he does not comment on the subject, and merely mentions it in passing in connection with a visit to France.[28]

Only later, when he had gained a more profound insight into European Imperialism, was his belief in a better, more humane Europe shaken. But his criticism of colonialism did not mar his admiration for European culture. To the end of his life he basically remained a nineteenth-century liberal who believed in the power of ideas and declared 'culture' as the highest human aim; who was convinced that only the educated, cultured man of 'good manners' could deliver the world from evil. His novels show this even more clearly. And it may already be said here in anticipation of later arguments that DuBois' changing preferences for democracy, socialism or communism respectively must also be seen in connection with his cultural ideal. These shifts have been wrongly denounced as opportunism; for him they merely offered different guises for the same ideals.

In an important diary entry of the night before his twenty-fifth birthday in 1893 Du Bois puts for the first time his life's maxim in the positively magic formula which was to run like a red thread throughout his writings :

What is life but life, after all? Its end is its greatest and fullest self – this end is the Good : the Beautiful is its attribute – its soul, and

Truth is its being. Not three commensurable things are these, they are three dimensions of the cube.

But in spite of his profound 'Europeanization' DuBois never ceased to feel as a black : 'The hot dark blood of a black forefather is beating at my heart.'[29] This expression of his allegiance to Africa appears abruptly after a passage describing an afternoon and evening spent at Potsdam, listening to classical music and drinking a bottle of Rüdesheimer wine; it is hence surprising and not very convincing, because DuBois's 'African soul' had not made itself felt on any previous page of his account of his stay in Europe. That he remembered his 'hot dark blood' none the less highlights DuBois's predicament and reveals the dichotomy inside the intellectual Afro-American who feels himself bound to 'white' culture, but is not allowed to identify with it and who channels his mental energies into the pursuit of emotional goals instead.[30] On his memorable birthday night he saw no possibility as yet of reconciling the two worlds : his personal ideals, which were those of the educated bourgeoisie, and the life-task which he had chosen at Fisk and Harvard, namely to free the black race from the dominance of the whites : 'God knows I am sorely puzzled. I am firmly convinced that my own best development is not one and the same with the best development of the world and here I am willing to sacrifice . . .'[31]

The year 1894 brought to an end not only DuBois's stay in Germany but also a momentous part of his life, his 'years of apprenticeship'. His versatile *vita activa* began after his return to America and made him one of the best-known Afro-American 'leaders' in a comparatively short time. This new task, which he took on willingly, resulted in a much more intensive preoccupation with the blacks, their position in the world, and above all with Africa, than had hitherto characterized his career. As his subsequent writings show, his thoughts revolved primarily around three subjects : first of all he wanted to show up the task or mission of the blacks, which included the idea of the importance of Africa to the world. Then he tried to analyse the existing conditions, and finally to demonstrate how the aim which he had outlined could best be reached. The first two points are not always clearly distinguishable. For only too often DuBois is unable to see what reality is like because he judges it by what he wants it to be. And yet these three aspects form a convenient scanning device for an understanding of his writings.

Not long after he had returned from Germany DuBois began to develop more concrete ideas about the first subject, the meaning of the black race. They are found in his well-known essay on 'The Conservation of Races' which appeared in 1897 in the journal of the American Negro Academy which had just been founded by Crummell.[32] In this article DuBois tried to apply the insights he had gained in Germany to the Afro-Americans. Nearly all the later themes which DuBois treated extensively in his novels are to be found here. The central problem of this article is the question of the 'real' meaning of 'race': 'What is the real meaning of Race; what has, in the past, been the law of race development, and what lessons has the past history of race development to teach the rising Negro people?' His main aim is to convey to the Afro-Americans a – positive – view of the racial theory which he had discovered in Europe. In this case too it is very likely that DuBois deceived himself, because as an Afro-American he could not free himself from the polarity of black and white, in terms of which he was used to interpret past and present events in the United States. He had already wrongly interpreted the anti-Americanism of the Germans as anti-materialism, that is as a 'higher' cultural stage which made German culture an allegedly positive pole *vis-à-vis* the negative, 'less civilised' culture of the Americans. He was similarly mistaken in his interpretation of European racism, which had not been primarily formulated against blacks, as being less 'racist'. This is implied at least in the first part of his article. There he said that Afro-Americans were wrong, albeit understandably so, in rejecting all racial theories because they had only come into contact with the racist ones of America which had the sole aim of marking the blacks as being eternally inferior. He maintained that no one could deny the fact that there existed different races, even that racial history was world history, 'the history, not of individuals, but of groups, not of nations, but of races, and he who ignores or seeks to override the race idea in human history ignores and overrides the central thought of all history'. As the situation in America showed all too clearly that the coexistence of different races presented problems, DuBois thought it very necessary to gain a deeper insight into the concept of 'race'. At the same time he advocated that future developments be planned, i.e.

> those large lines of policy and higher ideals which may form our guiding lines and boundaries in the practical difficulties of every day. For it is certain that all human striving must recognize the hard limits of natural law, and that any striving, no matter how intense and earnest, which is against the constitution of the world, is vain.

In his subsequent analysis of 'race' DuBois starts off by examining, in reaction to contemporary racial theories, the purely biological aspect of his concept and concludes that criteria which had previously been used, such as skin colour, hair, skull lengths, etc., are no longer sufficient. If they were, there would be only two races, namely a white and a black one, and possibly a third, the yellow race. But these provided an insufficient explanation for the very varied developments of all races, especially of all those mixed, 'intermediate' races which had their origins in those two or three races. To DuBois this rather proved 'that great as is the physical unlikeness of the various races of men their likenesses are greater, and upon this rests the whole scientific doctrine of Human Brotherhood.' – and, as has been shown above, present-day anthropologists would agree with him there. The principle of the equality of all races postulates at the same time their equal worth and thus their claim to equal rights. In order to be able to explain the divergent development of the races which did, after all, exist, other factors had to be taken into consideration : 'The deeper differences are spiritual, psychical, differences – undoubtedly based on the physical, but infinitely transcending them.' In the manner typical of racial theorists of the nineteenth and early twentieth centuries DuBois combined biological and cultural criteria; he himself said it marked the influence of Europe on him.

According to these criteria he distinguishes between eight races, with Britain and America on the one hand, and the 'Teutons of middle Europe' on the other, representing two different 'races'. For him each race is not only characterised by a 'race identity and common blood', but also by the more important criterion of 'a common history, common laws and religion, similar habits of thought and a conscious striving together for certain ideals of life. The whole process which has brought about these race differentiations has been a growth, and the great characteristic of this growth has been the differentiation of spiritual and mental differences between great races of mankind and the integration of physical differences.' DuBois thought, as did Blyden before him, that the 'race idea' inherent in every race would fulfil a very positive function : 'The race groups are striving, each in its own way, to develop for civilization its particular message, its particular ideal, which shall help to guide the world nearer that perfection of human life for which we all long, that *one far off Divine event*.'[33] During this process the relationship between the races need not be hostile, but should rather be compared to a sportsmanlike and noble contest, and be seen as 'a matter of clear, fair competition', as DuBois says elsewhere,[34] in which each race gives its best for the good of the noble aim.

This idealism, which distinguishes DuBois from nearly all other black nationalists, could hardly be based on events in America, where the number of lynch-murders and other acts of terrorism were reaching a climax. DuBois's idealism must clearly be seen in connection with his stay in Europe. Later he realised that his contact with the European whites had given him the impression that 'the eternal walls between races did not seem so stern and exclusive'.[35] During the later course of his life he came to the bitter and resigned conclusion that his idea of a peaceful and fair coexistence of the black and white races was merely an illusion. But it is one reason, to which other, weightier ones were added later, why DuBois categorically rejected the emigration of the blacks from America. He thought they were Americans 'not only by birth and by citizenship, but [also] by [their] political ideals, [their] language, [their] religion'. As there was general agreement on these important points, he saw no reason 'why, in the same country and on the same street, two or three great national ideals might not thrive and develop, that men of different races might not strive together for their race ideals as well, perhaps even better, than in isolation'. Apart from the fact that the concept of culture on which DuBois based these ideas is no longer tenable and would be intelligible only if cultures were conditioned purely by genetic factors, a far-reaching congruity such as this one seems to leave almost no room for independent racial ideals. But DuBois was not troubled by this; he demanded that the aim of the blacks should not be 'a servile imitation of Anglo-Saxon culture, but a stalwart originality which shall unswervingly follow Negro ideals'.[36] And DuBois did take pains to define the pure Negro ideal in greater detail, even if it proved somewhat difficult as long as he lacked a point of reference.

At the time of writing the article on 'The Conservation of Races', DuBois knew too little about Africa, the cradle of the black race. All he could do was to fall back on a favourite nineteenth-century argument and refer to the negroid elements in ancient Egypt as proof that the black race was capable of creating a culture. And DuBois also shared the widely-held contemporary view that since that time the black race had existed 'half awakening in the dark forests of its African fatherland'. He therefore did not expect a rebirth of the black idea to emerge from Africa, but from among the blacks of America, 'the first fruits of this new nation'. According to him they merited a place 'in the van of Pan-Negroism', for the Afro-Americans were 'the advance guard of the Negro people'. This key concept which appears for the first time in this article and which was later to be replaced by 'Pan-Africanism', was DuBois's adaptation of the 'Pan-Germanism' and its organisation, the 'Pan-German League', which he had encountered in Germany. And just as the Pan-Germans sought to unite all people of German origin, so DuBois called upon the blacks to organise themselves, for 'only Negroes bound and welded together, Negroes inspired by one vast ideal, can work out in its fullness the great message we have for humanity'. The blacks should uphold their belief in their great future even if the present situation, like the German one, was not encouraging. Any renaissance could thus be brought about only as a result of their own efforts, through firmly held convictions : 'Our one haven of refuge is

ourselves, and but one means of advance, our own belief in our great
destiny, our own implicit trust in our ability and worth.'[37]

This racial theory of DuBois – and generally, as has been mentioned,
of the black nationalists of the late nineteenth century – mirrors the
Afro-Americans' longing for a history of their own. As being without
history meant being without culture, even being incapable of producing
culture (an argument which was much favoured by the supporters of
slavery), they looked for a past in which they would find themselves
as intelligent and cultured beings, so that they could not only be conscious of their worth in the present, but would also be in a position to
open up a future for themselves. But DuBois's racial theory also demonstrates the great danger of this search : the cultural restoration which
he visualised is not based on existing traditions. DuBois, a product
of Western culture through and through, was completely alienated
from his group; and so he puts myths in the place of traditions, yet in
establishing them has to use such cultural 'matter' as was familiar to
him : the Anglo-Saxon one. In the process he put himself and his
theory at odds with Afro-American reality. What is more : he even
impeded the discovery of true African–Afro-American traditions. This
tendency to idealise which became even more pronounced later on,
is manifested in 1897 by the aim on which, as DuBois declared,
all energies should be centred : 'We are that people whose subtle sense
of song has given America its only American music, its only American
fairy tales, its only touch of pathos and humor amid its mad money-
getting plutocracy. As such, it is our duty to conserve our physical
powers, our intellectual endowments, our spiritual ideals.' The mission
of the blacks, in DuBois's poetical image, was 'to soften the whiteness
of the Teutonic today'.[38] Thus DuBois reverts back to the traditional
black-white symbolism, which Melville in particular had enlarged upon,
and provides an exhaustive interpretation. In his scheme the blacks
assume the role of a corrective. But this means that their ultimate
point of reference is again provided by the whites, and the sought-
after cultural independence does not go beyond the existing framework.

A very early DuBois poem, written in 1899, interprets the black-
white symbolism in this sense :

## The Song of Smoke

I am the smoke king,
I am black.
I am swinging in the sky,

    I am ringing worlds on high;
    I am the thought of the throbbing mills,

I am the soul of the soul toil kills,
I am the ripple of trading rills,

Up I'm curling from the sod,
I am whirling home to God.
I am the smoke king,
I am black.
. . .

Dark inspiration of iron times,
Wedding the toil of toiling climes,
Shedding the blood of bloodless crimes,
Down I lower in the blue,
Up I tower toward the true,
. . .

I am darkening with song,
I am harkening to wrong;
I will be black as blackness can,
The blacker the mantle the mightier the man,
My purp'ling midnights no day dawn may ban.

I am carving God in night,
I am painting hell in white.
. . .

Souls unto me are as mists in the night,
I whiten my blackmen, I blacken my white,
What's the hue of a hide to a man in his might!
. . .

Hail to the smoke king,
Hail to the black![39]

The poem tries to uphold the justification, necessity and beauty of the black existence in a world in which the blacks were degraded to the position of animals and described as ugly, soulless and stupid. The anaphoric, active 'I am' and the oft-repeated first two lines, the key lines of the poem, strengthen DuBois's proud assertion of his black ego. The smoke symbolises the inspiration of the world through the blacks. DuBois gives a very concrete interpretation to this image as a symbol of human labour. The smoke which rises from the chimneys of factories and ships bears witness to the ubiquitous labour force of the blacks who thus represent the heart of the world and fulfil a vitally important function. At the same time the dark smoke is associated with the mission of the blacks : they, the suffering and the honourable, who have had artistic temperaments from ancient times – 'Dark inspirations of iron times' alludes to the African cultures of the Iron Age which were far ahead of comparable contemporary Western cultures – will ascend to (their black) God and discover Truth. This is again DuBois's principal ideal. And finally it lays bare one of the roots of his racial theory, i.e. 'the "Myth of the Wonderful Oppressed" – the notion that because a group suffers from persecution it automatically encompasses all virtue and is purged of all faults.'[40]

The second part of the poem in particular marks an attempt to move away from the traditional black-white polarity : black is conjured up as a symbol of the power which enables the blacks to recreate the world 'according to their own image'; henceforth God is to be black and hell will be white. With this image DuBois anticipates the cosmology of the Black Muslims with their 'white devils' and 'black angels'. And yet, so he seems to say in the last three lines of the penultimate stanza, a forceful, humane black culture will not create a new, reversed racism : black and white will be interchangeable and hence unimportant.

When DuBois wrote 'Smoke King' he had already been living in Atlanta for two years, where he was a lecturer in sociology until 1910. During this time he published what is probably his most famous work, a volume of essays, called *The Souls of Black Folk*. It was mainly directed at Afro-Americans and tried to make them understand their difficult present predicament as being the disastrous consequence of slavery. This volume is widely admired to this day as 'a revolutionary contribution both to Negro letters and to Negro history'.[41] A more critical reading combined with an attempt to trace the criteria on which DuBois based his assessment of the black community ought really to have dampened this enthusiasm. The ideas expressed in this volume are best illuminated by the second, very personal, purpose behind *The Souls of Black Folk*; for these essays are at the same time a *plaidoyer* for DuBois's 'Talented Tenth' theory designed to make a wider public familiar with the aims and tasks of the blacks which DuBois had evolved during his student years and defined in 1897. Above all, DuBois wanted to delimitate his own ideas from those of Booker T. Washington, who in 1903 was still the undisputed leader of the Afro-Americans and a protégé of the whites enjoying their generous support. In this sense DuBois's volume may be seen as 'revolutionary'. Not only did it dare to attack the all-powerful 'Booker T.' for the first time, but it also emphasised the superiority of education and culture over wealth : 'The function of the university is not simply to teach bread-winning . . . The need of the South is knowledge and culture . . . Patience, Humility, Manners, and Taste, common schools and kindergartens, industrial and technical schools, literature and tolerance, – all these spring from knowledge and culture, the children of the university. So must men and nations build, not otherwise, not upside down.'[42] Thus DuBois's belief in the value and usefulness of an academic education did not diminish during the many years of his life in the South. It is very probable that DuBois was strengthened in his convictions by the evident need of the Afro-Americans to make up for their lack of schooling and academic training after their emancipation as well as by Booker T. Washington's pronounced anti-intellectualism.[43] This is why he puts his claim to leadership by a spiritual élite rather bluntly :

> This is an age of unusual economic development, and Mr. Washington's programme naturally takes an economic cast; becoming a gospel of Work and Money to such an extent as apparently almost completely to overshadow the higher aims of life . . . In the history of nearly all other races and peoples the doctrine preached at such crises has been that manly self-respect is worth more than lands and houses, and that a people who voluntarily surrender such respect, or cease striving for it, are not worth civilizing.

DuBois is not primarily concerned with an improvement of material conditions but with an appeal to 'all honorable men of the twentieth century to see that in the future competition of races the survival of the fittest shall mean the triumph of the good, the beautiful, and the true; that we may be able to preserve for future civilization all that is really fine and noble and strong'. He imagines the implementation of such ideals to take place in a cultural Eden in which all men share their cultural heritage and live in unity, truth and beauty, ennobled through culture and unheedful of any differences in colour.[44]

However, DuBois did not strive for an abolition of racial distinctions. As in 'The Conservation of the Races' and in 'The Song of the Smoke' he stated in *The Souls of Black Folk* 'that Negro blood has a message for the world'. The task of the black man thus was 'to be a coworker in the kingdom of culture'; his 'soul beauty', that is, his artistic talents, made him receptive to beauty and protected him against the base materialism of white Americans; for 'all in all, we black men seem the sole oasis of simple faith and reverence in a dusty desert of dollars and smartness'. By the same token he emphasised that the 'Negro ideal' should be realised 'not in opposition to or contempt for, other races, but rather in large conformity to the greater ideal of the American Republic, in order that some day on American soil two world-races may give each to each those characteristics both so sadly lack' There appears in these words a trend which was to become even clearer in DuBois's later writings : he is not really concerned with cultural pluralism; his belief is really in one culture, i.e. occidental, humanist culture, which he raises to the level of a 'world culture', of a culture transcending the races. But he remains unaware that by upholding this notion he places himself firmly in the tradition of those Anglo-Saxons and those European colonialists whom he despised so much. The development of distinctive races which he demands does not serve to create or strengthen different cultures, but merely to enrich or 'realise' the one and only culture which is the point of reference for all races.[45]

His vision of a world of humanist aesthetes, his frequent call for asceticism ('Entbehren sollst du, sollst entbehren' or 'life is more than meat and the body more than raiment'[46]) which is scarcely comprehensible in the face of the situation of the Afro-Americans at the turn of the century, show again that he was miles apart from the army of poor, even starving, largely illiterate blacks who still lived lives in slave-like dependence.[47] The intellectual ideal of an academic who had studied at Harvard and Berlin could hardly cater for the needs of most Afro-Americans. Above all, it narrowed DuBois's vision. He was unable to arrive at a realistic appraisal of the situation and tended to distort observable reality. Thus, in his above-mentioned 'Negro ideal' he had wrongly taken for anti-materialism what was really an involuntary asceticism generated by economic poverty; at other points he tries to counter the frequently heard allegation of black 'shiftlessness' and 'laziness' and to idealise them.[48] For example, he reports an encounter with a number of young Negroes who had passed him with a mule-drawn cart. Presumably overtired from long, heavy work, they were dozing and failed to notice the slipping bales of straw. DuBois tried to indicate them :

And yet follow these boys : they are not lazy; to-morrow morning they'll be up with the sun; they work hard when they do work, and they work willingly. They have no sordid, selfish, money-getting ways, but rather a fine disdain for mere cash. They'll loaf before your face and work behind your back with good-natured honesty. They'll steal a water-melon, and hand you back your lost purse intact.

His bias, which resulted from his understandable desire to counter the widespread racism, similarly influenced his image of Afro-Americans in his other writings. One of his biggest worries was the family and above all single women; in this problem, he believed, 'lies the seat of greatest moral danger'. The supposed 'sexual immorality' which could already be observed in parts of the rural population disturbed the puritanical moralist in him, and it was with a sigh of relief that he said :

There is little or no prostitution among these Negroes, and over three-forths [*sic*] of the families, as found by house-to-house investigation, deserved to be classed as decent people with considerable regard for female chastity. To be sure, the ideas of the mass would not suit New England, and there are many loose habits and notions. Yet the rate of illegitimacy is undoubtedly lower than in Austria or Italy, and the women as a class are modest.

Taking his standards, his general impression of the black rural population is relatively positive. Most of them are 'poor and ignorant, fairly honest and well meaning, plodding, and to a degree shiftless, with some but not great sexual looseness'. He had a worse impression of the urban poor. As far as they are concerned, DuBois completely shares the contemporary views of the white middle class, their appreciation of the so-called educated class, and their contempt of the 'masses' whom he also terms as 'mob'. While the black middle class represents 'good' Afro-America, the slum-dwellers form the dregs of society, living wretched lives on the verge of crime : 'The criminal and the sensualist leave the church for the gambling-hell and the brothel, and fill the slums of Chicago and Baltimore, the better classes segregate themselves from the group-life of both white and black, and form an aristocracy, cultured but pessimistic . . .'. Had the 'good' whites had more contact with the 'good' blacks, prejudices would hardly have arisen, but a 'Negro slum' was often 'in dangerous proximity to a white residence quarter', while it was also usual 'to find a white slum planted in the heart of a respectable Negro district'. The 'best' of the whites and the 'best' of the blacks seldom lived closely together. And the consequence of this situation : 'in nearly every Southern town and city, both whites and blacks see commonly the worst of each other'.

Inevitably DuBois's puritanical analysis of a social structure in which poverty and ignorance are equated with criminality and evil elements, but affluence and education – he does not censor the middle classes for their materialism – with positive values must lead to a curious reversal of moral standards. For he adds :

This is a vast change from the situation in the past, when, through the close contact of master and house-servant in the patriarchal big house, one found the best of both races in close contact and sympathy, while at the same time the squalor and dull round of toil among the field-hands was removed from the sight and hearing of the family.

Can one interpret this statement in any other way than in support of our central argument that DuBois's fight for equal rights did not break away from the traditional order of white America; nor did it affect his hierarchical world-view. He did not strive for a fundamental change of the situation which would have freed the blacks from their economic, political, and also spiritual bondage; rather he was of the opinion that what was lacking was 'not cash, but character. It was not and is not money these seething millions want, but love and sympathy . . .' He thus warned against a 'cheap and dangerous socialism', speaking of it and 'crime' in one breath, and he was convinced that 'no secure civilization can be built in the South with the Negro as an ignorant, turbulent proletariat'. He speaks of the development of the individual towards a 'better and truer self', that is towards an educated and cultured man, and juxtaposes this with the mobilisation of the masses through socialism : 'Above our modern socialism and out of the worship of the mass, must persist and evolve that higher individualism which the centres of culture protect.' DuBois's highest commandment is thus education, which will lead – as has been shown above – to the realisation of the inherent qualities of the 'Negro race'.

## II THE GENESIS OF THE 'PAN-AFRICAN'

The picture which DuBois painted of the black masses hardly seems to justify the notion of 'soul-beauty'. Consequently he had to create a frame of reference on to which he could project his 'white', occidental, ideals but which nevertheless allowed him to remain within the black world. He achieved this by creating a fictive black man, or more exactly an '*Ur*-African' who is not only hidden within Afro-Americans in the shape of an 'innate love of harmony and beauty', but also within the Africans themselves, who appear more prominently in *The Souls of Black Folk* than in the earlier writings. There is a close connection between the two : in his view Africans were equally underdeveloped : 'Civilisation flourished in Europe, and flickered, flamed, and died in Africa.' His image of the African sold into captivity in colonial times, whom he also calls 'African savage', mirrors, a number of correct observations notwithstanding, the general lack of knowledge characteristic of his time. It emerges very clearly in his ideas about the mysterious, gruesome activities of the heathens which he had met in the South in connection with the Voodoo cult :

> The Negro has already been pointed out many times as a religious animal, – a being of that deep emotional nature which turns instinctively toward the supernatural. Endowed with a rich tropical imagination and a keen, delicate appreciation of Nature, the transplanted African lived in a world animate with gods and devils, elves

**D**

and witches; full of strange influences, – of Good to be implored, of Evil to be propitiated . . . He called up all the resources of heathenism to aid, – exorcism and witchcraft, the mysterious Obi worship with its barbarous rites, spells, and blood-sacrifice even, now and then, of human victims. Weird midnight orgies and mystic conjurations were invoked, the witch-woman and the voodoo-priest became the centre of Negro group life, and that vein of vague superstition which characterized the unlettered Negro even to-day was deepened and strengthened.[49]

In spite of all this 'primitivism', elements of DuBois's 'ideal Negro' do transpire : his 'emotional nature', 'tropical imagination' and his 'keen, delicate appreciation of Nature' which make him capable of 'goodness, beauty and truth'. He cited as proof an 'ancient African chastity' and ancient African civilisations which he presumed to have existed : 'The shadow of a mighty Negro past flits through the tale of Ethiopia the Shadowy and of Egypt the Sphinx.'[50]

If one takes the presentation of Africa and of contemporary Africans in *The Soul of Black Folk* into account, one would not suspect that three years previously, in 1900, DuBois had had the opportunity of meeting a number of leading Africans at the first Pan-African Congress which he attended as Secretary; these encounters ought to have let a generalising definition of Africans as 'savage' appear unjustified. That his experience, however limited, did not leave a trace in DuBois's writings indicates that his ideas about Africa were based on other sources than observable reality. This is shown even more clearly in an early poem of 1908, dedicated to Africa :

### A Day in Africa

I rose to sense the incense of the hills,
The royal sun sent crimson heralds to the dawn
She glowed beneath her bridal veil of mist –
I felt her heart swell whiles the king
Paused on the world's rough edge,
And thousand birds did pour their little hearts
To maddened melody.
I leapt and danced, and found
My breakfast poised aloft
All served in living gold.

In purple flowered fields I wandered
Wreathed in crimson, blue and green.
My noon-tide meal did fawn about my feet
In striped sleekness.

I kissed it ere I killed it,
And slept away the liquid languor of the noon;
Then rose and chased a wild new creature
Down the glen, till suddenly
It wheeled and fetched its fangs
Across my breast. I poised my spear :
Then saw its fear-mad piteous eyes,
And gave it life and food.

The sun grew sad. I watched
The mystic moon-dance of the elves
Amid the mirth-mad laughter of the stars;
Till far away some voice did wind
The velvet trumpet of the night –
And then in glooming caves
I laid me with the lion,
And I slept.[51]

In order to understand this poem it is useful to remember that DuBois had been informed about Africa and the general situation there at the above-mentioned congress in 1900. Moreover, in 1906, i.e. again before the date of the poem, he got to know the anthropologist Franz Boas, who told him for the first time about Africa's history, its kingdoms and its states which had been destroyed in the late nineteenth century.[52] His poem does not reflect this directly, but does so indirectly, as will be seen. DuBois's Africa is not of this world; it is an Eden where beauty and goodness still exist in unsullied purity. DuBois likes to use – here and also in his novels and fables – the image of the red and golden glowing sun to symbolise African purity and beauty. In this paradise there is no sweat and toil, no materialistic acquisitiveness : food is there to be taken; there is no struggle for survival; injustice and evil are banished. Man and animal live together in complete harmony : the animal is either reconciled by a kiss before the slaughter – the alliteration helps to make the killing appear harmless – or it is mercifully spared if it does not voluntarily offer itself as food. There is no enmity : man and lion trust each other. Life consists of dancing, sleeping and walking, and is entirely in harmony with the rhythm of nature. And the theme of the mysterious moonlight dance of the elves also recurs in this poem. But this time the elves do not appear as an embodiment of superstition and the uncanny, presumably because the image of harmony would be disturbed by this. It is characteristic of DuBois's shyness that he does not present his African man within human society, but as an individual who is completely absorbed by himself and by nature.[53] His yearning for a peaceful, 'natural' order in which all differences are resolved is directed towards Africa, the haven of beauty and peace.

This idealisation of Africa, which is quite different from the Africa portrayed in *The Souls of Black Folk*, indicates that DuBois's image of Africa had meanwhile undergone a change. This was to be important for his 'Negro ideal'. He had thought of Africa as dark and 'savage' and was thus forced to refer the blacks back to themselves to achieve the renaissance which he advocated. But now he had been very impressed and stimulated into making intensive enquiries into African history by the knowledge of a continent with a rich culture and past of which Franz Boas had told him.⁵⁴ Even if his picture was anything but realistic, Africa from now on became a home with which he could identify and which seemed to justify the hopes he cherished for the 'Negro race'. Henceforth he projected his ideal picture of the black race on to Africa and the Africans, and he could do so in a more direct way than had been possible with his vague concept of the '*Ur*-African', supposedly dominant in all blacks. But it was of decisive importance that his Negro ideal did not arise from an acquaintance with the real Africa, but was moulded by the values of nineteenth-century liberalism. His narrow perspective gave him – as in the case of *The Souls of Black Folk* – a distorted view of reality. 'My ship seeks Africa', DuBois said many years later when at last he touched African soil in 1923 for the first time in his life;⁵⁵ but even then he was in search of his dream, was looking for a confirmation of his ideal. Thus his descriptions of the real Africa evoke the same atmosphere of a fairy-tale paradise as his poems, fables and, as will be seen later, his novels :

When shall I forget the night I set foot on African soil? I am the sixth generation in descent from forefathers who left this land. The moon was at the full and the waters of the Atlantic lay like a lake. All the long slow afternoon as the sun robed herself in her western scarlet with veils of misty cloud, I had seen Africa afar . . . The spell of Africa is upon me. The ancient witchery of her medicine is burning my drowsy, dreamy blood. This is not a country, it is a world, a universe of itself and for itself, a thing Different, Immense, Menacing, Alluring. It is a great black bosom where the spirit longs to die. It is life so burning, so fire encircled that one bursts with terrible soul inflaming life. One longs to  leap against the sun and then calls, like some great hand of fate, the slow, silent, crushing power of almighty sleep – of Silence, of immovable Power beyond, within, around. Then comes the calm. The dreamless boat of midday stillness at dusk, at dawn, at noon, always. Things move – black shiny bodies, perfect bodies, bodies of sleek unearthly poise and beauty. Eyes languish, black eyes – slow eyes, lovely and tender eyes in great dark formless faces . . .

The aim and the circumstances of DuBois's journey contributed to reality becoming submerged in his dream : DuBois made the journey in the solemn role of a delegate sent by the President of the United States, of an 'Envoy Extraordinary and Minister Plenipotentiary to Liberia – the highest rank ever given by any country to a diplomatic agent in black Africa', as he does not omit to add. His task was to convey to the Liberians 'a personal word of encouragement and moral support'.[56] Although this was hardly more than rather an empty gesture as far as the President was concerned, it was of the utmost personal importance to DuBois. This mission symbolised his life's dream – a Pan-Africa led by black Americans. He, an Afro-American, hurried to Africa to support his 'brothers' and received over there the reverence which was due to a 'leader' and served to sanction his role. 'The élitist' was, as Isaacs remarked, 'gratified by the rituals of power'.[58] As the preceding chapter has shown, Liberia had had great symbolic import-ance for the Afro-Americans since its inception; this was still the case in 1923, as DuBois emphasised in his address to the President of Liberia. The Afro-American, he said,

> knows that in the great battle against color caste in America, the ability of Negroes to rule in Africa has been and ever will be a great and encouraging reenforcement. He knows that the unswerving loyalty of Negro Americans to their country is fitly accompanied by a pride in their race and lineage, a belief in the potency and promise of Negro blood which makes them eager listeners to every whisper of success from Liberia.

In other words, the help which the Afro-Americans offer does not serve so much to support the liberation of Africa for its own sake, but rather helps to improve the status of the Negroes in America.[59] This gave the Africans a great responsibility! DuBois thus went to Africa with high expectations. He hoped to find that the Africans embodied in an exem-plary way those qualities which made up the 'Negro message' and which in his opinion had been largely suppressed in Afro-Americans. For this reason he closed his eyes to the sometimes very unpleasant reality and ignored things such as the obvious enslavement of the indigenous African population by the immigrant Afro-American settlers which would have enraged him greatly in a Western country.[60]

Beyond its Pan-African significance, the image of an idealised Africa had become possibly even more important for DuBois in other respects. He had by then developed into a sharp critic of the West, Europe included. In earlier years he had looked upon Europe as the positive factor, as the haven of culture and humanitarianism *vis-à-vis* materialistic and racist America; but now he, like so many intellectuals of his time, had become profoundly disillusioned by the World War and the obvious inability of the West regardless of all technical advances to master even its most urgent problems. 'After all, the darker world realizes the industrial triumphs of white Europe . . . it sees how the world might enjoy these things and how it does not, how it is enslaved by its own ingenuity, mechanized by its own machinery. It sees Western civilization spiritually-bankrupt and unhappy.'[61]

DuBois, who thought that 'the contact of living souls' was one of the most essential elements of social life, denounced the alienation among men as a particularly grave consequence of this development. For

> all these things we have – we have in such crushing abundance that they have mastered us and defeated their real good. We meet human beings in such throngs that we cannot know or even understand them – they become to us inhuman, mechanical, hateful. We are choked and suffocated, tempted and killed by goods accumulated from the ends of the earth.

But he did not resign himself and retained his 'dream of a world greater, sweeter, more beautiful and more honest than ever before, a world without war, without poverty and without hate'. He thought that this dream was realised by Africa : 'Africa is happy. The masses of its black folk are calmly contented, save where what is called "European" civilization has touched and uprooted them.'[63] The reasons for this contentment as enumerated by DuBois tell us more about his own thought categories than about those of the Africans. He thought to have discovered that 'efficiency and happiness do not go together in modern culture'. Blissfully ignorant of African life, DuBois presumes that Africa owes its happiness to its 'laziness: divine, eternal, languor is right and good and true'.[64] As in *The Souls of Black Folk*, this 'laziness' has to be spiritualised in order not to come into conflict with his rather rigorous ethics of achievement to which he also adhered. DuBois stylised it into a conscious renunciation of material affluence and accuses the West of failing to realize 'that lazy enjoyment and silent contemplation of life, without a surplus or even a sufficiency of modern comfort, may for a moment be held an end and ideal of existence; or that the efficient West and North can learn of the lazy South and sleepy East.' He argues that Western civilisation had not made men happier, but 'by exchanging European efficiency for African leisure and Asiatic contemplation they might gain tremendously in happiness' and – he adds naïvely – 'the world might be less afraid to give up economic imperialism'.[65] DuBois concludes that by renouncing materialism and 'efficiency' the Africans had won for themselves 'the leisure of true aristocracy, leisure for thought and courtesy, leisure for sleep and laughter'. Thus DuBois looks for, and finds, in the Africans all those virtues which he had seen the West betray :

> The primitive black man is courteous and dignified . . . [His] manners were better than those of Park Lane or Park Avenue. Oh, much better and more natural. They showed breeding . . . They have time for their children – such well-trained, beautiful children with perfect, unhidden bodies. Have you ever met a crowd of children in the east of London or New York . . . and fled to avoid their impudence and utter ignorance of courtesy? Come to Africa, and see well-bred and courteous children, playing happily . . .

In order to prove that the African is even morally superior DuBois, the Puritan, strips him of his blemishing sexuality and presents him as a sexless being or one who is at least not conscious of his sexuality and thus 'naturally innocent' :

> I have read everywhere that Africa means sexual licence . . . I was in West Africa only two months, but with both eyes wide. I saw children quite naked and women usually naked to the waist – with bare bosom and limbs. And in those sixty days I saw less of sex dalliance and appeal than I see daily on Fifth Avenue.[66]

Isaacs comments pertinently on these passages : "So much of DuBois is here in this brief African interlude . . . the daydreamer won by languor; the poet swooning on Africa's black bosom; the rhapsodist celebrating color, curve, and form; the aristocrat pleased by dignity, deference, order and gentility, the Puritan alert to any nonpoetic licence.'[67]

Not only the perspective from which DuBois judges Africa, but also his suggestions for an 'improvement' of African culture betray that his bitter criticism of the West remained superficial and that he continued to regard its ideals as generally valid and as the ultimate aim to be pursued by all peoples. His admiration for the humane African who had not yet become alienated from himself and from nature had its limits. DuBois found himself in a dilemma over this. On the one hand, he had seen the African way of life in a positive light : 'African life with its isolation has deeper knowledge of human souls. The village life, the forest ways, the teeming markets, bring in intimate human knowledge that the West misses, sinking the individual in the social. Africans know fewer folk, but know them infinitely better'; on the

other, this idyll had its negative sides : the Africans 'are vastly ignorant
of what the world is doing and thinking, and of what is known of its
physical forces. They suffer terribly from preventable disease, from
unnecessary hunger, from the freaks of the weather'. He goes on to
say that these are aspects where Africa has to learn; 'and Africa is
eager, breathless, to learn'.[68] He explains that a knowledge of technology is necessary because, among other things, it would put Africa
in a position to meet the more developed West on its own terms and
to escape colonialism. To him this is a strong reason 'to give black folk
a knowledge of modern culture'.

DuBois leaves no doubt about who would be best suited to transmit
this knowledge. It is the 150 millions of blacks throughout the world
who 'are gaining slowly an intelligent thoughtful leadership. The
main seat of their leadership is to-day the United States'.[69] And it is
not difficult to guess whom he would wish to be entrusted with the
leadership. He is not troubled by the contradictions within his scheme
– the incompatibility, which he himself points to, of a democracy of
'leisure' as well as of 'efficiency', of anti-materialism and industrialisation, of African 'communism' and Western individualism. On the contrary, he believes that the positive aspects of African life could unite
with the greater 'education' of the Afro-Americans to help create a
utopian 'Pan-African'. And this is where his literary work becomes
important.

DuBois's two novels must be interpreted as an attempt to create this
new, better, Pan-African man, if not in reality, at least in a fictional world,
in order to direct the blacks on their way into a better future. His first
novel, *The Quest of the Silver Fleece*, was published in 1911, a year
after DuBois had left Atlanta and had moved to New York as the
'Director of Publications and Research', of the NAACP. For several
years he had been politically active. In 1906 he had founded the Niagara
Movement, which merged with the NAACP in 1909. His interest in
the political and economic development of the blacks also finds its
expression in *The Quest of the Silver Fleece*. Cotton plays a major
role in DuBois's work, just as wheat does in Frank Norris's. But, says
Robert Bone, 'while Norris used the wheat as a symbol of the vast, im-
personal forces which determine the destiny of man, DuBois invaded
the cotton belt in order to expose the economic roots of the American
caste system'.[70] Yet Bone's politico-economic interpretation alone is
inadequate for an understanding of the novel; he pays too much attention to events on the surface and ignores DuBois's basic intentions.

Other critics have said that the novel consists of several themes which
are but loosely connected.[71] But this view is also rather too narrow.
If one looks at DuBois's novel from the perspective of his earlier writings
and the ideas developed in them, there clearly is a structure in it

which holds the various themes together and in spite of its manifold strands produces a unified effect. The key to this structure is again to be found in DuBois's principal aim, i.e. to show the blacks a way out of the darkness of their African slave past towards the light of education and culture as a necessary precondition for all political and material progress. It is noteworthy in this context that DuBois re-read this very novel on board ship on his way to Africa and remarked that '. . . it has points', thereby drawing attention to the African–Afro-American context of the work.

The plot is easily told : Bles Alwyn ('Blessed' [!] is his full name), an Afro-American yearning for knowledge, wins a place at a Negro school in Alabama led by a New Englander. In the forest next to the school he meets Zora, the daughter of a woman who had been a slave and still is a witch. A close friendship develops between the children. Bles teaches Zora to read and write and eventually she even gives up her free and easy life in  the forest to go to school, because Bles has convinced her of the necessity of learning. To finance their education they plant cotton deep in the forest; this cotton becomes the symbol of their friendship and of the striving for achievement of the blacks generally; but it also serves to exemplify their oppressed situation and sharpens their political consciousness, for the owner of the plantation brutally cheats them of the proceeds of their harvest. In the course of the years the friendship develops into love, but neither is mature enough for a union yet; they have to 'earn' their happiness first, i.e. they must recognise that their personal happiness has to take second place to the task of helping their people. Bles learns that as a child Zora has been raped by the owner of the plantation, and thus is no longer 'pure'. He is indignant – about her – , leaves her and goes to Washington where the black élite instructs him in matters of genteel living. He learns good manners, elegant clothes and conversation, but is also introduced to the problems facing the blacks in America. Eventually he becomes an influential politician. But before he can get corrupted by the 'machine', he returns to Alabama after he has come to realise that his true vocation lies in the deep South. There he meets Zora again, who has meanwhile grown into an active, intelligent, and above all well-educated young woman. She too has gone through her 'years of apprenticeship' and lived in New York and Washington as the maid of Mrs Vanderpool, a rich New Englander. And thanks to the care of Mrs Vanderpool she has been able to acquaint herself with art and literature, and to broaden her mind through journeys and contacts with 'cultured' people. None the less she has come to the conclusion that her talents were most needed in the South, and has returned to her home town. As her new deeper knowledge has taught her to 'see', she becomes active politically and founds a cooperative of tenant farmers in the forest in order to break the power the plantation owner has acquired through organised cotton production. In this meritorious manner she has atoned for her 'impurity' and the path is clear for a union with Bles, who now admires her whole-heartedly.

This story of the development of Zora and Bles Alwyn is interwoven with a presentation of the economic interests of the whites revolving around cotton. But it must be repeated that DuBois's novel is meant to be more than an 'economic tract', as Broderick maintains.[72] The development and 'cultivation' of the protagonists is always in the foreground. Broderick's interpretation is further weakened by the 'dematerialization' of the cotton which will be explained below. DuBois rather uses the description of a ruthless white capitalism and the resulting oppression of the blacks to demonstrate the contrast between black and white 'races'. This novel makes the same consistent use of the polarity of black and white which characterises DuBois's other writings. But while there – above all in his fables – he does not rise above an abstract colour symbolism often but poorly animated by the plot, he tries in this novel to visualise the two polar modes of existence through events and the differing behaviour of the characters. But apart from the one imposed by DuBois there is often no inherent logic in the behaviour of his white characters in particular, who appear wooden and unconvincing. Except for the understanding, warm-hearted headmistress Miss Smith, a representative of the 'best traditions of New England' which had been praised already in *The Souls of Black Folk*,[73] all whites are cold-hearted, calculating, superficial and lacking imagination; their materialism has dried up their feelings so that they are incapable of true love – except for their love of money. Nor do they have a deeper interest in their fellow human beings and their surrounding world. They lack 'immaterial' values which could give warmth and meaning to their lives. The white men who are the executives of a capitalist system surpass the women in toughness and lack of consideration. The coldness of their character is symbolised by the colour of their skin and their grey eyes. Correspondingly their voice has a 'keener, more metallic sound' as against the 'soft, rollicking laughter of black men'. The women have retained a certain sensitivity; at least they are aware of the emptiness of their lives, as Mrs Vanderpool for instance shows in a conversation with Zora :

'What is the world like?' asked Zora. Mrs. Vanderpool smiled. 'Oh, I meant great active cities and buildings, myriads of people and wonderful sights.' – 'Yes, but back of it all, what is it really? What does it look like?' – 'Heavens, child ! Don't ask. Really, it isn't worth while peering back of things. One is sure to be disappointed.' – 'Then what's the use of seeing the world?' – 'Why, one must live;

and why not be happy?' answered Mrs. Vanderpool, amused, baffled, spurred for the time being from her chronic *ennui*.

'Are you happy?' retorted Zora, looking her over carefully, from silken stockings to garden hat. Mrs. Vanderpool laid aside her little mockery and met the situation bravely. 'No', she replied simply. Her eyes grew old and tired. Involuntarily Zora's hand crept out protectingly and lay a moment over the white jewelled fingers . . . Mrs. Vanderpool's eyes became dim, 'I need you, Zora,' she said . . . 'Yes, and you need me; we need each other. In the world lies opportunity, and I will help you.'[74]

This sentimental scene summarises much of DuBois's world-view : the understanding, warm humanity of the blacks, the poverty of soul of the whites reflecting the futility of their material wealth, and finally the enrichment which the two 'races' could gain from each other and which would facilitate the creation of a new world. Mrs Vanderpool gives expression to DuBois's dearest wish, that the whites should recognise their own inadequacy and the value of the blacks and change their behaviour accordingly, like Mrs Vanderpool when towards the end of the novel she saves Miss Smith's school from financial ruin.

DuBois thus still believed that discrimination was the result of ignorance on the part of the whites about the 'true' character of the blacks, since the 'best' of both groups had so little opportunity to get to know each other. It is no accident that Mrs Vanderpool owes her 'conversion' to Zora; Zora is the purest representative of DuBois's 'New Negro' who, so DuBois hoped, would have a revolutionising effect on the behaviour of the whites. Zora's positive character traits reflect qualities peculiar to the black race and she has retained them almost in their undiluted original form. Her 'Africanism' sets her clearly apart from Bles, who has come into contact with Western culture; he is an enlightened, 'progressive' Afro-American, but one who has lost direct contact with his 'racial' roots; only through Zora does he rediscover them. It is true that he 'awakens' Zora and shows her the way, thereby fulfilling the function which the Afro-Americans have in DuBois's Pan-African system. But Zora outgrows him and in the last analysis possesses more knowledge and moral force. *She* becomes the leader in the end. It is difficult to say how far DuBois at this stage in his development wished this particular consequence of his racial ideal to be interpreted politically. In his later, purely 'Pan-African' novel *Dark Princess*, the claim to leadership still rests entirely with the Afro-Americans. It was only many years later, towards the end of his life, that DuBois came to realise that Africans, too, were capable of leading Pan-Africa. But in this context it is interesting to start with an examination of what the figure of Zora tells us about DuBois's ideas concerning the Pan-African.

To anticipate the conclusion : Zora shows how at least in his fiction he tried to give shape to his life's dream, i.e. the idea of bringing together Western cultural concepts with a nationalism founded on an idealised 'African race'.

One of the basic characteristics of the Pan-African – his 'Africanness' – is emphasised in Zora's case by her physiognomy. Unlike most heroines of early Afro-American novels she has a black skin and conspicuously negroid features.[75] DuBois thought it was one of the main tasks of the Afro-Americans to 'let us train ourselves to see beauty in black'.[76] Time and again and in ever new variations he tries to suggest to the reader that Zora is beautiful. To write the following passage in 1911 required considerable courage and a good deal of self-confidence :

> She was black, and lither, and tall, and willowy. Her garments twined and flew around the delicate moulding of her dark, young half-naked limbs. A heavy mass of hair clung motionless to her wide forehead. Her arms twirled and flickered, and body and soul seemed quivering and whirring in the poetry of her motion. As she danced she sang. He heard her voice as before, fluttering like a bird's in the full sweetness of her utter music. It was no tune nor melody, it was just formless, boundless music. The boy [Bles] forgot himself and all the world besides. All his darkness was sudden light; dazzled he crept forward, bewildered, fascinated, until with one last wild whirl the elf-girl paused, The crimson light fell full upon the warm and velvet bronze of her face – her midnight eyes were aglow, her full purple lips apart, her half hid bosom panting . . .

An African atmosphere is evoked here and earlier through the images of the 'elf-girl's' wild dance and the 'crimson light' which DuBois had used before in direct connection with Africa. Above all there is the obviously African music of which DuBois had said earlier on : 'It was human music, but of a wildness and a weirdness that startled the boy as it fluttered and danced across the dull red waters of the swamp.' Yet Zora not only possesses the 'primaeval' artistic talents of the African race which have been mentioned above; she also shares with her race a mentality which is based on intimate bonds with Nature and is distinguished above all by great powers of imagination.[77] DuBois endows Zora with all those characteristics which he tried to define as the 'peculiar spiritual quality' of the blacks in his famous volume, *The Gift of Black Folk*, published thirteen years later :

> The Negro is primarily an artist. The usual way of putting this is to speak disdainfully of his 'sensuous' nature. This means that the only race which has held at bay the life destroying forces of the

tropics, has gained therefrom in some slight compensation a sense of beauty, particularly for sound and color, which characterizes the race . . . It is . . . a certain spiritual joyousness: a sensuousness, tropical love of life, in vivid contrast to the cool and cautious New England reason; a slow and dreamful conception of the universe, a drawling and slurring of speech, an intense sensitiveness to spiritual values – all these things and others like to them, tell of the imprint of Africa on Europe and America.[78]

No definite conception of a 'race theory' can be abstracted from these lines. It is not clear whether the Africans have acquired their artistic sensibility despite their dangerous and wild tropical surroundings, thereby making it a 'racial' characteristic, or whether this sensibility was precisely a product of living in the wilderness. In this novel at least DuBois tries to show that it resulted from a mixture of the two. On the one hand Zora's 'great and awful visions' are explained by something like a milieu theory; on the other hand, DuBois moves within the framework of accepted racial categories of the time; he sees character- istics, acquired in tropical surroundings, as 'racial' features which have become fixed genetically and thus survive even against new cultural influences or other, non-tropical, surroundings. Accordingly DuBois begins his novel by putting Zora into a setting which is strongly reminis- cent of Africa to justify her 'Africanness'. Zora's good qualities, her 'natural', worldly wisdom which makes her appear so much more socially mature than her New England teachers, her fresh, alert intelli- gence, her intuitive knowledge of people, her spontaneity and her contempt for material goods, are shown to be products of her and her mother's life in the swamp forest far away from civilisation. These were the very qualities which DuBois 'rediscovered' in the Africans a good ten years later, and again he thought them to be the result of their isolation. But it is not merely her life in the forest which brings Zora's 'Africanness' to light; her surroundings, 'the swamp', are in themselves a section from an African world. At least DuBois uses the same images to describe the swamp as those which he associates elsewhere with Africa.[79]

However, the connection with Africa as it emerges from the accounts of the 'swamp' is made not merely by association. There is also a direct and tangible link, i.e. the cotton which Zora and Bles grow in the fertile soil of the black swamp. The seeds for this cotton, which is of course of the highest quality, come from Africa, 'the old land'.[80] This reference intended to show that cotton 'belongs' to the blacks; that it was 'stolen' from them by the whites and that it must be recaptured by the blacks. To DuBois this argument is of such central significance that again he invests it with a mythical force. As shown by the title of the novel and even more clearly by the title of an essay in *The Souls of Black Folk* which contained a nucleus of the later novel, he conceived of it as a 'black' saga of the Argonauts.[81] It is characteristic of DuBois that he gives a purely idealistic reason to justify the black's claim to cotton : they alone are receptive to the poetry of a cotton field, since the beauty of Nature is revealed to the sensitive soul of the Negroes alone. Their more humane nature prevents the blacks from desecrating cotton through a base hankering after profit, typical of the whites; rather they cultivate cotton as a disinterested service to their fellow-humans, conserving at the same time its immaterial value and, through their loving care, refining its quality.[82] Cotton becomes the symbol both of the integrity and 'beauty' of the black race and of their promising future. This is why it is important that the cotton is returned to them; for it is to become the basis of a new black world in the United States which draws its strength from Africa and thus acquires African qualities. The 'Cotton Belt' or 'Black Belt' is therefore seen as the cradle of a new Pan-Africa – Zora's cooperative – and of a more humane world in which the dualism of spirit and matter no longer exists and all ugliness is banished.

However not only will beauty and poetry prevail in DuBois's Pan-Africa, but 'culture' and bourgeois propriety as well. This is why DuBois did not transpose his Utopia to Africa. He wanted a fusion of the positive African qualities with those of Western culture, and contemporary Africa did not meet his ideal in this novel. There is the ugly witch-like figure of Elspeth who joins in the orgies of the white plantation owners and represents a black corrupted by slavery (or rather colonisation). Her imagination has turned into superstition which is evil and 'uncivilized'. It is true that Zora, who is forced by her mother to participate in the orgies, has also lost her 'African chastity'. But 'civilizing' Afro-American influences have come to bear on her in time. They prevent her utter corruption and free her from her mother, i.e. free her from her immediate past and thus from barbarism and ignorance. In a symbolic scene at the end of the novel the hut of Zora's dead mother is pulled down and the above-mentioned cotton cooperative is erected under Zora's leadership in its place : Africa becomes civilised, the cultured Pan-Africa has conquered the 'wild' Africa, the Africa which had been corrupted by the whites. In short, it is blacks like Zora who embody the (supposed) synthesis of African and European, Western, values. On her rests DuBois's great dream of the economic and political development of a new black world, which has been traced only in broad outline here.

Yet Zora's qualities can hardly be called 'African'. In fact, DuBois's aestheticism and idealism are of a purely European nature. Consequently Zora merely represents occidental cultural ideals shot through with a strong puritanical, moralistic bias. She is industrious, disciplined, has acquired a certain book-learning and knows how to dress and behave correctly – a prime virtue in DuBois's eyes; the characters in his novels show how cultured they are by the way they dress.[83] Because of her great mission Zora is willing to renounce and to forgo sexual fulfilment. Put briefly, it is 'a Zora made eminently respectable'[84] who marries Bles, the Afro-American, and together with him sets out on the great task to liberate the black race. DuBois is thus a long way away from his own demand 'to see beauty in black'. The 'black' in this novel is not inherently 'beautiful', but only after it has undergone a process of purification.

## III    THE MESSAGE OF PAN-AFRICA

How persistently DuBois was influenced by the – strongly formal – categories of Western culture is evidenced by his novel *Dark Princess*, published seventeen years later, in 1928. In it DuBois is unaffected by the general feeling of deep crisis which characterises the 1920s, and propagates the superiority of Western, European culture. He still regards occidental culture as the 'world culture' which has been corrupted by the 'white' race and which the 'black' race, with its superior human qualities, has been charged to revive in its original form. DuBois's unrealistic attempt to divorce certain forms of social life from their substance and invest supposedly African modes of existence with concepts of Western culture can only be understood in the context of his static idea of a 'mono-culture'. As Africa's significance cannot be separated from DuBois's notion of culture (and the one can only be understood in relation to the other), both elements have to be examined again in his next novel, *Dark Princess*.

*Dark Princess* has a structure very similar to that of *The Quest of the Silver Fleece*. Once more the spiritual development of the protagonists is the main concern. The plot is determined by the search for a black 'counter-world'. Again it revolves around two protagonists, the Afro-American Matthew and the Indian princess Kautilya of Bwodpur. As before the woman embodies the 'African' element; she – like Zora – is the truly active character directing the man's actions towards the right goal. She stands for his future as well as his past. When he wins her in the end he finds his true self as well as his new world, his 'Pan-Africa'. Beyond the personal education of the protagonists *Dark Princess* again includes political elements in the plot, and this time in a much more decisive and assured manner than in the earlier novel. In this respect the novel benefits from the experience DuBois had meanwhile gained in the field of politics. The scope is on the whole much larger, even 'world-wide'. In fact the novel deals with the fate of the entire coloured world. *Dark Princess* can be interpreted as an apotheosis of Pan-Africanism, for which this novel seeks to provide a philosophical basis. The politically desirable united front of coloured peoples is thus made to appear a 'natural' necessity beyond a momentary situation and presented as a permanent state of affairs. The front which was an attempt to counteract the weight of white predominance in the world is to be given a positive *raison d'être* in the hope of creating greater cohesion among the opposing forces within this 'counter-world'. This is of course a problem which has lost nothing of its relevance to the so-called Third World of today. But in focusing on this problem, *Dark Princess* becomes a novel *à thèse*, and as in the earlier novel this proves to be detrimental to its artistic value. However, in contrast to his first novel DuBois, who again propounds his 'great visions' at the expense of the laws of probability, does not try to express his ideas in terms of a plot. Rather he puts a fairy-tale-like and often trivial frame around the realistic and successful main part of the narrative. And – what is no less unfortunate – there is no logical connection between the two. He called the novel a 'romance', but this term applies only to the frame and does not vindicate the structural weakness of the whole. Even so, if one overlooks the unconvincing representation of most of the characters and of the frame, *Dark Princess* is an interesting document illustrating not only the new stage which DuBois's image of Africa had reached by 1928, but also the history of the Afro-American Pan-Africanist ideology and its literary expression.

The Afro-American Matthew, who is a young frustrated student of medicine, turns his back on America. He is very bitter because, his outstanding performance notwithstanding, he has been refused admission to a course in medicine at New York University. He goes to Europe and to Berlin, just as DuBois had done. But even there he cannot escape from his enemies, the whites: 'Sitting in the Viktoria Café, on the Unter den Linden, Berlin, Matthew looked again at the white leviathan – at that mighty organisation of white folk against which he felt himself so bitterly in revolt. It was the same vast, remorseless machine in Berlin as in New York.' It is true that he is not openly snubbed in Europe, but he remains suspicious of the whites even if he 'was treated as he was dressed, and today he had dressed carefully . . . Yes, these folks treated him as a man – or rather, they did not, on looking at him, treat him as less than a man. But what of it? They were white. What would they say if he asked for work? Or a chance for his brains? Or a daughter in marriage?' And to prove the corruption of white civilisation, to show that he was right in assuming that not the daughters but only the prostitutes are accessible to coloured people, he continues: 'There was a blonde and blue-eyed girl at the next table catching his eye. Faugh! She was for public sale . . .' In these cold white surroundings he yearns for the 'soft, brown world' which he had left behind him in America.

DuBois's antinomic world-view is in harmony with his renewed use of the colour symbolism of the earlier works and the old stereotyped figures of speech. As before, the whites are cold, 'spare, and fair, with cool grey eyes'; they live in a 'dead, white world' and subject the dark peoples to 'the dead, white light of European tyranny'. The same applies in reverse to his dark-skinned characters. While Matthew is still dreaming of dark beauties in the café, he suddenly sees his ideal before him :

First and above all came that sense of color : into this world of pale yellowish and pinkish parchment, that absence of negation of color, came, suddenly, a glow of golden brown skin. It was darker than sunlight and gold; it was lighter and livelier than brown. It was a living, glowing crimson, veiled beneath brown flesh. It called for no light and suffered no shadow, but glowed softly of its own inner radiance. Then came the sense of the woman herself : she was young and tall even when seated, and she bore herself above all with a singularly regal air. She was slim and lithe, gracefully curved. Unseeing, past him and into the struggling, noisy street, she was looking with eyes that were pools of night – liquid, translucent, haunting depths – whose brilliance made her face a glory and a dream.

Kautilya is thus an ideal type of Zora. As her personal maturing to a – as we may suppose – cultured coloured woman has already taken place, this novel stresses above all the development of her political consciousness, an element which the preceding novel had merely discussed in the vaguest terms.

Matthew succeeds in making her acquaintance by knocking down a rude white American who molests her – the Afro-American frees himself from his castration complex, the trauma of the period of slavery. But Matthew's behaviour, which would have been considered heroic in the American South, acquires a slightly grotesque symbolic significance in front of that Berlin café with Kautilya saying, 'it had never happened before that a stranger of my own color should offer me protection in Europe. I had a curious sense of some great inner meaning to your act – some world movement'. His chivalrous deed wins Matthew acceptance into a circle of ambassadors of the 'Darker Peoples' which meets in Berlin to prepare for the emancipation of these peoples under Kautilya's leadership. Apart from Kautilya there are a Japanese, two Chinese, an Egyptian, two Indians and an Arab. 'Indeed', says Kautilya, 'when all our circle is present, we represent all of it, save your world of Black Folk.' This strongly autobiographical novel shows how important his own person and his role as a 'black leader' was to DuBois. It not only unites Afro-Americans and Africans under the heading of 'Black Folk' but also has the young Pan-Africa represented by an Afro-American. There is no single African in the whole novel – the Egyptian has to be exempted since a distinction is generally made between Egyptians and 'Black Africans'. Nor does Africa itself, modern Africa, play a role; it does not even seem to exist. But this does not diminish its importance. As further analysis will show it is continually present as an 'idea', as an '*Ur*-culture'. An indication of this – tacit – function of Africa is given at the very beginning of the main plot when Kautilya says in reply to the Egyptian's observation that Matthew is not truly black but merely a half-caste : ' "Like all of us, especially me," laughed the Princess . . . , "as our black and curly-haired Lord Buddha testifies in a hundred places." '

But at first it is only Kautilya who believes 'that Pan-Africa belongs logically with Pan-Asia'. The aristocratic Asians have strong doubts about 'the ability, qualifications, and real possibilities of the black race in Africa or elsewhere'.[85] It is easy to see that DuBois deliberately tries to provoke the Afro-Americans who had so far hardly responded to his Pan-Africanism.[86] The suspicion of the Asians is fed by the contempt of the upper strata of society represented by them for the masses to which the majority of blacks belong. Thus the liberation of the 'Darker Peoples' which they are planning is not seen in terms of a social revolution. It is designed to assist the breakthrough of the 'natural inborn superiority' of the dark-skinned élite 'which the present color bar of Europe is holding back'. DuBois takes an obvious pleasure in describing the claim of the coloured peoples to superiority : 'How contemptuous was the young Indian of inferior races! But how humorous it was to Matthew to see all tables turned; the rabble now was the white workers of Europe; the inferior races were the ruling whites of Europe and America. The superior races were yellow and brown.' The matter is explained to Matthew like this : ' "You see, . . . the darker peoples are the best – the natural aristocracy, the makers of art, religion, philosophy, life, everything except brazen machines!" ' The basis of this superiority is likewise explained to the enquiring Matthew : ' "Because of the longer rule of natural aristocracy among us, we count our millenniums of history where Europe counts her centuries. We have our own carefully thought-out philosophy and civilisation, while Europe has sought to adopt an ill-fitting mélange of the cultures of the world!" ' How ironic does this contempt for European culture sound! After all, the discussions (held during the preceding dinner in several European languages to prove the extraordinary learning of the coloured élite) revolve exclusively around cultural events in Europe; not a word is said about oriental cultures, let alone African cultures. It is hard for the Afro-American to hold his own in the face of these self-confident

Asians. While animated discussions about the latest cultural happenings in Europe take place all around him, he feels 'his lack of culture audible, and not simply his own culture, but of all the culture in white America which he had unconsciously and foolishly, as he now realized, made his norm. Yet withal Matthew was not unhappy . . . Here were culture, wealth, and beauty. Here was power, and here he had some recognized part. God! If he could just do his part, any part!' But his acceptance by the others as a man who is equally capable of culture is slow. When he asks: ' "And suppose we found that ability and talent and art is not entirely or even mainly among the reigning aristocrats of Asia and Europe, but buried among millions of men down in the great sodden masses of all men and even in Africa?" ', the Egyptian exclaims contemptuously: ' "Pah! . . . what art ever came from the canaille!" ' In answer to this provocation Matthew intones the spiritual 'Go down, Moses' as the demonstration that the desire for liberty is just as strong and the artistic potential just as great among the blacks as among other races. In the end he receives the applause he has been hoping for. The others agree when he concludes ' " that ability and capacity for culture is not the hereditary monopoly of a few, but the widespread possibility for the majority of mankind if they only have a decent chance in life".'

These words by Matthew, and also the general discussion, reveal a peculiar idea of democracy, but one which is characteristic of DuBois: there is no natural right to an equality of chances which democracies cover with a basic guarantee. Such a right has to be won through 'culture' or at least through proving that one is capable of culture. Yet this élitist cultural ideal which DuBois shares, as has been explained above, with the German bourgeoisie of the nineteenth century, does not lead him to reject democracy as the Germans had done, even if he talks occasionally of the spiritual shallowness and lack of culture among American workers. For him as a black a more democratic society was of vital importance. As most blacks belong to the lower and lowest social strata and, thus being identified with the 'masses', have to cope with twofold prejudice and discrimination, i.e. that against the proletariat in general and that against blacks in particular, an improvement of the position of the masses through democracy was tantamount to an improvement of the predicament of the blacks. What is more: an increasingly democratic world also promised liberation from the predominance of the whites – an indispensable premise for the success of DuBois's cultural ideal. Yet this ideal had in turn been shaped by his own aristocratic ways of thinking. In the course of the novel DuBois tries to synthesise these contradictory elements of his theory of a black society. The fate of his two protagonists is intended to show that his ideal can be achieved theoretically as well as in practice.

The committee convened under Kautilya's leadership had been impressed by Matthew's artistic performances and had eventually decided to consider concerted action by Pan-Asia and Pan-Africa. However, as doubts continued to linger about the present level of consciousness of the Afro-Americans Matthew is sent back to the United States to inform himself about the situation. In subsequent episodes he works as a Pullman porter, later as a politician and almost loses sight of his original task. He apparently allows himself to be corrupted by the party machine and is almost beyond redemption when he marries a woman, the attractive Sara, he does not really love. She is an Afro-American of unbridled political ambition, cold and calculating, and of course almost white, with a predilection for grey dresses. She plans to use Matthew for her own ends, i.e. her material and social rise. (Together with the burly and scheming black lobbyist Sammy she may be considered the most successful character in DuBois's novels.) But Kautilya appears in time; she had shadowed him all the time so that she might save his soul. The two experience an idyllic time in the slums of Chicago where he has kept a flat from his bachelor days. But their happiness does not last long. They separate 'to get down to reality' as Kautilya puts it.[87] Their personal happiness has to take second place behind their task to emancipate the black peoples. Each is to work in his or her own sphere, Kautilya as Maharanee of Bwodpur, Matthew as a construction worker, a consciously symbolic activity to 'get to the bottom of things' by hard and honest digging. In their talks in Chicago and in their correspondence after their separation Matthew and Kautilya discuss at length the shape and function of the better, black world they want to build.

DuBois was an eclectic, and before the publication of *Dark Princess* he had stayed in the Soviet Union for some time and had been so enthusiastic about developments there that he became an admirer of Russia to the end of his life;[88] the concept of the new world which Kautilya and Matthew expound reflects some of the 'insights' gained in Russia. DuBois revels in revolutionary rhetoric and even adopts a militant tone reminiscent of his vehement quarrels with Booker T. Washington :

> Yes, Kautilya, I believe that with fire and sword, blood and whips we must fight this thing out physically, and literally beat the world into submission and a real civilization. The center of this fight must be America, because in America is the center of the world's sin. There must be developed here that world-tyranny which will impose by brute force a new heaven on this old and rotten earth.[89]

These few lines show that it is not a change in the social situation which is envisaged. Rather 'culture' is to be forced on to the people by means of a revolution. DuBois's attitude towards Communism need not be gone into in any detail here;[90] but his cultural ideal which is interesting in this context and his contempt of the 'uncivilized' masses which also had a negative effect on his relation with Africa show how far he was from being a Marxist : 'Gentle culture and the beauty and courtesies of life – they are the real end of all living. But they will not come by the dreaming of the few. Civilization cannot stand on its apex. It must stand on a broad base, supporting its inevitable and eterenal apex of fools.' And in the interest of culture these 'fools' cannot be left to their own devices :

> Whether we will or not, some must rule and do for the people what they are too weak and silly to do for themselves. They must be made to know and feel. It is knowledge and caring that are missing. Some know not and care not. Some know and care not. Some care not and know. We know and care, but, oh ! how and where? I am afraid that only great strokes of force – clubs, guns, dynamite in the hands of fanatics – that only such Revolution can bring the Day.

The claim to leadership by an élite is thus upheld very emphatically. In DuBois's system democracy is merely a means of facilitating a natural principle of selection' : 'It is democracy, if only the selection of the oligarchs is just and true'; and a means of preventing an élite which is composed in the traditional pattern of aristocracy and wealth : 'Only Talent served from the great Reservoir of All Men of All Races, of All Classes, of All Ages, of Both Sexes – this is real Aristocracy, real Democracy.' 'Aristocracy by birth' or 'by wealth' is to be supplanted by an 'aristocracy of the spirit'. Spirit and power are thought identical in a way characteristic of DuBois and the educated bourgeoisie of the nineteenth century. The intellectuals, the artists – in a word, DuBois's Talented Tenth' – are to govern; 'the wise rule of the gifted and powerful' is sought. This construction of a 'democratic aristocracy' or an aristocratic democracy' allows DuBois to connect the two main aims which he had formulated in 1893, i.e. the ideal of an educated élite and the emancipation of the blacks; he can now demand in one breath the abolition of the white rule and legitimise the rule of a black élite. At the centre of DuBois's system is European culture, but it is not seen as such. *Dark Princess* shows even more clearly than *The Quest of the Silver Fleece* that this culture is seen rather as possessing an absolute value; it is not defined as the expression of one particular society or people and their system of norms and values which gives this expression its 'inner' meaning. DuBois's 'absolute' culture cannot be 'occupied' by one group alone. On the contrary, blacks throughout the world have the same right to 'culture' as the whites who in turn can no longer refer to the superiority of 'their' culture to justify the oppression of the blacks. Of course a mere condemnation of racism and colonialism would not have needed such an elaborate counter-argument. Its construction by DuBois can only be explained by the fact that he operated with the same ideas as his opponents. In his eyes, too, the worth of a human being is determined by the degree of his 'culture', and 'culture' justifies, and even demands, the government of the 'most cultured'.

If the problem is looked at from this angle, it becomes understandable why DuBois should be so passionately interested in proving the black race's 'capacity for culture' and in reinterpreting the manifestations of African and Afro-American culture which he encountered to suit his own concept of culture. Although he postulates that all races are equal he leaves his readers in no doubt that the African 'character' is in the final analysis superior to the 'white' one. In order to call the supremacy of the whites in question they are shown to be decadent, corrupt and unworthy of power; the blacks, on the other hand, are seen as the restorers of culture and thus of the world. It is significant that often poets and artists rather than intellectuals are singled out explicity as the true carriers of culture and identified as the 'rulers'. For, as we have shown, it was their characteristics above all which DuBois thought to be typically African.

Unlike DuBois's earlier writings *Dark Princess* lends a wider significance to African culture and fuses it with Asiatic culture in order to build up, with the help of this culture of all 'darker peoples', a black counter-world. It is an attempt to give a philosophical basis to a political cooperation of Pan-Asia and Pan-Africa. This idea of a fusion explains why DuBois observed the rise of Japan with deep and uncritical admiration, and why Gandhi's sensational campaign against British colonialism in India in the 1920s epitomised his dream of a black fight for liberation. As there were no comparable events in Africa around this time or none known at least, DuBois did not hesitate to link Africa and Asia through a common '*Ur*-culture' which enabled Africa to share Asia's glory. But DuBois takes care not to stipulate a similarly direct connection (which according to the ideas of the times would have involved showing racial as well as cultural correspondences) with Japan. He merely retains the vague notion of 'darker peoples' and thus invests all dark-skinned peoples with the superiority of Japan, if only by way of association. This superiority is exemplified in *Dark Princess* by the figure of a 'Japanese baron'(!):

'He is civilization – he is the high goal toward which the world blindly gropes; high in birth and perfect in courtesy, filled with wide, deep and intimate knowledge of the world's past – the world, white, black brown, and yellow : knowing by personal contact and acquaintance-ship the present from kings to coolies. He is a man of decision and action. He is our leader, Matthew, the guide and counselor, the great Prime Minister of the Darker World.'[91]

But wherever the external appearance allows it, Africa is evoked. Kautilya for instance reports about the 'first great congress of the darker nations' which had taken place before Matthew was accepted into their circle : 'Your people were there, Matthew, but they did not come as Negroes. There were black men who were Egyptians; there were black men who were Turks; there were black men who were Indians, but there were no black men who represented purely and simply the black race and Africa.' The higher degree of 'genuineness' clearly implies a higher worth. Africa becomes the 'essence', the centre of the coloured world. The same trend is shown in Du Bois's attempt to trace back the culture of India to African roots and to mythologise it into the '*Ur*-mother' of the whole world : 'Out of black India the world was born. Into the black womb of India the world shall creep to die. All that the world has done, India did, and that more marvellously, more magnificently.' DuBois thus clearly tries to counter the evolutionary axiom of the 'Aryan' origin of culture. The descent of ancient India from Africa is first of all 'proven' by Kautilya's origins : 'We came out of the black South in ancient days and ruled in Rajputana; and then, scorning the yoke of the Aryan invaders, moved to Bwodpur, and there we gave birth to Buddha, black Buddha of the curly hair.' But as DuBois is only indirectly interested in Africa and Asia, and as his prime aim is to establish Afro-American leadership, he moves this Indo-African culture to America and even manages to raise its value in the process : the humanitarian principle of the great black Buddha is not manifested in the Indian Kautilya, but in Matthew's mother, and in a more perfect form than in Buddha himself : 'Your mother is Kali, the Black One; wife of Siva, Mother of the World !' She represents love, motherly tenderness and understanding : 'In the door stood a woman; tall, big, and brown. Her face seemed hard and seamed at first; but upon it her great cavernous eyes held in their depths that softness and under-standing which calls to lost souls and strengthens and comforts them . . . [Kautilya] strained up into the love of those old, old eyes.' She is at once the guardian of a great past and, by her dignified calm, the guarantor of a better future :

'. . . when I saw that old mother of yours standing in the blue shadows of twilight with flowers, cotton, and corn about her, I knew that I was looking upon one of the ancient prophets of India and that she was to lead me out of the depths in which I found myself and up to the atonement for which I yearned . . . We prayed to God, hers and mine, and out of her ancient lore she did the sacrifice of flame and blood which was the ceremony of my own great fathers and which came down to her from Shango of Western Africa.

In this way Asia and Africa gain a new cultural unity in America.[92]

It is remarkable how often 'old' and 'ancient' are used, the latter here in connection with 'lore' and 'prophets'. At another point the mother is called 'ancient priestess', and Kautilya once laments: 'I wanted to clean the slate and go back to the ancient simplicity of Brahma. But ah! Who can attack the strongholds of superstition and faith!' These references are meant not only to demonstrate the historicity and the existence of ancient traditions which the whites deny, but from which the superiority of the dark races is deduced at the beginning of the novel; they also mirror DuBois's yearning for elementary innocence, purity, simplicity and integrity, a yearning which had earlier led him to deplore the loss of 'African chastity'. Yet again this question is seen in terms of a black-white antinomy: the blacks are much nearer to the state of 'Grace' than the whites, as the term 'Mother of the World' in connection with Matthew's mother – and by proxy, in connection with the dark races – is meant to show. They, and the Afro-Americans in particular, are the carriers of the mission of the coloured peoples. It is their task 'to raise out of their pain, slavery, and humiliation, a beacon to guide manhood to health and happiness and life and away from the morass of hate, poverty, crime, sickness, monopoly, and the mass-murder called war'. This battle must be fought 'where beats down the fiercest blaze of Western civilization, and pushing back this hell, [we must] raise a black world upon it', i.e. in the United States. In America lies the new cultural centre of the 'darker peoples' as well as the political one. DuBois turns unequivocally against the 'Back-to-Africa' movement of the Garveyites when he puts the following words into Kautilya's mouth: 'In Africa and Asia we must work, and yet in Africa and Asia we are outside the world . . . In America your feet are further within the secret circle of that power that half-consciously rules the world.' She thinks that this is also to the advantage of the Afro-Americans: 'They are standing here in this technical triumph of human power and can use it as a fulcrum to lift earth and seas and stars.' But, she continues, to be at the centre of power is not enough:

'You must be free and able to act. You are not free in Chicago nor New York. But here in Virginia you are at the edge of a black world. The black belt of the Congo, the Nile, and the Ganges reaches by way of Guiana, Haiti, and Jamaica, like a red arrow, up into the heart of white America. Thus I see a mighty synthesis: you can work in Africa and Asia right here in America if you work in the Black Belt . . . Your heart of hearts is Africa . . . You may stand here, Matthew – here, halfway between Maine and Florida, between the Atlantic and the Pacific, with Europe in your face and China at your back; with industry in your right hand and commerce in your left and the Farm beneath your steady feet; and yet be in the Land of the Blacks.'[93]

The emphasis with which DuBois presents the Southern states of America as the centre of his Pan-Africa explains his positively furious rejection of a return to Africa. It is not that he was not 'romantic' enough or that he thought a 'Back-to-Africa' movement on a large scale to be 'impractical' and unwelcome to the Africans.[94] These are reasons which he himself put forward with a certain vehemence; but they are only used to conceal his real aim. His novels, which expose his hidden trains of thought more than any of his other writings, show that DuBois was above all concerned, if not with his own claim to power, with the claim of the Afro-American élite which was 'more progressive' and 'more educated' in his eyes than other black élites. He makes quite clear that he feels called upon to lead the black and thus the Third World. His speeches, such as the one 'To the people of China and Africa and through them to the world'[95] show that he was convinced of the global importance of his person. This claim to leadership by the Afro-Americans could not possibly have been realised from Africa. He did acquire Ghanaian citizenship shortly before his death, but this was only because he was deeply disappointed with the Afro-Americans who had not accepted his cultural ideal and now wanted to win over the Africans for a realisation of his ideals.[96]

But if DuBois opposed a mass return to Africa, the question remains of what he offered in its place as a solution inside America. Like several other black nationalists, such as the adherents of the 'Republic of New Africa',[97] DuBois chose the 'Black Belt', that is a predominantly agricultural region, as his base. It is not difficult to see that behind this return to the country – which had featured earlier in *The Quest of the Silver Fleece* – is the traditional town-country antagonism. It appears in a form typical of DuBois's black and white world-view: the city dwellers are to the country people what the colonial masters are to the people they colonised; the city is seen as the seat of the white oppressors (and thus of evil) who have become rich at the expense of the country, which is the home of the oppressed, but spiritually superior blacks. Connected with this is the yearning for a 'return to the Mothers', for a liberation from an evil, materialistic, complicated technical world and for a new beginning, a 'resurrection' in 'Beauty, Truth and Goodness'. In *Dark*

*Princess* too DuBois pays homage to the cult of the black earth as a symbol of fertility and renewal :

> 'The wide black earth around me is breathing deep with fancies . . . I seem to see salvation here, a gate to the world. Here is a tiny kingdom of tree and wood and hut. Oh, yes, and the brook, the symphony of the brook . . . I am beginning to feel that this place of yours may be no mere temporary refuge. That it may again be Home for you [Matthew]. I see this as yet but dimly, but life here seems symbolic. Here is the earth yearning for seed. Here men make food and clothes. We are at the bottom and beginning of things . . . On such deep founding-stones you may perhaps build. I can see work transformed. This cabin with little change in its aspect can be made a place of worship, of beauty and books . . . for life with music and color floating in it. Perhaps a little lake to woo the brook.[98]

DuBois does not go beyond this rather idyllic image of a black world dedicated to the cultivation of beauty; *Dark Princess* does not answer the question of the future of the blacks, and of whether it was really possible to establish a 'Pan-Africa' on American soil.

The end of the novel prudently takes refuge in the realm of the fairy-tale : after Matthew and Kautilya have agreed on the aims and location of the black world to be constructed, she calls him to Virginia ( !), where she has been staying since their separation and where she has given birth to a son. Significantly enough they are now to be married 'with a proper Christian knot'[99] to make 'dis little man an hones' chile'. After the exotic wedding ceremony there sounds 'from the forest, with faint and silver applause of trumpets : "King of the Snows of Gaurisankar !" – "Grand Mughal of Utter India !" – "Messenger and Messiah to all the Darker Worlds !" ' The union of Pan-Africa and Pan-Asia is thus secured by a threefold tie, cultural, political and physical. This final scene uses DuBoi's favourite colour symbolism to excess, and in its concentrated form its potential for *Kitsch* is revealed only too clearly :

> He saw her afar; standing at the gate there at the end of the long path home, and by the old black tree – her tall and slender form like a swaying willow. She was dressed in eastern style, royal in coloring, with no concession to Europe. As he neared, he sensed the flash of great jewels nestling on her neck and arms; a king's ransom lay between the naked beauty of her breasts; blood rubies weighed down her ears, and about the slim brown gold of her waist ran a girdle such as emperors fight for . . . a naked baby . . . lay upon her hands like a palpitating bubble of gold, asleep . . . the child awoke; . . . it cooed and crowed with joy on her soft arm and threw its golden limbs up to the golden sun . . .[100]

But there is more than mere bad taste in these lines; they mirror a flight from ugly reality into a fantastic world, into the beautiful kingdom of the imagination which is symptomatic of DuBois's attitude. Even his purely sociological writings are invaded by pathos and bombastic descriptive passages. It is no less characteristic that in *Darkwater*, the volume of personal reminiscences, DuBois inserted poems and parables in between essays of primarily sociological bent. There is an obvious psychological interpretation for this. It is reasonable to assume that DuBois's indulging in a fairy-tale world for the fulfilment of his dreams acted as a kind of drug which made him forget the hopeless reality for a short while at least. His search for a sound world of eternal beauty accordingly expresses a fear of reality which early on led him to an unrealistic assessment of Africa and of black behaviour in general.

His last major work, the autobiography which he finished at the age of ninety-two, shows that he never questioned his own premises, but thought that the reasons for his growing isolation within Afro-American society lay in the lack of understanding and goodwill on the part of his contemporaries alone. It is astonishing with what tenacity he clung to the idealism and élitism which he had formulated in his youth, retaining his original ideas even if they took on a slightly different complexion; and this he did in the face of the many social and spiritual upheavals which he witnessed during his long life. This is particularly true of his ideas about Africa. The thoughts on this subject expressed in the autobiography further corroborate the observations made in our analysis of his writings. Thus he deplores in his autobiography the materialism spreading even among the Afro-Americans and Africans :

> The very loosening of our racial discriminatory pressures had not, as I once believed, left Negroes free to become a group cemented into a new cultural unity, capable of absorbing socialism, tolerance, and democracy, and helping to lead America into a new heaven and new earth. But rather, partial emancipation is freeing some of them to ape the worst of American and Anglo-Saxon chauvinism, luxury, showing-off, and 'social-climbing'.

But this 'failure' does not lead him to a renewed examination of his 'racial ideal' or to an analysis which could have provided an explanation for the behaviour of the blacks. Instead he replaces rational thought by wishful ideas based on his dream of a society without conflict :

> I have long noted and fought this all too evident tendency, and built my faith [ !] in its ultimate change on an inner Negro cultural ideal. I thought this ideal would be built on ancient African communism, supported and developed by memory of slavery and experi-

ence of caste, which would drive the Negro group into a spiritual unity precluding the development of economic classes and inner class struggle. This was once possible [ !], but it is now improbable. I strove hard to accomplish this . . .[101]

In view of such comments it seems wrong to call DuBois a 'racist', as his critics consistently do. He did not dedicate his life's work to the preservation of a 'race'. His only concern was with 'culture' and the 'spirit' which he sought to defend and protect against the growing materialism throughout the world.[102] When he had to abandon his hope of building a community of the spirit with Afro-Americans he turned to a new area of activity, Africa, the country of origin of his 'Negro ideal'. It was there that a new, better, world was to arise, with the aim 'to teach mankind what Non-Violence and Courtesy, Literature and Art, Music and Dancing can do for this greedy, selfish, and war-stricken world'.[103]

DuBois thought that the only way for Africa to reach this goal was through socialism, the Eastern socialism which – as he believed since his contact with the Soviet Union – implemented his ideals. This is why a short final note must be added on the connection between his turn to the East and his concept of Pan-Africa; for this connection once again reveals the continuity of his missionary world view. And again his blind enthusiasm for socialism which seemed to promise fraternisation among all men also shows his lack of realistic appraisal – a lack which arose from a fear to face up to the desperate situation of the blacks and to become conscious of their desolation and loneliness.[104] This fear caused him to stop half-way through his rational analysis of the possibilities of overcoming racial problems by way of socialism in order to 'save' himself literally through an irrational belief in a better world. Thus DuBois's addresses to Africa and 'to the world'[105] in particular exhibit the same garbled Marxism which he had propagated thirty years previously in *Dark Princess* as a means of saving humanity, i.e. through culture. He had practically nothing in common with orthodox Marxists, save his contempt for occidental capitalism. But it must be emphasised again that this contempt was primarily based – in DuBois's case – on a concern for culture, on a fear of spiritual shallowness and loss of ideal values at a time of an apparent, menacing spread of materialism. His interest in an economic and political change of the situation was only secondary and was entirely dependent on his cultural ideal. Had he been a genuine Marxist, he would have had to revise this very ideal which had no social relevance whatever and merely aims at a completely a-political 'cultivation of beauty'; he would have had to recognise that this ideal was itself the product of a certain social order and hardly desirable in a socialist society. Because of his peculiar point of view DuBois time and again came to erroneous conclusions about the socialist states, even if his actual observations are frequently correct. Thus he mistook their anti-capitalism for anti-materialism, their economic backwardness for asceticism. He thought that the aim of these countries was 'the cultural progress of the mass of workers and not merely of an intellectual élite'. His assumption in itself may be correct; but his conclusion again betrays his peculiar concept of democracy which has been discussed above. For he continues : '. . . in return for all this, communist lands believe that the cultivation of the mass of people will discover more talent and genius to serve the state than any closed aristocracy ever furnished.' He therefore believes that with the help of socialism he will be able to fulfil the dream, formulated in *Dark Princess*, to supplant the 'closed aristocracy' of the Anglo-Saxon countries by an 'aristocracy of the spirit'. He continues to put much emphasis on education : '. . . that there merge on earth a single unified people, – free, well and educated.' This was an important point of contact with the so-called socialist states. Their authoritarian concept of leadership coincided with his own conviction that only education and leadership, even coercion if necessary, could help man to a better self. He advocates abolition of individual rights in favour of the 'state', which has to be understood as the embodiment of the 'cultural élite', of the 'educated group' often mentioned by him. He was closer to Lenin than to Marx : But what is Socialism? It is disciplined economy and political organisation in which the first duty of a citizen is to serve the state . . . the African tribe, whence all of you [Africans] sprung, was communistic in its very beginnings. No tribesman was free. All were servants of the tribe of whom the chief was father and voice.' Accordingly he calls for asceticism (as he had already done in *The Souls of Black Folk*) :

Live simply . . . You can starve a while longer rather than sell your great heritage for a mess of western capitalistic pottage . . . As I have said, this is a call for sacrifice. Great Goethe sang, 'Entbehren sollst du, sollst entbehren' – 'Thou shalt forgo, shalt do without'. If Africa unites it will be because each part, each nation, each tribe gives up a part of his heritage for the good of the whole . . . Your local tribal, much-loved languages must yield to the few world tongues which serve the largest numbers of people and promote understanding and world literature.[106]

Particularly the last part of the quotation shows at the same time how little conscious DuBois was of his problematical position. To demand giving up indigenous languages and cultures in favour of a 'world literature' meant precisely to perpetuate the cultural, and with it the political, dependence of the 'Third World'. DuBois's socialism thus led him to make similarly mistaken judgments about Africa as his earlier

idealism had done. This was to be expected. His socialism is basically
only the continuation of his idealism by other means. He failed to
appreciate the obstacles which stood in the way of socialism in Africa
ignored the economic dependence of the African states on the West,[10]
was struck with blindness as far as Chinese and Russian political aim
were concerned,[108] and simplified the solution of all problems by think
ing that, as Kautilya had said, 'it is simply a matter of wanting to'.[10]
Not only that, his repeated, much emphasised call on Africa to learn
from Russia and China also results in a strange picture of Africa : 'Thi
China knows. This Africa must learn . . . Come to China, Africa, and
look around. Invite Africa to come, China, and see what you can teach
by just pointing . . . All I ask from you [Africa] is the courage to know
to look about you and see what is happening in this old and
tired world . . .' There are confessions, such as : 'Once I thought of
you Africans as children, whom we educated Afro-Americans would
lead to liberty. I was wrong. We could not even lead ourselves, much
less you. Today I see you rising under your own leadership, guided
by your own brains . . . '; or similarly : 'American Negroes had too
often assumed that their leadership in Africa was natural. With th
rise [!] of an educated group of Africans, this was increasingly un
likely', or there are observations such as '. . . above all, the new Pan
Africa will seek education for all its youth on the broadest possibl
basis . . . for making [!] them modern, intelligent, responsible men of vision
and character'.[110] Such comments not only disregard long-standing
traditions of the African struggle for emancipation completely,[111] bu
imply at the same time that the Africans of the colonial era remain, al
protestations notwithstanding, 'children' in his eyes – ignorant, back
ward, *not* intelligent or responsible.

It is true that DuBois's lack of understanding of the indigenous valu
of African forms of life which is again apparent, and which originate
from his rigid Eurocentricity, was not very surprising in his writing
of around 1900; but that it should persist virtually unchanged for th
following sixty years is startling. At least it reveals DuBois as the oppo
site of what he is consistently considered to be by literary critics. He i
certainly not the father of a revolutionary black consciousness. It is tru
that because of his rigidly anti-white attitude he could be called
'nationalist'; but basically he wanted to build up with blacks a whit
culture, whose components would have been mostly 'European'. As thes
components were non-American, he thought they were also non-white
His hatred of white Americans made him myopic and prevented hir
from seeing the weaknesses of his own world view at an objective dis
tance. Moreover, his hatred chained him to the white world, which
fascinated him so much that he ultimately failed in his search for alter
natives. In so far as one wants to make value judgements at all, it ma

be said that DuBois is presumably much less to blame than the social order in which he lived and which moulded him.[112]

This extensive examination of DuBois's ideas about Africa seemed to be justified by the great importance which DuBois not only thought himself he had, but which he in fact did have for the liberation movement of the Afro-Americans. Furthermore the difficulties of establishing a rational relationship with Africa which DuBois's writings exhibit are symptomatic of all Afro-Americans who want to adopt an alien Africa, estranged from them by racist ideologies, as a new spiritual, often even cultural, home. DuBois's difficulties must therefore be kept in mind in subsequent analyses. His own premises caused DuBois to fail as far as his Pan-Africa was concerned. But his attempts to rehabilitate Africa and his repeated pleading against injustice helped others to establish a more positive relationship with Africa. This is particularly true of the poets of the Harlem Renaissance who will now be discussed. DuBois helped them through lively criticism and encouragement and in the periodical *Crisis* provided a public platform for them, thereby promoting their ideas. The following chapter will therefore deal with this new phase of Afro-American literary development and its connection with Africa.

# 4 The 'Harlem Renaissance'

As we have seen, Afro-American nationalism grew noticeably stronger towards the end of the nineteenth century. This trend was characterised above all by a feeling of greater 'racial solidarity' and by a keen interest among a number of blacks in Afro-American and African history. Their activities contributed to the emergence of a new type of Afro-American who was becoming increasingly conscious of his value as a black person. Harlem, where not only Afro-Americans but also West Indians and Africans came together in great numbers, soon turning it into the largest metropolis of the black world, became the rallying-point for this 'New Negro'. It was here that blacks were given a feeling of belonging together. It is therefore no coincidence that Harlem with its newly-won self-confidence and its Africa-orientated 'racial feeling' stimulated a rich literary activity which reached a first climax in the so-called Harlem Renaissance.

## I THE HARLEM MOVEMENT

The Harlem Movement has been called 'literary Garveyism'.[1] But it is easy to be misled by this term since it assumes a much closer connection between Marcus Garvey and the writers of the 1920s than actually existed. Garvey, it is true, influenced the cultural climate of this period and did much to make the large majority of Afro-Americans aware of their African origins which they had preferred to ignore for so long. But equally there was much that separated him from the representatives of the Harlem Renaissance. Garvey's attitude towards Africa was above all pragmatic. His enthusiasm for the 'homeland' with which he captured his audiences had no intellectual depth and was designed first and foremost to push them into action. The intellectuals and writers of the Harlem Renaissance, on the other hand, were too deeply rooted in Western literary and intellectual traditions whose imprint can be traced through their works to feel much enthusiasm for Garvey' emigration programme. On the contrary, as far as can be ascertained none of the New Negroes has ever given an indication that they wished to settle in Africa. Nor did they find it easy to identify with Garvey' 'African consciousness' which his movement proclaimed with naïve pomposity. Their attitude towards Africa was both more detached and more differentiated.[2]

## (a) ALAIN LOCKE'S 'MANIFESTO' OF THE HARLEM RENAISSANCE

A certain affinity, however, can be discovered between Garvey and one of the leading black intellectuals of this time : Alain Locke, the actual mentor of the Harlem Renaissance. Like Garvey he preached the political and cultural 'rebirth of the black race' under Afro-American leadership. Locke has defined his ideas in an introductory essay to a volume entitled *The New Negro* and edited by him. This essay is generally considered to be the manifesto of the Harlem Renaissance. It maintains that the blacks are about to emancipate themselves intellectually from the psychological ravages of slavery and to follow the West on its path into modernity. This New Negro, Locke continues, has gained a completely new consciousness of his worth as a black human being. He sees this 'as an augury of a new democracy in American culture'. Henceforth blacks are to be considered not only serious partners of white Americans on their way towards democracy, but – Locke added in reference to Garvey – they are also conscious 'of acting as the advance-guard of the African peoples in their contact with Twentieth Century civilization'. According to Locke, the most important task of the Afro-Americans was to rehabilitate the black man throughout the world, and to demolish the prejudices which had been carried over from slavery. This mission was to be fulfilled through achievements in the fields of art and culture. This at any rate is the area where Locke believed the greatest concentration of black talent to exist. A policy of this kind, he argued, would strengthen black group cohesion and, above all, convince the whites that there is no justification in looking down on the black race. Like DuBois, Locke is full of regret that 'the more intelligent representative elements of the two race groups have at so many points got quite out of vital touch with one another.' He finds his arguments supported by the fact that, for the first time in Afro-American history, black writers had achieved a decisive breakthrough and succeeded in making a deep impression on the whites.[3]

The linking of a political renewal with a cultural one, which came to be an important propellant in Afro-American literary production, was not simply a product of Locke's idealism. In fact he had specific examples in mind, namely the nationalist movements of the nineteenth and twentieth centuries. His Harlem Renaissance was moulded on these precedents when a lively cultural life went hand-in-hand with national liberation – with Irish and Czech nationalism being, in Locke's view, two good cases in point.[4] He was, to be sure, everything but a radical nationalist. What Locke aspired to was to extend democratic rights and

E

liberties to the Afro-American minority in the United States. He was certain that they were on their way towards this goal which, considering that the black predicament worsened in the 1920s, must be regarded as surprisingly optimistic.[5]

It is more appropriate to use 'Renaissance' as a term to circumscribe the *cultural* movement of this period. Although this term is employed widely and almost as a matter of course, it is useful to examine its precise meaning, the more so since the movement of the 1960s and early 1970s has been described as 'Renaissance II'.[6] On a very general level the term 'Renaissance' might be defined in the sense of Littré as a 'lively intellectual movement following a period of oppression' as evidence of the 'spiritual emancipation' of the blacks from slavery and its repercussions. But, as Wagner has pointed out, the Harlem Renaissance is comparable also in the narrower sense to the Renaissance of the fifteenth and sixteenth centuries :

> Like the great European Renaissance, the Negro's 'Little Renaissance' had, in addition to an Antiquity to excavate and extoll, a Middle Ages to repudiate. Africa, whose artistic treasures were only currently being discovered, was its Antiquity, and slavery its Middle Ages, whose shadows were at last being dispersed in the dawn of a new age.[7]

By publishing his anthology Locke intended to inform a wider audience that this new era had already begun. At the same time he wanted to give a few pointers as to the direction which any future development of black culture ought to take.[8] Like some of the leading Afro-American intellectuals of the nineteenth and twentieth centuries, Locke and the other contributors to the volume emphasise that the first task was to gain a positive attitude towards black history, American as well as African. Schomburg expresses this imperative most clearly in his contribution :

> The American Negro must remake his past in order to make his future. Though it is orthodox to think of America as the one country where it is unnecessary to have a past, what is a luxury for the nation as a whole becomes a prime social necessity for the Negro. For him, a group tradition must supply compensation for persecution, and pride of race the antidote for prejudice. History must restore what slavery took away, for it is the social damage of slavery that the present generation must repair and offset.[9]

Locke was most interested in a revision of 'black antiquity', that is of African art. He was encouraged in this by the enthusiasm with which artists in Western Europe – Picasso, Bracque and Matisse among them – rediscovered African sculptures for themselves. It was their own turning to abstract art which had opened their eyes to the beauty of stylised African sculptures.[10] If even European artists were inspired by this kind of art, there was no reason why they should not also have as much or greater influence 'upon the blood descendants, bound to it by a sense of direct cultural kinship, than upon those who inherit by tradition only, and through the channels of an exotic curiosity and interest.' Of course, the artistic temperament of the Afro-Americans had moved a considerable distance from that of their African ancestors. 'What we have thought primitive in the American Negro – his naïveté, his sentimentalism, his exuberance and his improvising spontaneity', Locke argued, 'are then neither characteristically African nor to be explained as an ancestral heritage. They are the result of his peculiar experience in America and the emotional upheaval of its trials and ordeals.' African art by contrast was 'disciplined, sophisticated, laconic and fatalistic'. And yet, he continues, there existed, thanks to a clearly perceptible 'deep-seated aesthetic endowment', a chance 'that the sensitive artistic mind of the American Negro, stimulated by a cultural pride and interest, will receive from African art a profound and galvanizing influence . . . , the lesson of a classic background, the lesson of discipline, of style, of technical control pushed to the limits of technical mastery'.[11] Locke's recommendations are obviously not without pitfalls. On the other hand, his ideas on the subject are not as extreme as they might appear at first glance.[12] The revival of the ancient period by the humanists of the fifteenth and sixteenth centuries was, after all, a deliberate act in the absence of a direct and traditional continuity. To this extent the Renaissance was no less 'artificial' than Locke's equally legitimate proposal that the New Negro should go back to his African heritage. One might even go so far as to argue that there existed less of a link between Erasmus of Rotterdam and some Greek philosophers of the ancient period than between a present-day Afro-American and an African.[13]

Apart from the very different historical significance of the two 'Renaissances' in question, they were separated by another essential point : the New Negro had no intention of assimilating African ideas, languages, literatures or music. What he had in mind was to define his own position *vis-à-vis* Africa. Afro-Americans did not possess, as Locke maintains, an 'ardent respect and love for Africa, the motherland'.[14] Consequently their first task was to put some order into their ambiguous feelings towards a continent which – unlike antiquity, which had always been treated with unlimited reverence – had been scorned as 'dark' and whose history was shrouded in prejudice. Moreover, the black intellectuals of the Harlem Renaissance knew too little about Africa not to be vexed by doubts about their 'revivalist' activities. A lack of self-assurance and false notions about Africa therefore characterise their literary endeavours. Locke was the exception. He moved in advance of his times as far as his theoretical writings and his appeal to embark upon stylistic experiments are concerned. His arguments might have met with a response some forty years later. The New Negroes of the 1920s, however, were too unsure of themselves to be able to question their own position in their literary experiments. With the exception of Toomer and possibly Hughes, they were all catholic in their literary tastes.[15] But this does not apply to their literary message. In this respect Locke belonged to the older generation of DuBois and Booker T. Washington, and the young black poets who contributed to Locke's anthology have little in common with him. What united the older and the younger generations was 'racial pride' – 'that wholesome, welcome virtue of finding beauty in oneself'.[16] But the more important among the New Negro movement did not share the élitism of DuBois and others, their craving for recognition by the whites and their optimistic belief that American democracy would be applied to Afro-Americans in the near future. Nor were they as convinced as DuBois, Garvey or Locke that it was the Afro-Americans who were destined to become the cultural 'leaders' of Africa.

It is easy to list what the poets of the Harlem Renaissance did *not* aim for. It is more difficult to analyse their positive objectives. This is because the Harlem Renaissance did not represent a coherent movement. It lacked a precise programme from which the intentions of its active members might be distilled. Those who came to be the New Negroes had met in Harlem rather by coincidence. It was the favourable external conditions there which gave cohesion to this group and left the impression that their work amounted to a 'movement'.[17] It was not some 'inner' necessity or the conviction that, in order to achieve permanence and substance, the new black culture required something like a 'cultural philosophy' which brought them together.[18] Historical factors such as a growing group consciousness, urbanisation, the rise of Harlem to the position of a Black-American metropolis with a lively intellectual sub-culture, and finally the awareness of the 'African heritage' created a framework within which black artists could develop. They had the good and rare fortune of finding themselves at one with the consciousness of the surrounding black environment.[19] They may not have reached many people since the masses continued to follow Garvey's movement.[20] But the New Negroes certainly gave the Harlem Movement a greater intensity and effectiveness than might have been possible in different circumstances, though the quality of their artistic production by and large did not surpass that of other periods.[21]

*(b)* THE ROLE OF THE WHITE PRIMITIVISTS

We have to include yet another element in our analysis of the origins of the Harlem Renaissance, namely the influence of white writers and patrons. They took an interest in the black artists of the 1920s such as one had not seen before or was to see later. The roots of this can be found in the popularity of primitivism which, although it was part and parcel of the Western tradition, came to dominate American thinking of the inter-war period. By this time the optimistic belief in progress of the nineteenth century had been replaced by a feeling of profound disillusionment. Industrialisation, it appeared, had not helped to solve the problems of mankind. On the contrary, the world seemed to have become a less secure and more complicated place as a result of the dissolution of traditional structures which accompanied the Industrial Revolution. People were overcome by a sense of *ennui* with modern society. It was reinforced by the argument that the moral rigidity of Puritanism and the invasion of technology into men's daily lives had alienated the individual from true humanity. The point is that many whites did not try to solve the problems of the technical age by rational means, but escaped into primitivism. Harlem suddenly became the meeting-place of all those frustrated white intellectuals who were hoping to forget the sterility of their own lives by attending floor-shows with blacks dancing on the stage against the backdrop of cardboard jungles. In this way they thought they might be able to recapture some of the lost spontaneous beauty of the body which the supposedly 'earthy' blacks had preserved in themselves. This was the time 'when the Negro was in vogue',[22] and the intellectuals of the Harlem Movement suddenly enjoyed a prestige among whites which they had not known before.

Yet it would be wrong to conclude from the dependence of the black authors on white patronage that there would have been no Harlem Renaissance had it not been for the whites.[23] After all, most artists are in one form or another dependent on outside financial support. But there is another point to be made about the Harlem Renaissance : as has been shown in the preceding chapters, it is not an isolated phenomenon in Afro-American history. On the contrary, it was deeply rooted in that history and had a number of precursors. It is true that without the support of the whites who either maintained the New Negroes or introduced them to influential publishers,[24] the Harlem Renaissance would have found it more difficult to make its impact. However, artists find themselves in a precarious position at all times and patronage does not necessarily lead to artistic corruption. In his autobiography one of them, Langston Hughes, has admitted that some authors 'ceased to write to amuse themselves and began to write to amuse and entertain white people'. 'Negroes', he added, 'have writer-racketeers, as has any other race. But I have known almost all of them, and most of the good ones have tried to be honest, write honestly, and express their world as they saw it.'[25]

Apart from active support in finding publishers, interested whites like Vachel Lindsay and Van Vechten obviously gave them encouragement and intellectual stimulation. But Hughes energetically refuted the notion that they worked under white tutelage. Rather their ideas were influenced by Charles S. Johnson, Jessie Fauset and Alain Locke. These men had first brought the New Negroes together, given them advice and opened the pages of *Crisis* and *Opportunity* to them. Only this had helped many of them to become known at all. Hughes himself severed links with his own patron, a mysterious Park Avenue millionairess when

> she wanted me to be primitive and know and feel the intuitions of the primitive. But, unfortunately, I did not feel the rhythms of the primitive surging through me, and so I could not live and write as though I did. I was only an American Negro — who had loved the surface of Africa and the rhythms of Africa — but I was not Africa. I was Chicago and Kansas City and Broadway and Harlem. And I was not what she wanted me to be.[26]

McKay spent much of his time in France and North Africa and more or less survived on his royalties. Cullen explicitly refused any help which Van Vechten had offered and earned his living as a teacher.[27] If nothing else, one will have to concede the protagonists of the Harlem Renaissance their integrity as artists. In analysing their works it is therefore safe to assume that their consciousness is authentically reflected in them. But this does not imply that the poems and novels of the New Negroes are not pervaded by primitivist elements. In this respect they were of course just as exposed to the *Zeitgeist* as the white authors of the inter-war period.

However, if one compares white and black primitivist literature, it is possible to discover differences which are characteristic of the image which the respective authors had of Africa and of black men. Without going into the large body of white primitivist literature, we must mention some of its features here. The most outstanding among these is the notion that blacks are still immature and the captives of natural 'animality'. This is because they are supposedly 'only a few generations removed from the jungle'.[28] There are now two different types of 'natural' human beings, depending on whether one saw 'good' or 'evil' forces at work in Nature. These two types had a firm place in Western thinking as we have seen above when discussing 'Sambo' and 'The Brute'. Gertrude Stein's 'negroes and all the kind of children', as depicted in *Melanctha*, with their 'wide, abandoned laughter that makes the warm broad glow of negro sunshine . . . the earthborn, boundless joy of negroes', fall into the first category.[29] Melanctha's warmth, intuition and capacity to follow the 'wisdom' of her body is due to her close contact with 'Nature' and stands in contrast to 'pensive' cold-blooded Jeff. Anderson's 'niggers' display a similar naturalness. In his novel *Dark Laughter*, which was widely read in the 1920s, they are charged with bringing an anaemic civilisation to life again. Their 'dark' laughter, their dark skin, their dancing and singing and their sexual prowess and promiscuity are seen as manifestations of an undiluted 'animality'. This enables them to establish a link with the 'ultimate truth of things' which the whites have lost because of their intellectuality and preoccupations with abstractions.[30] Child-like simplicity, peaceableness and instinctive behaviour are also the features which recur in Frank's *Holiday* as well as in most of Faulkner's novels.[31]

In *Nigger Heaven* Van Vechten similarly gives a positive weight to the origins of the blacks : 'This primitive birthright which was so valuable and important an asset, a birthright that all the civilized races were struggling to get back to . . . this African beat . . . this love of drums, of exciting rhythms, this naïve delight in glowing colour – the colour that exists only in cloudless tropical climes – this warm, sexual emotion . . .' Primitivism assumes the significance of an abstract ideal in Van Vechten's novel, however. The blacks are depicted as children, but as naughty ones. They are much more 'savage' than 'noble'. *Nigger Heaven* is hence more accurately to be counted among the primitivist literature of our second category. Being primitive has a positive connotation only if it has no more than a decorative function as in the case of Mary, the cultured and puritanical heroine. Being primitive is acceptable only if it has been 'defused' by the regulative mechanisms of bourgeois conventions. The less 'civilised', i.e. the more 'African' the blacks are, the more they are captives of their instincts and passions, displaying all that is threatening and evil in their African character : 'The girl . . . was pure black, with savage African features, thick nose, thick lips, . . . while her eyes rolled back so far that only the whites were visible. And now she began to perform her evil rites . . .' The African element is, in other words, manifested first and foremost in the sexuality of the blacks and this sexuality is, in line with puritanical tradition, bound up with vice and viciousness emerging 'from the depths of hell'.[32]

At the same time Van Vechten's widely-read novel reflects the influence of two other well-known works of the 1920s : Lindsay's 'The Congo' and O'Neill's *The Emperor Jones*.[33] Both Lindsay and O'Neill expose the 'basic savagery'[34] of the blacks and the destructive, menacing and vicious force of the pagan 'Congo Civilization'. By accepting Western values and Christianity to which they are introduced during the period of slavery in the United States, the blacks in 'The Congo' succeed in ridding themselves of their African savagery. They turn Africa into a paradise and, with the proclamation of the Gospel, civilisation can at last also strike roots in the 'Dark Continent' :

> . . .
> And they all repented, a thousand strong
> From their stupor and savagery and sin and wrong
> And slammed with their hymn books till they
>     shook the room
> With 'glory, glory, glory',

> . . .
> There, where the wild ghost-gods had wailed
> A million boats of the angels sailed
> With oars of silver, and prows of blue
> And silken pennants that the sun shone
>     through.
> 'Twas a land transfigured, 'twas a new
>     creation.

> Oh, a singing wind swept the negro nation
> And on through the backwoods clearing
>     flew : —
> 'Mumbo-Jumbo is dead in the jungle.
> Never again will he hoo-doo you.'[35]

O'Neill likewise uses traditional white stereotypes in his drama. It appears as if the figure of Brutus (i.e. 'the Brute' !) is designed to underline that 'the modern black man is a walking savage thinly disguised by western culture and religion'.[36] Yet O'Neill did not have Lindsay's rather naïve juxtaposition of African primitiveness and Western culture in mind. Brutus Jones is not intended to portray a typical representative of the black race, but to describe the general predicament of man; he wants to demonstrate 'how a superficially acquired and corrupted "civility" threatens to disintegrate under the impact of *Angst* and how the subconscious can gain the upper hand'.[37] It is nevertheless significant that O'Neill took a black man to unmask the 'innate savagery'[38] of all human beings. Apparently, blacks are closer to this state of mind than whites, as far as he is concerned.

It is not necessary to discuss further examples. The works mentioned here can be regarded as representative of primitivist currents in early twentieth-century white literature in the United States. There are minor discrepancies between them, but the general picture of blacks is fairly uniform. They represent intuitive and emotional men who, depending on whether the author's basic attitude was negative or positive, lived either in a state of infantile and 'natural' innocence or of bestial savagery. Africa is more a place of hell than a part of this world, 'a vacuum of savagery and decay'. It is easy to project white anxieties and guilt-feelings onto this continent. The blacks, as children 'of that violent nothingness',[39] do not appear as real persons with complex characters, but as 'images of comfortable white sexual fantasy and assuagement of guilt'.[40] What is reflected in them is the existential fears of the whites when they saw themselves confronted with the dissolution of traditional society. They believed to recognise in the 'hell of Africa' and in the 'primitive blacks' the bottomless pits of their own soul, 'The Heart of Darkness' from which – were it not for 'civilising', i.e. disciplining, influences – irrational and frightening forces seemed to ascend.

(*c*) THE BLACK POETS OF THE HARLEM RENAISSANCE AND AFRICA

It is not surprising that the Afro-Americans found it impossible to identify themselves with such a frightful image of Africa. Their literature, it is true, contains a strongly primitivistic streak. But their attitude towards Africa was more discriminating and, of necessity, more positive. Unlike the white authors, many of them no longer considered the United States as their spiritual and emotional home. It was from Africa that they expected a new legitimation of their identity. Their writings revolve around four or five themes from which the various aspects of their attitude towards Africa can most usefully be analysed.

One group of poems still reflects the 'colonial image', as one might call it, of 'Dark Africa'. It emerges from an early poem by McKay which appeared in his collection *Songs of Jamaica*, published in 1912 :

> Seems our lan' must ha' been a bery low-do'n place,
> Mek it tek such long time in tu'ning out a race,
> . . .
> But I t'ink it do good, tek we from Africa
> An' lan' us in a blessed place as dis a ya.
>
> Talk 'bouten Africa, we would be deh till now,
> Maybe same half-naked – all day dribe buccra cow,

An' tearin' t'rough de bush wid all de monkey dem,
Wile an' uncibilise', an' neber comin' tame.[41]

Neither in McKay's nor in the writings of other representatives of the Harlem Renaissance does the theme of 'Dark Africa' recur with such bluntness. Rather we find a revealing variation of it which has been encountered before in DuBois's attitude towards Africa : even if Africa is now backward and primitive, there was a time when it was great and culturally more advanced than the Western world. Africa's present state, in short, is merely a recent phenomenon. It was presumably under the influence of DuBois, whom he greatly admired, and of Garvey, to whose journal, *Negro World*, he contributed,[42] that McKay changed his mind. Ten years later, at any rate, in his second volume of poems, entitled *Harlem Shadows*, the early rejection of Africa has been replaced by a positive view of that continent :

### Africa

The sun sought thy dim bed and brought forth light,
The sciences were suckling at thy breast;
When all the world was young in pregnant night
Thy slaves toiled at thy monumental best.
Thou ancient treasure-land, thou modern prize,
New peoples marvel at thy pyramids ![43]

The poem shows that Africa is now much closer to his heart. In another poem in this volume he even goes so far as to call Africa his 'mother-land' and Africans 'my brothers and my sisters'. Shattered by the events of the 'Bloody Sunday' of 1919,[44] he calls on Africa to follow in Russia's footsteps and to shake off its century-old powerlessness by means of a revolution. However, he continues to adhere to the image of a 'Dark Africa' :

Africa ! long ages sleeping, O my motherland,
    awake !
From the deep primeval forests where the crouching
    leopard's lurking,
Lift your heavy-lidded eyes, Ethiopia ! awake ![45]

His attitude towards 'Dark Africa' is more favourable in his poem 'Outcast' :

For the dim regions whence my fathers came
My spirit, bondaged by the body, longs.
Words felt, but never heard, my lips would frame;

My soul would sing forgotten jungle songs.
I would go back to darkness and to peace,
But the great western world holds me in fee,
And I may never hope for full release
While to its alien gods I bend my knee.
Something in me is lost, forever lost,
Some vital thing has gone out of my heart,
And I must walk the way of life a ghost
Among the sons of earth, a thing apart.
For I was born, far from my native clime,
Under the white man's menace, out of time.[46]

Africa has by now assumed a very different quality. Loneliness and
the feeling of living as an outcast in white society have turned Africa
into a haven of peace, beauty and protective warmth. His earlier naïve
admiration for the West which had supposedly saved him from African
primitiveness, on the other hand, has given way to a profound disillusionment with occidental civilisation. McKay's protest songs of the
1920s testify to this change of heart, which finally makes him cry out in
a fit of powerless hatred :

The white man is a tiger at my throat,
Drinking my blood as my life ebbs away.
. . .

My heart grows sick with hate, becomes as lead,
For this my race that has no home on earth.[47]

With his militancy McKay was far ahead of the other New Negroes.[48]
He had spent his youth in Jamaica relatively protected from racism.
It is possible that he was, for this reason, struck all the more sharply
by racist feelings in the United States while his fellow-blacks in America
had learned quite early on to smother or suppress their own feelings of
hatred.

Even if other poets of the Harlem Renaissance thus found it more
difficult to articulate their hatred as openly as McKay did, there are
a number of poems which reflect the sense of alienation which they all
experienced. Slavery had thrown them into a hostile environment
which made them feel ugly and inferior, 'being born "out of time" '.
This is how Cuney expressed it in what is one of the most famous
poems of the Harlem Renaissance :

She does not know
Her beauty,

> She thinks her brown body
> Has no glory.
>
> If she could dance
> Naked,
> Under palm trees
> And see her image in the river
> She would know.
>
> But there are no palm trees
> On the street,
> And dishwater gives back no images.[49]

To be sure, white Americans shared this feeling of alienation with the black poets of the Harlem Renaissance. But if sentiments of this kind are at all comparable, it might perhaps be said that the experience of alienation was more direct, more personal and hence also more intense in the case of the Afro-Americans. It was, after all, one of the basic bitter experiences with which all blacks were confronted. And as several poems related to this theme show, this feeling of emptiness, of an inner void, could not simply be removed by a fresh awareness of Africa. McKay, for example, relates in his 'On a Primitive Canoe' how he once discovered a tastefully carved African canoe in a shop-window. It made him faintly aware of the beauty of his ancestors' homeland and caused him to feel something like homesickness. Yet at the same time Africa is too unknown to him, too remote to generate more than a vague feeling of belonging inside him :

> . . .
> Why does it thrill more than the handsome boat
> And fill me with a rare sense of things remote
> From this harsh life of fretful nights and days?
> I cannot answer but, whate'er it be,
> An old wine has intoxicated me.[50]

The New Negroes thus accept Africa as being the *Ur*-homeland of all blacks and express a longing for that continent where 'black is beautiful'. But they are also aware of the fact that it is a lost paradise :

> . . .
> Subdued and time-lost
> Are the drums – and yet
> Through some vast mist of race
> There comes this song

I do not understand,
This song of atavistic land,
Of bitter yearnings lost
Without a place —
so long,
So far away
Is Africa's
Dark face.[51]

In short, the New Negroes lost Africa the moment they discovered it. Their feeling of alienation from Africa and America became total, intensifying their sense of sadness and rootlessness. There are so many poems of this period which mirror the loneliness and desperation of the Afro-Americans that it is surprising that this important element should not have been given greater attention in literary criticism, where the overriding theme has been that of the exotic character of the Harlem Renaissance. Loneliness and desperation transpires not only through the above-mentioned poems, above all through McKay's 'Outcast',[52] but also through the following lines by Hughes, entitled 'Afraid' :

We cry among the skyscrapers
As our ancestors
Cried among the palms in Africa
Because we are alone,
It is night,
And we're afraid.[53]

Feelings of sadness, helplessness and despair, stimulated by thoughts of Africa, are probably best brought to life in Cullen's famous poem 'Heritage'. Here the author asks himself, implicitly voicing the feelings of many Afro-Americans : 'What is Africa for me?'[54] Cullen is unable to give a clear-cut answer. His relationship with Africa has many layers. In this poem there are two, the conscious and the subconscious one, between which he is moving back and forth. These vacillations imbue the poem with an ambivalence which is both characteristic of Cullen and symbolic of his position and that of the Harlem Renaissance in general. On a realistic level he feels hardly any affinity towards Africa, as described in this poem. Some three hundred years have passed since his ancestors were enslaved and shipped across the Atlantic. His knowledge of the continent is scant and he is also not terribly interested in it :

. . .

Africa? A book one thumbs
Listlessly, till slumber comes.

. . .
> What is last year's snow to me,
> Last year's anything? The tree
> Budding yearly just forget
> How its past arose or set—

. . .
> *One three centuries removed*
> *From the scenes his fathers loved,*
> *Spicy grove, cinnamon tree,*
> *What is Africa to me?*

These sceptical questions, which apparently leave no  scope for an affirmative answer, are toned down by the context in which they are embedded. They are interrupted by longer passages in which diametrically opposed and irrational feelings rise to the surface and undermine the author's earlier rational considerations :

> So I lie, who always hear,
> Though I cram against my ear
> Both my thumbs, and keep them there,
> Great drums throbbing through the air.
> So I lie, whose fount of pride,
> Dear distress, and joy allied,
> Is my somber flesh and skin,
> With the dark blood dammed within
> Like great pulsing tides of wine
> That, I fear, must burst the fine
> Channels of the chafing net
> Where they surge and foam and fret.

What vexes him and makes him so restless is that his pent-up emotions, the 'paganism of blood' as Locke called it,[55] are being prevented from asserting themselves owing to the strictly Methodist education which his foster-parents gave him.[56] As a result he is permanently haunted by guilt-feelings.[57] As Cullen once remarked himself : 'My chief problem has been that of reconciling a Christian upbringing with a pagan inclination'.[58] In other words, he juxtaposes pagan Africa with Christianity. For him Africa represents all that his education forces him to suppress, which is giving free expression to his sexuality and to his *élan vital* in general. The Africa of 'Heritage' and some of his other poems are therefore associated with a rich tropical world of plants and animals :

So I lie, who all day long
Want no sound except the song
Sung by wild barbaric birds
Goading massive jungle herds,
Juggernauts of flesh that pass
Trampling tall defiant grass
Where young forest lovers lie,
Plighting troth beneath the sky.

Cullen, by contrast believes that religion has made him a sexual and emotional cripple. It has deprived him of his 'pagan' vitality as well as his African Gods :

Quaint, outlandish heathen gods
Black men fashion out of rods,
Clay, and brittle bits of stone,
In a likeness like their own,
My conversion came high-priced ;
I belong to Jesus Christ,
Preacher of humility,
Heathen gods are naught to me.

There is hence only one way of ridding oneself of one's frustrations : to rebel against the Christian God and to identify with the African Gods who might be able to save him. Yet, this road is closed to him. To make things worse : this Christian God, to whom he feels tied, obliges him to show humility and to accept his unacceptable predicament. Towards the end, Cullen's poem thus acquires a political undertone. He allows himself to be carried away by his protest, albeit vexed by feelings of guilt, and begins to long for a Black Jesus who is like him and who can share with him his outrage as well as his knowledge of what it means to be black in a white world.

The last lines of the poem give us an inkling of how much it must have cost him to 'tame' his rebellious 'African' ego and not to allow his anguish and hate against the 'white' God burst forward :

*All day long and all night through*
*One thing only must I do:*
*Quench my pride and cool my blood,*
*Lest I perish in the flood,*
*Lest a hidden ember set*
*Timber that I thought was wet*
*Burning like the dryest flax,*
*Melting like the merest wax,*
*Lest the grave restore its dead.*

At the time of his writing 'Heritage' Cullen's attitude towards Africa was thus ambiguous. On the one hand, he was emotionally attracted by Africa, because it gave him liberties of which his puritanical Western education had deprived him. On the other hand, he fears the 'African within himself'. For this African represents everything he has to suppress if he wants to survive in a 'white' world. Open rebellion might have offered a solution. But his Christian God and his consciousness proscribed this. His education stood in the way of his identifying more closely with Africa. Africa, as it appears in this poem, cannot therefore be described as opium, as Wagner has maintained.[59] On the contrary, the growing feelings of hatred which become more and more difficult to suppress, seem to indicate that Africa did not necessarily have a healing and intoxicating effect. Rather it was salt on the psychic wounds under which Cullen like most other Afro-Americans had to suffer.

There is, however, a group of poems and novels in which the relationship with Africa appears less conflict-laden and which reflect primitivist currents more clearly than the above-mentioned works. McKay's *Home to Harlem* may serve as an example :

> Howard University was a prison with white warders . . . Now he was a young shining chief in a marble palace; slim, naked negresses dancing for his pleasure; courtiers reclining on cushions soft like passionate kisses; . . . and life was all blue happiness. Taboos and terrors and penalties were transformed into new pagan delights, orgies of Orient-blue carnival, of rare flowers and red fruits, cherubs and seraphs and fetishes and phalli and all the most-high gods . . .[60]

In fact, there is hardly an author who did not set out to paint a naïvely romantic picture of Africa. And yet there are important changes of emphasis if one compares black and white primitivism. These differences seem to place the writings of the New Negroes much more into a literary Afro-American tradition. As in the early poetry and the spirituals, Africa is regularly described as a land of freedom, a land which offered its inhabitants an inner peace unknown to the Afro-Americans. The notion of 'freedom' as it appears in these poems in connection with Africa does not imply liberation from moral codes and internalised social taboos for which the white primitivist were longing. It means first and foremost relief from the permanent psychological pressure under which Afro-Americans were forced to live in the United States. This pressure made their life seem grey and joyless and caused Africa to appear in a glowing light.

> . . . these alien skies
> Do not our whole life measure and confine.

No less, once in a land of scarlet suns
And brooding winds, before the hurricane
Bore down upon us, long before this pain,
We found a place where quiet water runs;
I held your hand this way upon a hill,
And felt my heart forebear, my pulse grow still.[61]

There are a number of indications that the authors knew about the artificiality of their African paradise. This may be deduced from the sub-titles of Hughes's 'Our Land' ('Poem for a Decorative Panel') and 'Poem' ('For the Portrait of an African Boy after the manner of Gauguin'[62]) which seem to indicate that Hughes preserved a certain detachment from the primitivist currents of his time and regarded it more as an aesthetic device. In McKay's 'North and South' the African paradise makes its appearance in a dream, and in his novels *Home to Harlem* and *Banjo*[63] it even takes the form of hallucinations under the influence of drugs. Africa itself turns into a drug; it is a dream-world into which the author tries to escape when he finds it too difficult to cope with reality. Such flights into the world of fantasy cannot, of course, absolve the poet from his fate. But they can at least temporarily soothe his pain. There is little doubt that McKay speaks his mind through Ray, the main character of his two novels. Thus he relates in his memoirs how he was almost speechless with anger, when he once went to see a play together with a white fellow-critic and was sent up to the upper circle, called 'Nigger Heaven',[64] although he had a ticket for the stalls. He then adds: 'Damn it all! Goodnight, plays and players. The prison is vast, there is plenty of space and a little time to sing and dance and laugh and love. There is a little time to dream of the jungle, revel in rare scents and riotous colours, croon a plantation melody, and be a real original Negro in spite of all the crackers.'[65] By taking refuge in a dream-world and in primitivist posturing he tries to compensate for the humiliation which he has suffered. This escapism may on occasion even fulfil a therapeutic function in that it helps the author to regain, albeit for a brief moment, his self-respect. An example of this is the magnificent poem 'The Shroud of Color' by Cullen, who suffered many agonies over his blackness.

'Lord, being dark', I said, 'I cannot bear
The further touch of earth, the scented air;
Lord, being dark forewilled to that despair
My color shrouds me in, I am as dirt
Beneath my brother's heel . . .'

. . .
> I strangle in this yoke drawn tighter than
> the worth of bearing it, just to be man.
> I am not brave enough to pay the price
> In full; I lack the strength to sacrifice.

His childhood and youth had shielded him against recognising his true predicament as a black man. But now, in his adulthood, the moment of truth has come. He can no longer dodge the issue. Nevertheless, he finds it impossible to abandon his youthful dreams of a life in freedom and happiness which would bring out the best in him. He refuses to sacrifice his dreams to the fact that, to the real world around him, he is a marked man – marked by the colour of his skin. In his utter despair he thinks of putting an end to his life. But before taking this step he asks God to give him a sign so that he would not die in complete hopelessness. He thereupon has those visions in which God tells him that, like all other beings, he will have to fight for his existence and assert himself. This is but small comfort to the poet and it is only when Africa appears before his inner eye that he finds fresh encouragement. It is the image of a once-free Africa which encourages him to believe that the blacks can look forward to a better future. The freedom of the past is his proof that their present status of inferiority and suppression is not going to be their 'natural', permanent fate.[66]

The consciousness which emerges from these attitudes towards Africa explains the peculiar character of the primitivism of the Harlem Renaissance. Few traces of this, if any, can be found in white primitivist literature. The 'primitive' man who appears in these poems is beautiful and proud, a man who has preserved his dignity in a hostile world around him. It is a man who is self-confident and filled with an unbroken desire to be free. This is why he has great difficulty in subduing his feelings of hatred :

> With subtle poise he grips his tray
>     Of delicate things to eat;
> Choice viands to their mouths half way,
>     The ladies watch his feet
>
> Go carving dexterous avenues
>     Through sly intricacies;
> Ten thousand years on jungle clues
>     Alone shaped feet like these.
>
> For him to be humble who is proud
>     Needs colder artifice;

> Though half his pride is disavowed,
>     In vain the sacrifice.
> Sheer through his acquiescent mask
>     of bland gentility,
> The jungle flames like a copper cask
>     Set where the sun strikes free.[67]

McKay takes up the theme of the 'basic savagery' of the black in a similar vein. And he, too, turns it into a stick with which to threaten the whites and to underline his rebellious thirst for revenge :

> Think you I am not fiend and savage too?
> Think you I could not arm me with a gun
> And shoot down ten of you for every one
> Of my black brothers murdered, burnt by you?
> Be not deceived, for every deed you do
> I could match – outmatch : am I not Afric's son,
> Back of that black land where black deeds are done?[68]

The word 'savage' thus has a connotation here which is very different from Van Vechten's and Lindsay's use of the word. It is an expression of the black's determination to survive and to voice his protest against an inhuman civilisation. It is not Africa and the blacks who are barbaric, but a civilisation which deprives them of their freedom and their human dignity.[69]

Criticism of Western civilisation was a standard feature of the literature of the Harlem Renaissance. Yet it cannot be separated from another theme which might be called the search for a new, black identity. The criticism of Western civilisation served as a kind of orientation point in this attempt at self-definition. This is true above all of the 'black-is-beautiful' theme which enjoyed considerable popularity. The first task was obviously to revive a sense of dignity in dark-skinned human beings which they were widely denied in occidental culture. Toomer's *Cane*, perhaps the greatest work of the Harlem Renaissance, is a case in point. In it, he tried to capture in the form of poetry and poetic prose the beauty of the American South and its people which he introduced with the following lines :

> Her skin is like dusk on the eastern horizon,
> O cant you see it, O cant you see it,
> Her skin is like dusk on the eastern horizon
> . . . When the sun goes down.

> Men had always wanted her, this Karintha, even as a child,
>     Karintha carrying beauty, perfect as dusk when the sun goes
>     down . . .[70]

Hughes has dwelt upon this theme in many of his poems. Thus he wrote in 'My People' :

> The night is beautiful,
> So the faces of my people.
>
> The stars are beautiful,
> So the eyes of my people.
>
> Beautiful, also, is the sun,
> Beautiful, also, are the souls of my people.[71]

These poems are strongly reminiscent of Garvey's slogans and may have been inspired by them. But this does not make them any less 'genuine'.[72] In fact, they appear to reflect a serious desire on the part of both Garvey and the poets of the Harlem Renaissance to gain a positive relationship *vis-à-vis* the notion of 'black'. They all hoped to destroy the negative connotations of the word and to feel 'at home' with it. For this reason 'black' is often associated with a feeling of warmth and belonging. It generates a sense of protection rather than fear such as can be found in the African jungle and its darkness.[73] The notion of 'white', on the other hand, is associated with cold and harshness, with a feeling of exposure and homelessness.[74] It is the same symbolic use of colour which DuBois adhered to and which pervades much of American literature, except that the traditional 'weighting' is reversed. However, to the writers of the Harlem Renaissance these colour symbols had much more than a literary significance. Here for the first time, an attempt was made on a large scale to profess acceptance of one's colour and one's African origins and hence of oneself. At the same time the New Negroes dissociated themselves from the dominant white colour :

> Black
> As the gentle night,
> Black as the kind and quiet night,
> Black as the deep and productive earth,
> Body
> Out of Africa,
> Strong and black . . .
> Kind
> As the black night
> My song
> From the dark lips
> of Africa . . .
> Beautiful

> As the black night . . .
> Black out of Africa,
> Me and my song.[75]

However irrational this reorientation and magic incantation may appear, they fulfilled an important function in the search for an identity in which the New Negroes were engaged. However, the process did not end there. It also involved an acceptance of one's history and the discovery of the past as a source of a new and reinvigorating self-respect :

> Now the dead past seems vividly alive,
>     And in this shining moment I can trace,
> Down through the vista of the vanished years,
>     Your faun-like form, your fond elusive face . . .
>
> I cannot praise, for you have passed from praise,
>     I have no tinted thoughts to paint you true;
> But I can feel and I can write the word;
>     The best of me is but the least of you.[76]

There were two spheres in this past with which the New Negroes had to come to terms : slavery and Africa. It is significant that they no longer feel ashamed of the humiliations they suffered. Compassion and respect for the suffering of their ancestors replaced the former feelings of shame. The suffering of the individual becomes submerged in the suffering of all black men. Individual pain thus loses its pungency and stimulates a fresh will to live. Cullen, for example, abandons his death-wish in 'The Shroud of Color' after God had sent him a vision of the fate of the blacks :

> The cries of all dark people near or far
> Were billowed over me, a mighty surge
> Of suffering in which my puny grief must
>     merge
> And lose itself; I had no further claim to urge
> For death; in shame I raised my dusty-grimed
>     head . . .[77]

In his famous poem 'The Negro speaks of Rivers' which he dedicated to DuBois, Hughes takes this theme one step further and derives the myth of the 'wonderful oppressed'[78] from the notion that all blacks are united in their fate. They have gained a new dignity by what they have all lived through. His soul had become as 'deep' as all those rivers which accompanied the black man's path throughout the history of mankind.

> I've known rivers :
> I've known rivers ancient as the world and older than the
>     flow of human blood in human veins.
>
> My soul has grown deep like the rivers.
> I bathed in the Euphrates when dawns were young.
> I built my hut near the Congo and it lulled me to sleep.
> I looked upon the Nile and raised the pyramids above it.
> I heard the singing of the Mississippi when Abe Lincoln
>     went down to New Orleans, and I've seen its muddy
>     bosom turn all golden in the sunset.
>
> I've known rivers :
> Ancient, dusky rivers.
>
> My soul has grown deep like the rivers.[79]

*Cane* may be taken to represent the sum total of the feelings and attitudes towards Afro-American history in the poetry of McKay, Cullen and Hughes. Toomer's autobiographical notes are interesting as an early source of his thinking. He had been asked to provide these notes in 1922 by Max Eastman, the editor of *Liberator*, and by Eastman's friend and collaborator McKay. Like others, Toomer had experienced the vitalising effect of an emotional identification with his 'Negro group', although this path was considerably more arduous for him than for McKay. Physically there was nothing that connected him with his black forebears. He could, without difficulty, move between the two ethnic groups and he did. He had always, it is true, tried to bring about a 'spiritual fusion analogous to the fact of racial intermingling' and to establish an inner balance between the various elements in his background. He wanted, as he put it, 'to let them function as complements'. Yet, so he continues,

> within the last two or three years, my growing need for artistic expression has pulled me deeper and deeper into the Negro group. And as my powers of receptivity increased, I found myself loving it in a way that I could never love the other. It has stimulated and fertilized whatever creative talent I may contain within me. A visit to Georgia last fall was the starting point of almost everything of worth that I have done. I heard folk-songs come from the lips of Negro peasants. I saw the rich dusk beauty that I had heard many false accents about, and of which till then, I was somewhat skeptical. And a deep part of my nature, a part that I had repressed, sprang suddenly to life and responded to them. Now, I cannot conceive of myself as

aloof and separated. My point of view has not changed; it has deepened, it has widened.[80]

But the joy of having a hitherto closed dimension of black life opened to him is quickly diluted by sadness which he feels when thinking about the imminent destruction of this Southern culture by migration and industrialisation. '*Cane* was a swan-song', Toomer commented, 'it was a song of an end',[81] the end of a black culture with its sorrowful beauty. He hoped to make 'that parting soul' visible and to record it for posterity :

> Pour O pour that parting soul in song,
> O pour it in the sawdust glow of night,
> Into the velvet pine-smoke air to-night,
> And let the valley carry it along.
> And let the valley carry it along.
>     . . .
>
> O Negro slaves, dark purple ripened plums,
> Squeezed, and bursting in the pine-wood air,
> Passing, before they stripped the old tree bare
> One plum was saved for me, one seed becomes
>
> An everlasting song, a singing tree,
> Caroling softly souls of slavery,
> What they were, and what they are to me,
> Caroling softly souls of slavery.[82]

But before transcending the experience of slavery in this way, Toomer apparently overcame a number of emotional barriers. Judging from the autobiographical passages in *Cane* it seems to have been a most painful process of maturing. And in the final analysis he probably failed to find what he was looking for, i.e. 'identity and personal wholeness'.[83] At least it is very doubtful if he ever achieved the reconciliation of the various elements inside him, a harmonious balance which included his black heritage. He crossed the 'color-line' for good and lived an existence in obscurity as a member of the white world, and only bits and pieces of his subsequent life have survived.[84]

*Cane* also contains references to Toomer's later decision to leave the black world; but even more clearly can one discern in this book the agonising conflicts which he must have experienced before taking it. 'Kabnis', the dramatic key piece in the volume, is of particular interest here. In it Toomer projects his own schizophrenic feelings onto two characters, Ralph Kabnis and Lewis. Kabnis is a black poet who has come to Georgia from the North and whose life had been uprooted and confused by life in the big Northern cities. His feelings of inferiority, self-hatred, and prejudice against his fellow blacks in the South, stemming from his unfamiliarity with their life, have filled him with scorn and fear of their customs. Yet he is ashamed of this : 'Singing from the church becomes audible. Above it, rising and falling in a plaintive moan, a woman's voice swells to shouting. Kabnis hears it. His face gives way to an expression of mingled fear, contempt, and pity.' His friends are given the following explanation of his version : 'Couldn't stand the shouting, and thats a fact. We dont have that sort of thing up North.' But in fact it is his refusal to accept the suffering which is reflected in the spirituals and shouts. It conjures up in him a shameful past – slavery to which he owes his existence as a mulatto. He rejects this part of his ego and projects his self-hatred on to his environment :

> God Almighty, dear God, dear Jesus, do not torture me with beauty. Take it away. Give me an ugly world. Ha, ugly. Stinking like un-washed niggers. Dear Jesus, do not chain me to myself and set these hills and valleys, heaving with folk-songs, so close to me that I cannot reach them. There is a radiant beauty in the night that touches and . . . tortures me. Ugh, Hell. Get up, you damn fool. Look around. Whats beautiful there?

However, by refusing to recognise the beauty of the South and the value of its black women and men, as celebrated in the spirituals, he deprives himself of what alone might be able to save him : 'Kabnis, a promise of a soil-soaked beauty; uprooted, thinning out. Suspended a few feet above the soil whose touch would resurrect him.'[85] His demora-lisation can no longer be stopped. Lewis, so to speak Toomer's 'better self', makes a last attempt to shake Kabnis out of his self-destructive state of mind by asking him a number of critical questions. They meet at a party in a cellar to which Toomer attaches a symbolic significance : it is the place of truth and passion where the ego finds itself and encoun-ters the past. It is the place where Father John is living in obscurity, an old blind man, a former slave. And just like slavery he is 'a mute witness, emblematic of the Negro's true and real past . . . It is clear that redemption is to be found through Father John.'[86] Significantly enough, Kabnis has always ignored him. But now Lewis brings them face to face :

> Lewis : The old man as symbol, flesh, and spirit of the past, what do think he would say if he could see you? You look at him, Kabnis.
> Kabnis : Just like any done-up preacher is what he looks to me. Jam some false teeth in his mouth and crank him, an youd have

God Almighty spit in torrents all around th floor. Oh, hell, an he reminds me of that black cockroach over yonder. An besides, he aint my past. My ancestors were Southern blue-bloods –

Lewis : And black. – Kabnis : Aint much difference between blue an black. – Lewis : Nough to draw a denial from you. Cant hold them, can you? Master; slave. Soil; and the overarching heavens. Dusk; dawn. They fight and bastardize you. The sun tint of your cheeks, flame of the great season's multi-colored leaves, tarnished, burned. Split, shredded : easily burned. No use . . .

Yet, nothing can liberate Kabnis from his self-hatred and self-rejection : 'Mind me, th only sin is whats done against th soul. Th whole world is a conspiracy t sin, espially in America, an against me. I'm th victim of their sin. I'm what sin is.' In a final fit of hatred, which can only be called masochistic, Kabnis denigrates Father John and with him his own past :

You know what hell is cause youve been there. Its a feelin an its ragin in my soul in a way that'll pop out of me an run you through, an scorch y, an burn an rip your soul. Your soul. Ha. Nigger soul. A gin soul that gets drunk on a preacher's words. An screams. An shouts. God Almighty, how I hate that shoutin. Where's th beauty in that? . . . Aint surprisin th white folks hate y so. When you had eyes, did you ever see th beauty of th world? Tell me that. Th hell y did. Now dont tell me. I know y didnt.

Lewis, on the other hand, succeeds in preserving his integrity. He accepts his past, i.e. slavery as his fate and identifies himself with, and thereby transcends, the suffering of the blacks. In this way he can experience the poetic quality of the South with its beauty born out of suffering and escapes the demoralization which is afflicting Kabnis : 'Lewis, seated now so that his eyes rest upon the old man, merges with his source and lets the pain and beauty of the South meet him there.'[87] 'The pain and the beauty of the South' – these words summarise the central theme of this volume and the meaning of its title : cane symbolises the ambivalence of the Afro-American predicament, 'the bitter-sweet qualities of the black American's African and Southern past'.[88] Cane embodies the enslavement and demoralisation of the blacks,[89] but at the same time the character of the South with its unspoilt beauty and liveliness.

It is close to Nature that the Afro-Americans are thought to have preserved traces of their African heritage to which they owe their vitality and their peculiar human dignity. The spirit of Africa lives above all in the spirituals which combine bitterness with the greatness of the past :

> . . .
> A feast of moon and men and barking hounds,
>> An orgy for some genius of the South
>> With blood-hot eyes and cane-lipped scented mouth,
> Surprised in making folk-songs from soul sounds.
> . . .

> Meanwhile, the men, with vestiges of pomp,
>> Race memories of king and caravan,
>> High-priests, an ostrich, and a juju-man,
> Go singing through the footpaths of the swamp.

There are even traces of this dignity to be found in the prostitutes – symbols of black degeneration and corruption – who, Kabnis hopes, will help him forget :

> The girls, before the mirror, are doing up their hair. It is bushy that has gone through some straightening process. Character, however, has not all been ironed out. As they kneel there, heavy-eyed and dusky, and throwing grotesque moving shadows on the wall, they are two princesses in Africa going through the early-morning ablutions of their pagan prayers.[90]

Toomer's descriptions of African greatness and beauty with all their suffering and bitterness in the daily life of the black Southerners do not contain any triumphant or optimistic elements. The keynote of *Cane* is that of resignation. All the stories in this volume revolve around the 'aching futility of the fecund that cannot bear, the empty sterile pointlessness of uprooted lives'; they are characterised by the impotence and sense of frustration of people who, faced with the disintegration of black culture and the advance of forces hostile to Nature, cannot activate the potential of talent in them.[91] Still, there is a hope of salvation through the rise of a new powerful African race. This, at least, is the vision of King Barlo, a black preacher who proclaims : ' "I saw a man arise, an he was big an black an powerful – " ' Barlo rises to his full height. He is immense. To the people he assumes the outlines of his visioned African. In a mighty voice he bellows : . . . "Open your eyes an see th dawnin of th mornin light. Open your ears – " '.[92] However, as far as *Cane* is concerned, Toomer did not intend to advocate a naïve Back-to-Nature solution. The characters in this book are neither happy nor simple-minded, nor 'virtuous'. Toomer himself confessed that 'back to Nature, even if desirable, was no longer possible, because industry had taken nature into itself'. This means that 'in *Cane* only those characters whose experience enables them to arrive at a higher level of consciousness of self manage to transcend the sufferings and limitations of their "natural" existence', as Bell rightly commented.[93] Lewis – the conscience of Kabnis (and Toomer) may be counted among the members of this new generation of blacks who will probably succeed in finding 'roots and sustenance, vitality and manhood'.[94]

This is also true of Dan Moore, the central figure of the other key piece in *Cane*, entitled 'Box Seat' : ' "I am Dan Moore", he says, "I was born in a canefield. The hands of Jesus touched me. I am come to a sick world to heal it." '[95] This story contains a more candid and clear-cut criticism of modern technological society than can be found in Toomer's other narratives. Here the North with its anonymous big cities embodies a sick and unhealthy world. The cities are seen as the petrified symbols of 'white' civilisation. They represent the whites' 'attachment to inorganic objects and property, . . . their enslavement to abstractions like civilization and its conventions, and . . . their alienation from the past which spawned them'.[96] For the blacks to accept the rules which govern this world would be tantamount to denying their innermost nature and to destroying themselves. Dan himself senses the paralysing effect of this environment which is so alien to his soul : 'Dan sings. His voice is a little hoarse. It cracks. He strains to produce tones in keeping with the houses' loveliness. Cant be done. He whistles. His notes are shrill. They hurt him.' But Dan succeeds in preserving the vitality of his Negro Soul. He is not prepared to identify himself with the rigid and sterile world of the whites. He feels akin to the world of the blacks and he gains an almost messianic strength from it. Muriel's soul, on the other hand, whom he loves and whom he hopes to save from self-destruction (the Lewis-Kabnis dichotomy!) has already been affected by the process of disintegration. There is, to be sure, a residue of 'animalism, still unconquered by zoo-restrictions and keeper-taboos' in her. But otherwise the puritanical civilisation of the whites has largely succeeded in smothering all spontaneous feelings inside her. Dan tries everything to break through the wall which Muriel has erected around her. But she is too much a prisoner of the 'system' whose ethos she has internalised. She even tries to impose it on Dan by admonishing him that he 'ought to work more and think less. Thats the best way to get along.' Diligence, efficiency and the pursuit of happiness are elements of her value system, values to which the puritanical society around her has given its blessing. Dan, however, replies that her 'aim is wrong. There is no such thing as happiness . . . Perfect joy, or perfect pain, with no contrasting element to define them, would mean a monotony of consciousness, would mean death.' After rejecting Muriel's work ethos because of its dehumanising effect on man, Dan sets out to subject her notion of happiness to criticism. This notion, he argues, is utopian and by-passes the realities of life; it fails to take account of the complexity of life of which one must accept both its negative and positive aspects – 'the pain and the beauty'. Muriel's striving for happiness, he feels, is alien to life and hence, in the final analysis, hostile to it. The actual task of man was to accept and to reproduce life in all its manifold aspects.[97] Dan wants this to be taken as a reminder to the whites, but even more so to the blacks. For the blacks to identify with this ethos is tantamount to rejecting their own reality and thereby destroying themselves. A society which negates suffering and is ashamed of ugliness will also deny the blacks their human dignity whose life consists of suffering.

It could be argued that McKay tried even harder than Toomer to help and direct the Afro-Americans (and himself) in their search for an identity. He certainly included Africa much more directly and openly in his concept of the New Negro than did Toomer. He, too, created 'his' ideal Negro who was diametrically opposed to everything white and who radically questioned the white value system. Time and again he assaults, in his three novels, the claim that Euro-American culture is superior to African. He tries to show that, quite to the contrary, blacks are superior to whites in their humanity. Like other primitivists, he considered emotionality, spontaneity and instinctiveness to be the paramount qualities of blacks. Whites, on the other hand, are characterised by their unnatural rationality. However, Western culture had no doubt had a profound influence on him and, being a writer, he also did not wish to abandon his intellectuality. His problem was therefore how he could avoid the supposed sterility of Western culture and absorb the allegedly un-intellectual features of African culture. If nothing else, it is this division of man's nature into an intellectual and an erotic sphere which shows how deeply McKay – unlike Toomer – was influenced by the occidental modes of thought. This influence on him was certainly stronger than he himself realised. His three novels testify to the great effort which uniting these opposites required. Here is Ray, the intellectual hero of *Home to Harlem* and *Banjo* who is McKay's proxy : 'Ray had found that to be educated, black and his instinctive self was something of a big job to put over.'[98]

The reader of *Home to Harlem* is taken through the world of 'primitive' blacks by Jake, himself a representative of that world. Ray, who met Jake on a train on which the latter was working as a pullman porter, acts as a kind of interpreter of Jake's life. In his attempt to establish the widest possible contrast between the blacks and the 'sterile' whites living in their 'well-patterned, well-made emotions of the respectable world' McKay's blacks are left without an opportunity to behave rationally. They live thoughtlessly from one day to the next; they act erratically. They possess a 'child-like capacity for wistfulness-and-laughter' and merely abide by their 'simple, raw emotions and real'. They exude an exotic 'savagery', directly inherited from Africa and expressed, *inter alia*, in 'pure voluptuous jazzing' :

> The piano-player had wandered off into some dim, far-away ancestral source of music . . . The notes were naked acute alert. Like black youth burning naked in the bush. Love in the deep heart of the jungle . . . The sharp spring of a leopard from a leafy limb, the snarl of a jackal, green lizards in amorous play, the flight of a plumed bird, and the sudden laughter of mischievous monkeys in their green homes . . . Black lovers of life caught up in their own free native rhythm, threaded to a remote scarce-remembered past . . .

In the face of so much animalism it is not surprising that Ray finds it impossible to do as Jake does. But Ray believes that this is because he has been 'civilized' too thoroughly. He regards himself as one of the 'slaves of the civilized tradition'. At the same time he feels a certain kinship tie with Jake. For Jake's world is a 'reservoir of that intense emotional energy so peculiar to his race. Life touched him emotionally in a thousand vivid ways. Maybe his own being was something of a touchstone of the general emotions of his race.' It is because of his Western intellectual education that Ray, paradoxically, possesses a sensibility which enables him to activate greater emotional resources than Jake is capable of raising. But what was he to do with all this surplus sensitivity and vitality? In *Home to Harlem* Ray does not see a way out of his dilemma yet. ' "The fact is, Jake", Ray said, "I don't know what I'll do with my little education. I wonder sometimes if I could get rid of it and go and lose myself in some savage culture in the jungles of Africa. I am a misfit . . ." ' So he signs on as a ship's steward and leaves the United States.[99]

In his next novel, more correctly called by McKay a 'Story without a Plot', we meet Ray again, this time in Marseilles. He is accompanied by Banjo, so called because he plays that kind of instrument. Banjo possesses the spontaneity and intuition of Jake, but lacks his 'savagery'. For in the meantime McKay has met many West Africans in the 'Ditch' of Marseilles and these encounters have changed his image of Africa. He admires 'their loose, instinctive way of living', the elegance of their movements and their way of dancing.[100] They are not the kind of purely sexual beings as which the white man likes to see them who like Busha Glengley in *Banana Bottom* 'had all his life been so absorbed in the bodies of Negroes that he had never had any time to find out anything about their souls'.[101] McKay believes that blacks are more intact spiritually and not 'crippled' by puritanical notions of morality. They are 'freer and simpler in their sex urge, and as white people on the whole were not, they naturally attributed over-sexed emotions to Negroes . . . It was as if the white man considered sex a nasty, irritating thing, while a Negro accepted it with primitive joy.'

Ray particularly enjoyed hearing 'the African dialects sounding around him. The dialects were so rich and round and ripe like soft tropical fruit, as if they were fashioned to eliminate all things bitter and harsh to express.' They gave him a homely feeling, human warmth which he was searching for :

> The Africans gave him a positive feeling of wholesome contact with racial roots. They made him feel that he was not merely an unfortunate accident of birth, but that he belonged definitely to a race weighed, tested, and poised in the universal scheme. They inspired him with confidence in them. Short of extermination by the Europeans, they were a safe people, protected by their own indigenous culture. Even though they stood bewildered before the imposing bigness of white things, apparently unaware of the invaluable worth of their own, they were naturally defended by the richness of their fundamental racial values.[102]

Thus McKay's process of identification with Africa is much more advanced than in *Home to Harlem*. And correspondingly his criticism of Western civilization is more radical and more to the point. It is this calling into question of occidental norms and values that differentiates both McKay and Toomer from the white primitivists. Thus Van Vechten could not do without a heroine who was a 'respectable, proper and moral lady'. Nor did he dare to touch the cornerstone of the Western capitalist ethic that 'commercial success was worthwhile – "to make it" was the idea.'[103] McKay, on the other hand, openly condemns this ethic as well as the materialism of the whites and their 'hypocritical' democratic and humanist ideals. According to the whites, these values are supposed to have universal applicability. But in fact they are merely design to buttress their hegemonic position in the world. McKay believes that blacks often do not appreciate this until it is too late. It is only after they have abandoned their own culture, adapted the 'superior' culture of the whites and begun to hate their own that

> you realize with a shock that you don't and can't belong to the white race. All your education and achievements cannot put you in the intimate circles of the whites and give you a white man's full opportunity. However advanced, clever, and cultivated you are, you will

have the distinguished adjective of 'colored' before your name. And instead of accepting it proudly and manfully, most of you are soured and bitter about it – especially you mixed-bloods.

In these circumstances, rejection of white civilisation is seen as the only way out. Within Western culture, 'you're a lost crowd, you educated Negroes, and you will only find yourself in the roots of your own people.'

It was not among the black middle-classes, however, that the revival of black culture, as pursued by the so-called 'racial renaissance' could be effected, nor among Afro-Americans in general. They were, McKay thought, 'long-deracinated, still rootless among phantoms and pale shadows and enfeebled by self-effacement before condescending patronage, social negativism, and miscegenation'. The avantgarde would be made up of those who had been least exposed to Western civilisation, i.e. 'the true tropical African Negro' and 'the common people . . . who furnish the bone and sinew and salt of any race or nation'. His faith in 'the simple, natural warmth of a people believing in themselves, such as he had felt among the rugged poor and socially backward blacks of his island home' leads him into the ambit of the socialist movements of his day, the Irish and Russian among others. In his view these movements provide models which he recommends to his fellow-blacks for their own renaissance. Speaking through Ray, he even indicates that he dreamed of an association between the blacks and the socialists.[104] But he soon came to realise that the latter were just as deeply imbued with the materialistic values of the West as the capitalists. Both socialists and capitalists adhered to the idea of progress and both threatened to impose 'the ever tightening mechanical organization of modern life'. Yet it was precisely industrialisation and technical society which deprived the blacks of their best qualities. Hence there was also no salvation in a progress of the left-wing variety. 'Perhaps they would have their best chance in a world influenced by the clamped on machine with a few screws loose and some nuts fallen off', McKay concludes. And finally he asks (hardly realising how topical his question would be half a century later) : 'But in this great age of science and super-invention was there any possibility of arresting the thing unless it stopped of its own exhaustion?' There is but one hope for McKay, i.e. the 'apparent failing under the organisation of the modern world' which would, at some future date, turn out to be a blessing in disguise : the failure of technological society might save the blacks from becoming the thing that was the common white creature of it'.[105]

In his last and perhaps best novel, *Banana Bottom*, [106] McKay finally develops his counter-model of a world which has not yet become alienated from itself. The duality of his earlier novel has been eliminated here : the character of Bita combines Ray's Western education with the spontaneous warmth and vitality of Jake and Banjo. After several years at a school in Britain Bita has gone back to her village in the hinterland of Jamaica. But she has no difficulty in readjusting to this environment, although she stays with a very puritanical British missionary and his wife who have no understanding for the distinctly African cultural peculiarities of the blacks around them. This couple had acted as Bita's foster-parents when she was little in order to make her into a 'civilised' woman who would act as an example to the other villagers. Bita, however, succeeds in escaping from this influence. In the end she gets married to a peasant. McKay has painted with much affection a picture of a humane village community – evidently taken from the one in which he once lived. The norms of this community are considerably more flexible than those of the West.[107] There are no hierarchies and privileges, and its members are subject to a bare minimum of conventions. Criminal offences are absorbed by the community. All inhabitants are fully integrated into it.

It is difficult to say if McKay's *Banana Bottom* was really meant to offer an alternative to the 'civilized machine' of the West. At least he ought to have realised that Bita's 'return to the village' could not possibly represent a solution to all the problems of a technological society. On the other hand, he certainly intended to refute, in *Banana Bottom* as well as in his two earlier novels, the claim that Western civilisation was superior to others. Its bureaucratism and its 'success ethic', he believed, had a dehumanising effect on man. At the same time, he wanted to generate an understanding for the idea that African cultures had a value of their own and that they were capable of creating more humane living conditions.


## II   SUMMARY

*Banana Bottom* stands at the end of the Renaissance period which McKay had been instrumental in initiating as one of its first representatives. His own development, which led him from a total rejection of Africa to a position of approval and admiration for African traditions, reflects the development which the Harlem Renaissance underwent as a whole. Of course, this does not mean to imply that the development was continuous. As has been shown, the idealisation of Africa stood side by side with exoticism, the notion of Africa as a 'dark continent' and a sense of alienation from both Africa and America. At the same time attempts were made to gain an objective picture of Africa and to accept a stigmatised past. This was to serve as the basis of a positive self-image. All these elements appeared simultaneously and were sometimes even to be found within one and the same author. It has been mentioned that contradictions between these various elements can be reduced to the ambivalent attitudes of Afro-Americans towards Africa. Nevertheless, a certain evolution is discernible. At least, it is significant that Johnson, for example, made decisive changes in his poem 'Fifty Years', first published in 1913, when he reissued it in 1935. He deleted the last two stanzas which contained the following devout words : 'That we may grow more worthy of / This country and this land of ours', and replaced 'From heathen kraals and jungle dens' by 'From slave and pagan denizens'.[108] Similarly, the other works discussed in this chapter display, as far as Africa is concerned, an early shift away from the notion of a barbaric and pagan continent. As time goes by, the determination to identify with Africa grows markedly. Although there was a decline in the interest in Africa in the period that followed, the continent continued to play an important role as a force which changed the Afro-American's consciousness, and this in turn was to exert a considerable influence on the literature of subsequent decades. It is to this question that we shall now have to direct our attention.

F

# 5 The Transitional Phase — Time of Scepticism

## I THE BACKGROUND

There are considerable differences of opinion among literary critics as to the causes of the marked change which took place in Afro-American literature in the 1930s. Those who identify the Harlem Renaissance with exoticism and see the white primitivists and patrons as the driving force behind the movement, argue that it experienced 'a spectacular demise'.[1] What is more : the quick collapse is taken as evidence of its superficiality.[2] Others – usually those who emphasise the Afro-American rather than the 'white' origins of the Harlem Renaissance – do not see the Great Depression as marking the end of the movement. They argue that there was a temporary recession in literary activity which had been fully overcome by the end of the 1930s.[3] However, the notion of 'renaissance' would lose all precision if one were to describe the following decades summarily as a 'second period of Renaissance', as Franklin has done.[4] Most authors of the generation between the 1920s and 1960s were guided by intentions which differed from those of the Harlem Renaissance. Yet, to attempt an exact analysis of the 'post-Renaissance'[5] generation was presumably not Franklin's main concern anyway. He wanted to draw attention to the continuity in Afro-American literature. To this extent he has certainly made an important point. But this continuity did not just consist of the fact that, as Franklin seems to think, there is a substantial volume of black American literature for this period. What is no less significant is that certain positions of the Harlem Renaissance were upheld and developed further while others were abandoned.[6] It was this thematic shift of emphasis which characterised Afro-American literature of the 1930s to the 1960s and which gave it a new quality.

The most remarkable difference between the 1920s and the following decades is the disappearance of primitivism. Africa in this period moves again to the periphery of Afro-American preoccupations. No doubt the waning interest of the white patrons is partly responsible. Following the Great Crash they could no longer afford to give their 'darkies' their liberal support.[7] But this is no more than a partial explanation.

Another reason appears to have been the growing economic and social crisis which hit the blacks even harder than the whites. It is this experience that led to a general sobering. The colourful life of the 'Jazz Age' was over. There was little room for primitivism with its dreams of distant paradises. Moreover, Roosevelt's New Deal resulted in a closer integration of the blacks into politics, on the one hand, and a rise in lynch-murders as well as incidents like the famous Scottsboro Case, on the other. The effect of this was a greater interest in problems of day-to-day politics and a shift away from the cultural national-ism of the Harlem Renaissance without altogether destroying its impact.

One way of looking at the 'post-Renaissance' period is by defining it as the epoch of 'literary isolationism'. It was in this period that the Afro-Americans became once again more acutely aware of their position within American society and tried to give it a constructive meaning. Certain basic attitudes however, which can be detected in this period, would not have been thinkable without the prior impact of the Harlem Renaissance. Thus without the movement of the 1920s the authors of the following decades would hardly have professed so uninhibitedly a belief in themselves and the history of the Afro-Americans. This is evidenced by the fact that they now make free use of 'race material'[8] and identify completely with the characters in their writings. One does not try to justify any more why the life of blacks, and particu-larly that of the lower classes, should be worth recounting, as McKay had felt obliged to do in some of his novels. The 'new consciousness' of the New Negro, which the writers of the Harlem Renaissance had still been grappling with, is now taken for granted, even if the old colour-based inferiority complex has not by any means been overcome. But the main task is now to learn to see the predicament of the black man as an individual within a broader framework and to arrive at a closer defini-tion of it. In attempting this, the black intellectuals leave no doubt whatsoever that Afro-Americans have a justified claim to a fair place in American society. There are no more appeals of the kind issued by John-son that the whites should show compassion and accept the blacks into their community. The New Negroes of the period of 'literary isolation-ism' did not abandon any of the 'relative' militancy which they had acquired in the 1920s. The difference was that, while the writers of the Harlem Renaissance had been orientated towards 'racial' problems,[9] their successors began to stress the importance of social questions. Nevertheless, even if this was a period of reorientation towards the United States, they could not avoid facing the problem of Africa. They all had to try to find an answer to Cullen's question of 'what is Africa for me'. The importance of this question emerges from the fact that traces of the Harlem Renaissance can be found in many poems.[10]

It must be emphasised, however, that these poems are not typical of the *Zeitgeist* of the post-Renaissance period. This *Zeitgeist* can be gauged more accurately from the writings of Richard Wright, Ralph Ellison and James Baldwin, who dominated the literary scene during this period.

## II   RICHARD WRIGHT

Richard Wright's writings deal with a facet of the Afro-American image of Africa which can be understood largely by reference to the changes which took place in the political and social position of blacks in the 1930s. It was in this period that Marxism, which appeared to offer a comprehensive explanation of the Great Depression, made considerable gains among intellectuals and also captured Wright's imagination. On the one hand, Wright identifies himself wholeheartedly with his 'racial past'[11] and to this extent reflects the repercussions of the Harlem Renaissance. In fact, in his early years he had even proclaimed the necessity of a moderate nationalism. But, on the other hand, his emphasis on social processes clearly points to a political consciousness which had been shaped by the Great Depression and its consequences and which took its tools of analysis, as is true of other writers of this period, from Marxism.[12]

Apart from his report on his journey to Ghana, which will be dealt with later, Africa does not play a prominent role in Wright's work. However, this does not mean to imply that it played an insignificant one. On the contrary, we shall see that his attitude towards the homeland of his ancestors offers an important key to his thinking. Another important point to emerge from a glance through Wright's works is that his attitude remained practically unchanged throughout his life. This fact has influenced the structure of this sub-chapter. The following examination of Wright's relationship with Africa does not proceed chronologically. Rather it attempts to put together in a systematic fashion all references to Africa which are scattered throughout his work. Our hope is that a fairly coherent picture will emerge in the end.

To begin with, it is typical of Wright's attitude towards Africa that he does not refer to it in his autobiography. But this is not because the question had never occurred to him. What he has done is simply not to mention various impressions which he gained in his youth. Only years later, when planning his trip to Ghana, he tells us all of a sudden that when the word 'Africa' came up 'something strange and disturbing stirred slowly in the depths of me'. He had a vague feeling that 'I am African! I'm of African descent . . . Yet I'd never seen Africa; I'd never really known any Africans; I'd hardly ever thought of Africa . . .' When Dorothy Padmore, the wife of the well-known 'father of Pan-Africanism' asked him, 'Why don't you go to Africa?', he felt he 'was on the defensive'. And when, while in Ghana, an African asked him 'what part of Africa' he came from, Wright's reaction was similar : 'I didn't answer. I stared vaguely about me. I had, in my childhood, asked my parents about it, but they had had no information, or else they hadn't wanted to speak of it.' In other words, Wright as well as his parents felt uncomfortable whenever the idea of their African descent came up. Their reaction to this complex of problems was one of defensive silence.[13] But some of Wright's novels contain information about the kind of early contact which he may have had with Africa and which may have led to his negative attitude towards that continent.[14]

In *The Long Dream*, for instance, Fishbelly, the hero, and his friends engage in a very heated debate about Africa. Sam, the son of an adherent of Garvey, asks the provocative question : 'Fish, you want to go to Africa?' But the reaction of his friends is one of outrage and hostility : ' "All I know about Africa's what I read in the geography book at school", Fishbelly mumbled, unwilling to commit himself. "Sam wants us to git naked and run wild and eat with our hands and live in mud huts!" Zeke ridiculed Sam's thesis.' Clearly, none of them wants to identify himself with this kind of image of Africa. They are ashamed of this unwanted heritage which weighs so heavily on their lives : ' "White folks say you bad 'cause you black", Sam analyzed. And there ain't nothing you can do about being black." ' And since the boys could not cast off this heritage, they tried at least to forget and to deny it. Sam's words strike a chord in their subconscious which they have kept carefully hidden from themselves. They did not wish to lose their emotional stability so carefully established with the help of a string of self-deceptions. They sidestep the problem of their identity and live under the illusion that they are 'ordinary Americans'. But Sam, influenced by his father, knows that this is a dangerous delusion. He finds it easy to make nonsense of Tony's argument by asking provocative questions like this one : ' "Why you put lye and mashed potatoes on your hair? . . . You kill your hair to make it straight like white folks' hair!" ' The tug-of-words which was touched off by Sam's provocation is worth quoting because it offers a good insight into the African problem and Wright's recurrent treatment of it :

'Fish, what your *color*?' – M-my color?' Fishbelly asked stammeringly. 'Hell, man, can't you s-see I'm *black*?' – 'Yeah?' Sam asked ironically. 'And *why* you black?' – 'I was born that way', Fishbelly said resentfully. – 'But there's a *reason* why you got a *black* color,'

Sam was implacable. – 'My mama's black. My papa's black. And
that makes me black', Fishbelly said. 'And your mama's mama and
your papa's papa was black, wasn't they? Sam asked softly. – 'Sure',
Fishbelly said with a resentful hum, afraid of the conclusions to
which his answers were leading. – 'And where did your mama's
mama's *mama* and your papa's papa's *papa* come from?' Sam next
wanted to know. – 'From A-Africa, I reckon', Fishbelly stammered. –
'You just reckon?' Sam was derisive. 'You know damn well
where–'. – 'Okay. They came from Africa.' Fishbelly tried to cover
up his hesitancy. Sam now fired his climactic question : 'Now, just
stand there and tell me what *is* you?' Before Fishbelly could reply
Zeke and Tony set up a chant : 'Fishbelly's a African! Fishbelly's
a African !' – 'Let Fish answer !' Sam tried to drown them out. – 'I'm
black and I live in America and my folks came from Africa', Fishbelly summed up his background. 'That's all I know'. – 'Your
folks was *brought* from Africa', Sam sneered . . . 'Fish is a African
who's been taken out of Africa . . . Fish thinks he's American, but
he ain't. Now my papa says all black folks ought to build up Africa
'cause that's our true home – '.

But the friends reject this idea vigorously. They feel they belong to the
United States, thus driving Sam into a final outburst of anger :

'You niggers ain't *nowhere*. You ain't in Africa, 'cause the white
man took you out. And you ain't in America, 'cause if you was you'd
act like *Americans* – . . . You ain't no American ! You live Jim
Crow. . . . You can't live like no American, 'cause you ain't no American ! And you ain't African neither ! So what is you? Nothing ! Just
*nothing* !'

This is the climax and the end of the discussion. The unmentionable
has been mentioned. The boys have been confronted with the truth
about their existence : they belong nowhere and they are, in the final
analysis, nothing. Yet this 'nothingness' is so terrible that they cannot
face it. They either retreat and cover the open wound with silence; or
they find a release for their pains and frustrations by turning their
feelings of hatred against themselves or against other blacks. Fish starts
a brawl with Sam and pours abuse over him : ' "You blacker'n me
so you more nigger'n me." ' And later, in a fit of self-hatred and shame
he spits at his mirror image.[15]

By describing the life of young Afro-Americans in this way, Wright
alludes to the psychological mechanism which, in his view, underlies
their attitude towards Africa, towards the whites and towards themselves. In his writings, the connection between these three aspects is

possibly even more explicit than in the works of the other authors which have been discussed so far. For this reason we shall now turn first of all to Wright's attitude towards whites and blacks in greater detail before going back to his image of Africa, which revolves very much around the above notion of the blacks not really having a place they belong to. As will be seen, his concept of the rootless outsider which he evolved in his work is a vital key to an understanding of his uneasy relationship with Africa.

To the extent that the characters in his novels reflect his ideas, Wright's early traumatic experiences appear to have been the result not so much of a growing consciousness of his African descent than of a sense of powerlessness *vis-à-vis* the whites. He had come to realise 'that those powerful, invisible white faces ruled the lives of black people to a degree that but few black people could allow themselves to acknowledge'.[16] Yet this realisation has a curious effect on Wright's characters, such as Fish, Bigger or 'Black Boy'.[17] They are so ashamed of the black predicament and so hate the whites as the root cause of their misery that they lapse into a deep inner crisis. This crisis leads to their alienation from their own group on top of their being excluded from the world of the whites. According to Fish, learning about the helplessness of the blacks forced them to become aware 'how black people looked to white people; he was beginning to look at his people through alien eyes and what he saw evoked in him a sense of distance between him and his people that baffled and worried him'.[18]

Fish shares this feeling of scorn for the blacks and of isolation from them with practically all other characters in Wright's novels. He tries to show through these characters how the Afro-Americans have become uprooted and dehumanised by the structure of American society.[19] They all, Wright argues – and he explicitly includes himself in this argument – 'felt tense, afraid, nervous, hysterical, and restless', because 'the civilization which had given birth to Bigger contained no spiritual sustenance, had created no culture which could hold and claim his allegiance and faith'.[20] Does this rejection of white civilisation imply that Wright regards black nationalism as an alternative? If one takes his 'Blueprint for Negro Literature', published in 1937, it is easy to gain this impression. In this essay Wright defends a moderate form of nationalism, but adds that 'no attempt is made to propagate a specious and blatant nationalism'. Of course, 'the nationalist character of the Negro people is unmistakable. Psychologically this nationalism is reflected in the whole Negro culture, and especially in folklore'. Wright goes on to exhort Afro-American writers to revive Negro culture and 'racial wisdom' and to teach their fellow Afro-Americans in the ghettos an awareness of this culture with its Southern roots. Furthermore he postulates that 'the presentation of their lives should be simple, yes; but all the complexity, the strangeness, the magic wonder of life that plays like a bright sheen over even the most sordid existence, should be there.'

However, it soon becomes apparent that Wright's conviction of the value of black cultural traditions was not particularly deep and that he at least considered it to be unsatisfactory. It is, he writes, the special task of the black intellectuals 'to do no less than create values by which their race is to struggle, live and die. They are being called upon to furnish moral sanctions for action, to give a meaning to blighted lives and to supply motives for mass movements of millions of people.'[21] Thus Richard Wright, the intellectual, has resolved to create 'a scheme of images and symbols whose direction could enlist the sympathies, loyalties, and yearnings of millions of Bigger Thomases in every land and race'.[22] This statement clearly demonstrates the influence of a 'colour-blind' Marxism–Leninism and of the Communist Party of which Wright was then still a member.[23] Accordingly he maintains that a Marxist analysis of society is capable of creating 'a meaning and significant picture of the world today . . . which, when placed squarely before the eyes of the writer, should unify his personality, organize his emotions, and buttress him with a tense and obdurate will to change the world'.

But just as he abhors an exaggerated nationalism – a 'black chauvinism', as he calls it – he is dissatisfied with orthodox Marxism–Leninism. Instead he propounds a 'nationalism carrying the highest possible pitch of social consciousness'.[24] This was a nationalism which did not deny Afro-American culture a value of its own. This position also emerges from Wright's first successful book, a collection of short stories published under the title of *Uncle Tom's Children*.[25] In this volume he urges fraternisation not only of all Afro-Americans but also of blacks and whites so as to enable them to fight together for a change of existing social conditions.[26]

However, Wright's enthusiasm for the Communist Party and a 'communist nationalism' soon began to wane. Although the Party became an intellectual and spiritual haven for him, he grew increasingly disillusioned with the orthodoxy of the party line. Ultimately he turned his back on Communism altogether, bitterly disappointed by the hostility with which his friends viewed his striving for artistic independence and integrity.[27] The coming of the final break transpires from Wright's *Native Son* and henceforth he seems to have lost all sense of commitment. After leaving the Communist Party he did not turn more clearly towards black culture. The 'transcendental nationalism' which he proclaimed[28] fell into a state of disarray. All that was left was to write about a black who had lost his sense of orientation and was totally lonely. Wright's blacks were without any ties :

His people possessed no memory of a heritage, of a glorious past to which he could cling to buttress his personal pride, and there was no clearly defined, redeeming future toward which he could now look with longing. He had only the flat and pallid present. He was unencumbered with emotional luggage, but there was no adventurous journey he wanted to make, no goal toward which he sought to strive. Other than a self-justifying yen for imitating the outward standards of the white world above him, there had not come within the range of his experience any ideal that could have captured his imagination. Other than a defensive callousness toward his own people which he practiced to be free to act out his own limited daily aims, other than the masked behavior he adopted toward the whites, other than the secret fantasy which he sought to realize while denying it, he had no traditions, no mores to sustain him.[29]

Wright called this kind of existence that of an 'outsider' which he made the basic theme of all his later works and which he equated with his own position after his break with the Communist Party. He even tried to give it a philosophical 'superstructure' whose contours can best be retraced from his novel *The Outsider*.[30] Its main character, Cross Damon, sees himself as a rootless intellectual who has nominated himself 'creator of himself'.[31] Damon believes that his intellect enables him to construct a new and personal system of values and symbols with which he will be able to fill the self-created vacuum around him. His being a Negro does not have a positive function in this context. Whatever group consciousness there may be, for Wright it was no more than 'a defensive solidarity that had, except for latent white hostility, no valid reason for being'. Only the colour of his skin possesses a certain importance in so far as it enables him to assume more easily than alienated whites can the posture of an outsider. This in turn leads Wright to believe that their predicament as blacks helps Afro-Americans to gain a deeper insight into social and cultural questions. They are more 'knowing' than whites.[32]

However, at this point a contradiction emerges between theory and practice. As Wright concedes in his autobiography, he owes the first insights into his predicament to whites. The same applies to Cross Damon. He first became aware of his situation in discussions with a white man, Houston, who also did much to reinforce Cross's views.[33] Closer examination likewise demonstrates that his supposed neutrality towards Western values is just as illusory as his theory of the greater insight of the black outsider. His criticisms of society as well as his ideals of rationality and the autonomy of the individual reflect a purely occidental tradition of thought.[34] This leads us on to the second aspect of his work, i.e. his attitude towards the white world.

It soon turns out that neither Cross nor any of Wright's other characters can be called 'free-floating outsiders'. They all have a fixation about the white world for which they opt – half-consciously or deliberately – by emulating its 'outward standards', i.e. by subscribing, without much reflection, to the American Dream. To put it into the words of Fishbelly : 'I don't want to read nothing about Africa. I want to make some goddam money.'[35] The awakening from this 'long dream' is rude and results either in flight or death,[36] since the return into the black world is blocked in view of the far-reaching identification with white standards : 'He was fatally in love with that white world, in love in a way that could never be cured. That white world's attempt to curb him had dangerously and irresponsibly claimed him for its own.'[37] And the more insurmountable the barriers became, the stronger grew his determination to assert himself in a totally hostile environment. Ultimately, identification with the white world was so complete that inferiority, 'that fantastic and fearful image' of one's self,[38] is accepted as valid and is perpetuated.[39]

Fish – and Wright himself – escaped from this vicious circle only by leaving the United States. Bigger, on the other hand, accepts his inferiority, 'the crime of being black',[40] to the hilt as he is barred from finding his identity through positive action, his hatred of the whites and of himself drive him into an act of destruction. But even this negative 'act of creation',[41] as Baldwin interprets Bigger's resort to murder, does not give him more than a sham liberty. 'They still ruled him . . . he had reached out and killed and had not solved anything.'[42] Nothing betrays the absurdity of Bigger's predicament more candidly than the reports which appear in the local press about his case. He had hoped, through these murders, 'to wring a meaning out of meaningless suffering'[43] and to find a measure of human dignity. But the press commentaries heap the most humiliating insults upon him, calling him 'a jungle beast . . . utterly untouched by the softening influences of modern civilization'.[44] They fail to appreciate how much he is, after all, a product of this 'modern civilization' and push him back into the pit from which he was hoping to escape. The circle of hopelessness closes.

Like other Afro-American writers, Wright resorts to a black-white symbolism which he turns into a recurrent theme and with which he tries to elucidate the fundamental dilemma of his characters. But unlike almost all authors who have been discussed so far and who, by moving away from the traditional pattern of polarity, hoped to up-value the 'black' world, Wright does not engage in a 'transvaluation' of colours. In his novels and short stories,[45] 'black' retains its evil and menacing quality. He describes the 'shadow-world' of the blacks and their desperation.[46] Rarely and as a last resort are they driven into rebellion against their oppressors and they regularly fail in the process. In the case of Bigger this is well expressed in his symbolic fight with a black rat which anticipates his own useless struggle and ultimate death.

'White', on the other hand, is equated by Wright with 'freedom' which has the highest rating on his scale of values. White are the clouds which drift effortlessly through the skies; white is the glittering hull of the aeroplane; greyish-white the body of the pigeon which is being envied by Bigger and his friends for its freedom of movement. Occasionally the white world is depicted as menacing and coldly repulsive. Snow offers Wright a welcome and frequently used symbol to demonstrate the loneliness of those blacks who have ventured out into the white world and are now being punished with exposure to an Arctic cold. Bigger almost freezes to death when trying to escape from the police on to a roof.[47] A *haiku* written by Wright might also be interpreted in this way :

> In the falling snow
> A laughing boy holds out his palms
> Until they are white.[48]

In the final analysis, therefore, he portrays both worlds, black and white, as being repulsive. Wright's Afro-American characters do not find peace in either. They live, as he called it, in a 'no-man's land'.[49] In this way Wright tries to support his concept of the outsider from various directions, surrounding it with an air of objectivity that was at least no more than his subjective perception. Clearly, it is only from the perspective of the white America that the black existence assumed a 'nothingness'. As early as 1951 Baldwin, in a critique of *Native Son*, reproached Wright with failing to deal with social reality and with perpetuating a myth which he had adopted from the whites. It was the myth that 'in Negro life there exists no tradition, no field of manners, no possibility of ritual or intercourse such as may, for example, sustain the Jew even after he has left his father's house'.[50]

There was now hardly a place for Africa in the world of 'nothingness' into which he thought the blacks had been thrown. But we have seen that the question of Africa arose for all Afro-American writers in one form or another, and even Wright could not escape it. One of the impulses which pushed Wright, if indirectly, into ruminating on the problem was, it seems, the Garvey Movement. This movement, to be sure, had by the 1930s lost much of its earlier splendour. But it did live on among the masses, among which the idea of a return to Africa as an alternative to a life of misery in the United States continued to exert on obvious attraction. Here the memory of the 'homeland' was kept alive.[51] This kind of a mass movement was bound to fascinate a Marxist, which Wright then professed to be. And indeed, the excerpts which Constance Webb has published from his diaries contain references to his encounters with Garveyites. The Garvey Movement, he recorded, had given him an idea 'of the potential strength of the American Negro'. He also believed to have understood their motives and feelings, 'for I partly shared them'.[52] However, this understanding does not appear to have gone very far. An identification with the African 'home-land' which Garvey propagated was at any rate totally alien to him. Marxism had influenced his perspective too strongly. Garvey's emigra-tion programme was, he thought, based on illusions. References to this attitude can be found in *Lawd Today*, Wright's first novel, published in 1937. In one of its key scenes, he describes a procession of Garvey and his 'troops', emphasising the *opera buffe* elements of the movement, its foible for uniforms and medals and the pompousness of its 'digni-taries'. Resorting to considerable exaggeration, he concentrates on the weaknesses of the UNIA programme and ridicules Garvey as 'Supreme Undisputed Exalted Commander of the Allied Imperial African War Councils unto the Fourth and Last Generations'. It is typical that he ignores Garvey's appeal to solidarity and 'racial pride', which was, after all, the basis of the entire movement. He allows him-self to be deceived by the external appearance of the movement with its uniforms. And he wrongly interprets the UNIA as a purely military phenomenon bent on the conquest of Africa and, ultimately, of the white world. Such misrepresentations are designed to expose the alleged absurdity of a 'Back-to-Africa' movement which did not offer a solution to the problems of the blacks in the United States. It is in line with this attitude that Jake has no desire to continue his contact with the UNIA after his first encounter with it. Only in a moment of extreme despair does he, the post office employee who feels frustrated by his boring job, allow himself to be lured by the 'Black Dream' :

If only there was something he could do to pay the white folks back for all they had ever done ! Even if he lost his own life in doing it ! But what could he do? He felt the loneliness of his black skin. *Yeah, some foreign country ought to do it!* He remembered the parade he had seen that morning when he was on his way to work. *Yeah, maybe they's right. Who knows?* He saw millions of black soldiers marching in black armies; he saw a black battle ship flying a black flag; he himself was standing on the deck of that black battleship surrounded by black generals; he heard a voice commanding : 'FIRE !' *BOOOOOOM!* A black shell screamed through black smoke and he saw the white head of the Statue of Liberty topple, explode, and tumble into the Atlantic Ocean . . . *Gawdamn right!* He had reached that point in his imagined epic where black troops were about to conquer the whole world, when a metallic gong boomed throughout the Mailing Division and a voice yelled : 'TWELVE-THIRTY, CLERKS, CHECKOUT FOR LUNCH !'[53]

The contrast between Jake's hallucinations and rough reality – a reality which dominates *him* and bosses *him* about – underlines the illusory basis of Garveyism. Although Wright regards its ideas as 'childish',[54] he does not fail to appreciate the social roots of the movement. In line with his Marxist beliefs of this time, he tries, as in *Uncle Tom's Children*, to 'transcend' black nationalism. He does so by referring to its origins and by labouring to bring about, through his writings, a change of social conditions in the United States. There are no traces in this book of his earlier position when he still thought it possible that nationalism might fulfil a positive role. Even his later personal contact with Africa did not affect his attitude towards the 'Back-to-Africa' movement. On the contrary, it probably reinforced his views. At any rate, in his last novel, which he wrote after his visit to Africa, 'Sam's wild ideas' are juxtaposed time and again with the alternative of America. But in the end Sam's solution is rejected by his friends. 'That black nigger's crazy', is their reply.[55]

Wright's denigration of Garveyism represents an indirect detraction of Africa. But already his *Lawd Today* contains a direct criticism. There is a scene in which Jake and his friends meet a quack who poses as a 'snake man' endowed with magic powers and born 'in the great COUNtreeeeey of AFRIKer, yo' COUNtreeeeey 'n' mah COUNtreeeeey – in tha' LAN' where, in the YEARs gone by, yo' FATHER 'n' mah FATHER ruled SUPREME !' He employs various tricks to sell his magic tonic, combining Christian religious elements with those of a snake cult and cunningly abusing the gullibility of his simple-minded audience.[56] In other words, Wright associates Africa not merely with wishful thinking here, but with superstition and charlatanism designed to keep people in ignorance and to impede a change of conditions through enlightenment and rationality.

It is against the background of what has been said so far about Wright's attitudes towards the world and Africa that we can begin to understand how ambiguous his feelings must have been when he finally did go to Africa. As a Marxist and, later, as a 'personalist' he had learned to think in terms of Western ideas, and his confrontation with Africa was rather forced upon him. In view of this it is not surprising that, when he asked himself : *'But, am I African? . . .* Was there something in Africa that my feelings could latch onto to make all of this dark past clear and meaningful? Would the Africans regard me as a lost brother who had returned?', his reply should be : 'I could not feel anything African about myself.' Indeed, how could he feel any affinity towards a distant continent if he did not even have feelings of solidarity with his own group in the United States? If the predicament of the

Afro-Americans filled him with shame and scorn, his reaction to his 'African heritage' was bound to be even stronger. On the one hand, Africa was a land of clowns and charlatans; on the other it raised in him 'associations of hatred, violence, and death'. What he seems to be alluding to is not just the violence to which Afro-Americans were subjected in the United States but also their violent enslavement in Africa which, in its turn, had generated hatred and brutality. Wright, rather summarily, considers his African ancestors to be those who are really responsible for the predicament of the blacks in the United States, for after all it was Africans who 'had sold their people into slavery; it had been said that they had had no idea of the kind of slavery into which they had been selling their people, but they had sold them . . .' And as Wright, after his arrival in Ghana, did not hesitate to voice his bitter feelings, it is not surprising that the Africans reacted to such accusations with embarrassed silence or even hostility. And this in turn merely reinforced Wright's feelings of animosity.[57]

Wright never made any bones about his ambivalent feelings towards Africa whenever he met Africans or other people of the Third World. This led to problems of communication which, in turn, had such a negative impact on his image of the continent.[58] It was a real vicious circle. However, it was not just the crude way in which he used to ask questions which made it difficult for him to make contact with Africans. He also made the mistake of attempting to apply his concept of the outsider rather uncritically to Africa. Of course, he tried to learn, for 'each hour events were driving home to me that Africa was another world, another sphere of being.' Yet, 'for it to become natural to me, I'd have to learn to accept without thought a whole new range of assumptions',[59] and this Wright was incapable of or not prepared to do. He still thought to be in the role of an 'impartial' and 'objective' observer, of an outsider who was able to gain deeper insights into African society than the Africans themselves.[60] We have seen how this notion proved to be problematical in his own, Afro-American context; it was even less tenable in an African one. Instead of helping him to overcome the confines of his own cultural background through critical reflection it made him a prisoner of his own prejudices.

If one tries to find an accurate term to define Wright's position *vis-à-vis* Africa, one might call him an *outcast*. This would explain both his precarious psychological predicament and his specific perspective which was conditioned by his predicament. As before in America, it was the same process of attraction to and repulsion by Africa which left deep scars on his psyche. All he could do in the end was again rationalise his existence as an outcast and give it, in retrospect, a positive meaning, that is that he *wanted* to live this kind of existence. Before setting out for Africa he asked himself if the Africans would welcome him as a 'brother'. What this question shows is how strong his desire was to be accepted. There are moreover a number of comments on certain African patterns of behaviour which represent crude generalisations and betray a degree of anger and irritation on his part. They seem to indicate that Wright did try to establish contacts and perhaps even friendships with Africans. But he was hurt when these attempts failed because of his own aggressiveness. Without ever suspecting that he himself may have provoked African reactions towards him, he makes allegations such as : 'I found that the African almost invariably underestimated the person with whom he was dealing; he always placed too much confidence in an evasive reply, thinking that if he denied something, then that something ceased to exist. It was childlike.' It is characteristic of the measure of his annoyance rather than of his objectivity that he denigrates as 'childish' an attitude which he does not understand. On other occasions he actually became conscious of this 'sense of uneasiness on levels of emotion deeper than I could control' : 'A protest against what I saw seized me . . . My protest was not against Africa or its people; it was directed against the unsettled feeling engendered by the strangeness of a completely different order of life.' And after having spent a longer period in the country, his main conclusion is a resigned admission of defeat : 'I had understood nothing. I was black and they were black, but my blackness did not help me.'[61]

This admission, as well as his resolution to take an unbiased look at the African world, was soon forgotten, however. Instead he set out to judge by purely Western standards a civilisation which, according to his own words, was alien to him and about which he even had feelings of revulsion. Again his categories of judgement are those of a radical individualist. He 'sensed', he said, 'that man – just sheer brute man, just as he is – has a meaning and value over and above all sanctions or mandates from mystical powers, either on high or from below'.[62] At the same time his Marxist background slips into his thinking. He adheres to the idea of rationality and unconditional progress which leads him to reject tradition and even the notion of 'culture'. They are to him an 'opium' which impedes the move forward; they are responsible, in his eyes, for the interference of irrational forces in rational processes; they put a smokescreen around the 'objective reality'.[63] Here Wright's Marxism, which continued to shape his views even after his break with the Communist Party, reinforced a strong childhood aversion to religion.[64] This aversion was then extended to apply to every kind of tradition-bound activity and put him in the position of denying all group consciousness and escaping all associations with other blacks.

It was therefore a considerable shock to him to discover in Ghana the existence of cultural affinities. Thus he sees African women dancing and suddenly remembers having seen similar dances in the United States. He is perturbed and asks himself :

> How was that possible? . . . I'd long contended that the American Negro, because of what he had undergone in the United States, had been basically altered, that his consciousness had been filled with a new content, that 'racial' qualities were but myths of prejudiced minds. Then, if that were true, how could I account for what I now saw?[65]

Wright has tried very hard to find a satisfactory answer to this problem, which evidently disturbed him profoundly. But he did not succeed and, given his premises, he could not succeed in finding one. He continued to insist on the view that Africa could expect salvation only from the West. Equally it was thanks to the West that many Africans had successfully shaken off the 'irrational ties of religion and custom and tradition'. 'In sum', as Baldwin put it, 'he felt that Europe had brought the Enlightenment to Africa and that "what was good for Europe was good for all mankind" '.[66]

It was in line with Wright's thinking that he should regard the colonial expansion of Europe as a positive historical force :

> 'I do say "Bravo!" to the consequences of Western plundering, a plundering, that created the conditions for the possible rise of rational societies for the greater majority of mankind . . . Thank the white man's God for that bit of racial and color stupidity! His liberating effect upon Asia and Africa would not have been so thorough had he been more human.'

However, if one follows Wright, the process of 'enlightenment' and destruction of African traditions has not yet reached its final conclusion. So far it is only the intellectual, Western-educated élite which – living in a 'spiritual void', 'stripped of the past and free for the future' – is capable of introducing rational change. Its members are 'the FREEST MEN IN ALL THE WORLD TODAY. They stand poised, nervous, straining at the leash, ready to go, with no weight of the dead past clouding their minds, no fears of foolish customs benumbing their consciousness, eager to build industrial civilizations.'[67] If there were ever any Africans with whom Wright felt able to identify, it was this élite.[68] But it was an élite which was no more than a projection of his own concept of the 'outsider'. Wright now found himself in a paradoxical situation. He thought he as the outsider was in a position to create a counter-world, governed by laws of its own, against that of the whites. Yet he was incapable of grasping the non-Western character of the African world with *its* specific laws.

In short, it is so obvious that Wright's attempt to solve 'the fearful conundrum of Africa' has failed that we need not draw up a list of all his errors here. On the occasion of Wright's death, Baldwin wrote an epilogue which may suitably be quoted here :

> I was always exasperated by his notions of society, politics and history, for they seemed to me utterly fanciful. I never believed that he had any real sense of how a society is put together. It had not occurred to me, and perhaps it had not occurred to him, that his major interests as well as his power lay elsewhere.[69]

Indeed Wright's great merit lies clearly in the powerful narrative with which he gave expression to the conflicts and pains of Afro-Americans, resulting from a confrontation with white America as well as Africa. Perhaps Wright's own predicament is best symbolised by the scene which appeared before his mind when he said farewell to Africa at Cape Coast Castle, once the assembly point of slaves :

> If there is any treasure hidden in these vast walls, I'm sure that it has a sheen that outshines gold – a tiny, pear-shaped tear that formed on the cheek of some black woman torn away from her children . . . a shy tear . . . on that black cheek, unredeemed, unappeased – a tear that was hastily brushed off when her arm was grabbed and she was led toward those narrow, dank steps that guided her to the tunnel that directed her feet to the waiting ship that would bear her across the heaving, mist-shrouded Atlantic . . .[70]

All his attempts at rationalisation notwithstanding, Wright turns his back on Africa, unreconciled and irreconcilable, and returns to his 'no-man's land between the black world and the white'.[71]

## III RALPH ELLISON

Alienation also characterised Ralph Ellison's attitude towards Africa. Yet, whereas Wright did at least try, albeit unsuccessfully, to overcome it, Ellison flatly denied 'that there is any significant kinship between American Negroes and Africans'. He has no interest in Africa whatsoever. For him that continent is 'just a part of the bigger world picture'; he has, he writes, great difficulty in 'associating [him]self with Africa'. This lack of interest does not, he protests, result from repressed feelings of shame about his 'forefathers'. At least he cannot remember that he was ever 'repelled' by the sight of Africans, for instance in films. He explains his attitude from the fact that Africans are totally alien to him. This fact, he says, in turn stems from the complete lack of a cultural connection between Africans and Afro-Americans. 'The African content of American Negro life is more fanciful than actual',[72] he maintains unceremoniously. The specificity of black culture can, according to Ellison, be derived only from the history of the Afro-Americans in the U.S. Black culture, he argues, does have various points of contact with Anglo-Saxon culture; but it also possesses a number of independent elements which derive from the historical development of black society in white America and which Ellison would like to see preserved. At any rate, he flatly rejects the idea of assimilating Afro-American culture into an all-American one; for he is convinced that black culture, despite certain negative and pathological features, has 'much of great value, of richness'. It is this wealth which could even prove to be an asset for the United States in the long run. 'What is needed', he goes on, 'are Negroes to take it and create of it "the uncreated consciousness of their race" '.[73] What this consciousness ought to look like, which cultural elements should be preserved and which should be demolished as 'Jim-Crow' products, Ellison does not dare to predict yet.[74] All that can be said with reasonable certainty is that Africa – in the shape of a Pan-African nationalism à la DuBois, for example – was not expected to play a role when it came to creating a new black consciousness.

But it would be a mistake to conclude from this that Ellison never concerned himself with the problem of Africa. As can be seen from our discussion of earlier authors, a negative attitude towards Africa does not mean that they had nothing to say on this subject. On the contrary, in one way or another Africa is a recurrent theme in Afro-American literature as a whole. It therefore hardly comes as a surprise to encounter it in *Invisible Man*, Ellison's first and only novel to date, in the shape of a grinning and 'ugly ebony African god'. It is kept together with other 'cracked relics from slavery time' in a room at the college which the main character of the novel is attending. 'Though I had seen them very seldom', he muses, 'they were vivid in my mind. They had not been pleasant and whenever I had visited the room I avoided the glass case in which they rested'.[75]

It was only in the course of his 'archetypal' journey from the South to the North[76] that he learns to accept the Afro-American part of his past. He discovers that deep down in this past there lies hidden his true self, and he puts it into the following characteristic formula : 'I yam what I am ! . . . To hell with being ashamed of what you liked. No more of that for me.'[77] Slowly he comes to realise that alienation from his black ego has turned him into a blind tool of various social forces which try to manipulate him in pursuit of their own selfish interests.[78] This applies in particular to those groups which pretend to act for and in the interest of, the Afro-Americans. In fact, however, these groups – such as the Liberals and the Communists – pursue their own aims and merely try to impose on him their own ideas about what his role shall be.

The revolt against these foreign influences on his ego is radical. It is directed against white and black political movements alike : 'It is not Black Nationalism Ellison is after, but American nationalism.'[79] And yet black nationalism, as proclaimed by Ras, occupies a special place among the movements which Ellison discusses. Behind Ras's racism (Ras=Race) lies a more realistic appraisal of the Afro-American predicament than the Communist Brotherhood is able to offer. There is a dramatic encounter between Ras and the protagonist of the novel which reveals the precarious position in which the latter finds himself due to his membership in the Brotherhood :

> You *my* brother, mahn. Brothers are the same colour; how the hell you call these white men *brother*? Shit, mahn. That's shit! Brothers the same colour. We sons of Mama Africa, you done forget? You black, BLACK! . . . You African, AFRICAN! Why you with them? Leave that shit, mahn. They sell you out. That shit is old-fashioned. They enslave us – you forget that? How can they mean a black mahn any good? How they going to be your *brother*?

These words clearly have a very profound effect on the hero of the novel and even more so on his friend, Tod Clifton. Their reaction is one of fear and hatred when Ras asks them :

> What you trying to deny by betraying the black people? Why *you* fight against us? You *young* fellows. You black men with plenty education; I been hearing your rabble-rousing. Why you go over to the enslaver? . . . Is it self-respect – black against black? . . . He got you so you don't trust your black intelligence? You young, don't play you'self cheap, mahn. Don't deny you-self! . . . You black and beautiful – don't let 'em tell you different! . . . Ras recognized your black possibilities, mahn.[80]

Ellison's 'ego' is too deeply rooted in the ideology of the Brotherhood, however, to see through Ras's rabidly nationalistic rhetoric and to take the criticism as a warning : 'The narrator obviously does not understand that the militant Ras is an alternative to his present existence.' It is only step by step that he comes to recognise how Harlem assumes for the Brotherhood the function of a 'political entity' within an abstract historical concept. This allows its leaders to wield, in the name of rationality, its authority over the 'living entities' controlled by them.[81] It takes him some time to recognise 'that Ras was not funny, or not only funny, but dangerous as well, wrong but justified, crazy and yet coldly sane . . . It was funny and dangerous and sad.' Yet this insight comes all too late. 'Ras the Exhorter [has] become Ras the Destroyer upon a great black horse' who organises a ghetto uprising. He leads a contingent of blacks, armed with sticks and rifles, into a battle against both the whites and the black members of the Brotherhood. But he does so without appreciating the discrepancy between his display of militancy and the power realities of American society.

Interestingly enough, Ellison has underlined this discrepancy as follows : Ras appears on the battle scene dressed as an African chief with 'a fur cap upon his head, his arm bearing a shield, a cape made of the skin of some wild animal around his shoulders'. On the protagonist he leaves the impression of 'a madman in a foreign costume . . . a figure more out of a dream than out of Harlem, than out of even this Harlem night, yet real, alive, alarming'. But unlike Wright, in whose *Lawd Today* Garvey is portrayed as a somewhat ridiculous and comic figure, Ellison takes Ras seriously. He knows that his hatred and violence as well as the absurdity of his battle-dress are expressions of a deep-seated feeling of frustration and stem from the hopelessness of the black predicament. To the observer Ras's actions seem absurd because he knows that the uprising has been provoked by the Brotherhood in furtherance of its own aims. This means that the blacks are being manipulated even when their hatred and resistance reaches its climax. For 'they counted on [Ras], too. They needed this *destroyer* to do their work.' And, turning to the inhabitants of the ghetto the protagonist continues, 'they deserted you so that in your despair you'd follow this man to your destruction. Can't you see it? They want you guilty of your own murder, your own sacrifice !'

It is characteristic of Ellison's attitude towards Africa that he describes Ras's attire and his Pan-African ideology as exotic, 'crazy' and 'funny', almost as if they had a pathological significance. His shield, spear and fur are evidently intended to indicate cultural distance and to demonstrate how inappropriate it is for the Afro-Americans, living as they do in an industrial society, to orientate themselves towards Africa. That continent cannot furnish the right weapons for the liberation struggle. Rather it is a leg chain, symbolising the period of slavery and given to the narrator as a present by a former prisoner, which is turned into a weapon. It becomes a knuckleduster which he uses against his enemies, among them Ras and his friends. It is this weapon which provides him with 'a certain new sense of self'. Thus the narrator finds his identity only inside the United States. Ras's black nationalism, the protagonist continues, merely tries to force an alien identity upon this self by turning the Afro-Americans into Africans : 'And I knew that it was better to live out one's own absurdity than to die for that of others, whether

Ras's or Jack's.'[82] This is obviously a rejection of Africa. Nevertheless, it is interesting that Ellison discusses the African problem at all and to see how he tackles it. No doubt his basic position is typical of the period of 'literary isolationism' during which a feeling of alienation from Africa became very marked, especially in comparison with the previous epoch.

## IV   JAMES BALDWIN

Compared with the attitudes of Ellison and Wright, Baldwin's relationship with Africa is more direct and more personal. At the same time, it displays the same tensions and ambivalences which are characteristic of most of the Afro-American writers analysed thus far. However, it is more difficult than in any of the other cases to define Baldwin's position *vis-à-vis* Africa, on the one hand, and *vis-à-vis* the West, on the other. The reason for this is that it is almost impossible to reconcile his various statements on the subject with one another. Some of these openly contradict each other and it is hence not easy to give this section on Baldwin a sort of 'red thread'. Fortunately there are a number of points of orientation, among them the central theme of his life and work, his relationship with his (step-) father.

Baldwin was frightened of him. But at the same time he admired him and tried, albeit unsuccessfully, to woo him. This conflict between him and his step-father had a profound influence on James's life. It can be traced throughout his work, in which David Baldwin is frequently 'resurrected'. Baldwin regarded his relationship with his step-father not merely as a personal problem. To him it was symbolic of the predicament of the Afro-Americans in general. It demonstrated his 'bastardization' and his alienation from his 'forefathers', American as well as African. Baldwin has always tried very hard to gain the love of his father. But his attempts met with nothing but refusal and hatred. It was because of this that he became finally convinced that he was inferior. Baldwin came to believe that he was too ugly and too evil to expect salvation through love. *Go Tell It On The Mountain*, Baldwin's first and distinctly autobiographical novel, describes how his father told him time and again 'that his face was the face of Satan'. The dramatic 'scenes of conversion', the key passages of the book, show, however, how strong John's inner resistance was to identifying himself with the image which his father tried to impose on him. Such an identification would have implied that he accepted his supposed inferiority as representing his true self. But it also meant subjugation to his father, who hated him, and to the world which he embodied. This was a world of 'utter darkness' in which, although love is being preached, men destroy themselves through hatred and self-hatred just as John's father and his aunt Florence destroyed each other. It was a world, in which biblical language is experienced directly and in which the manifold associations of 'black' with 'dirt', 'evil' or 'sinner' are evidence of damnation. It is, finally, a world which is filled with

> rage and weeping from time set free, but bound now in eternity; rage that had no language, weeping with no voice – which yet spoke now, to John's startled soul, of boundless melancholy, of the bitterest patience and the longest night; of the deepest water, the strongest chain, the most cruel lash; . . . Yes, the darkness hummed with murder : the body in the water, the body in the fire, the body on the tree. John looked down the line of these armies of darkness, army upon army, and his soul whispered : 'Who are these? Who are they?' And wondered : 'Where shall I go?'

There was no chance for John to escape this darkness which was his fate. 'His strength was finished, and he could not move. He belonged to the darkness – the darkness from which he had thought to flee had claimed him.' He had no choice but to identify himself with the suffering of all black men and to accept despair and misery as God-given. This was the God who spoke to him through his father, a preacher invested with divine authority. 'His father's will was stronger than John's own. His power was greater because he belonged to God. Now, John felt no hatred, nothing, only a bitter, unbelieving despair : all prophecies were true, salvation was finished, damnation was real !'

In order to impart some kind of sense to the misery of the blacks for which they were so obviously not responsible, John subjected himself reluctantly to Noah's Curse. This, he hoped, would make the suffering more tolerable. In this way he came to see the present predicament of the blacks as a penance for past crimes, i.e. for the sins of Ham, who, according to the Bible, was the *Ur*-father of the Africans. These sins had been conferred on to subsequent generations and were now living on inside John. Thus John is faced with the paradoxical situation that John's father – himself a 'son of the devil' – bequeathes his 'black' sinfulness to his son, but, at the same time, hates him for his inherited wickedness.[83] On top of it all, he demands John's subjugation to his fate and thus to him as offering the only path of redemption. Rejection and attraction accompanied by an acceptance of his own inferiority represented therefore the sum total of Baldwin's contradictory feelings which circumscribed his relationship with his father as well as other blacks, as will be seen later.

His attitude towards his African ancestry which is similarly ambiguous is directly connected with his views on sin. Africa embodies for him the 'dark', mysterious and 'sinful' past of the blacks. He associates it with a very dark man, 'much blacker than me, naked, very romantic, very banal, sweat, something very sensual, very free, something very mysterious. It intrigues me. Also frightens me.'[84] It was through books and films that Baldwin gained this impression of Africa. He was told in school 'that Africa had never contributed "anything" to civilization. Or one was taught the same lesson more obliquely, and even more effectively, by watching nearly naked, dancing, comic-opera, cannibalistic savages in the movies.'[85] And it was his step-father, David Baldwin, with his dark skin, filled with hatred and pride alike, who seemed to represent to James what he had learned from books and films about his ancestors : 'He looked to me, as I grew older, like pictures I had seen of African tribal chieftains : he really should have been naked, with war-paint on and barbaric mementos, standing among spears.'[86] Just as he was ashamed of 'African savages', he despised his father and his parishioners whom he compared with those 'savages'.

Baldwin at first refused to identify with these men who appeared to be primitive and African to him. After all, they merely confirmed people in their 'general attitude . . . of uneasy contempt' for Africans and blacks in general.[87] However, the boy had no possibility of finding more positive models which he could look up to. They simply did not exist in the world in which he grew up. He could only accept as true what he read about his ancestors. Wherever he turned, the more 'civilized', more beautiful, wealthier and cleaner world of the whites merely underlined the 'primitiveness' and inferiority of the blacks. Ultimately, he made his 'worst discovery' : 'It was not only that society treated me like a *nigger* and thought of me as one, but that *I myself* believed – that I believed what *white* people said to me.'[88]

This meant that he had now accepted the 'white image of the "nigger" ' just as he identified himself with the 'black' and equally negative image of his father. It also implied his acceptance of his African past in which the 'sinfulness' and 'savagery' of the Afro-Americans was rooted.[89] All he had to do was to learn to live with it. His African past, he feels, is still a part of himself, and he is made aware of this whenever he meets Africans. Africans, those of the present not excepted, embody for the Afro-American 'the unspeakable, dark, guilty, erotic past which the Protestant fathers made him bury – . . . but which lies in his personality and haunts the universe yet'.[90] Pagan sensuousness, a concern for life in this world and a Christian sense of sin are closely intertwined here and become the sources of serious inner conflicts in those blacks who have been converted to Christianity. To resist the will of God would disqualify him from redemption; to subject himself to the will of God, on the other hand, was tantamount to renouncing worldly pleasures and fulfilment. Knowing the 'truth' is consequently not a cause for rejoicing and liberation, but is seen to be a burden. He almost seems

to envy those 'African savages' who do not have to bear this responsibility.[91]

In his earlier writings Baldwin considered Africans 'at once simpler
and more devious, more directly erotic and at the same time more subtle,
and they were proud'; they are oblivious of the 'profound, almost
ineradicable self-hatred' that harrows the Afro-Americans. He even
envies Africans for their comparatively intact self-confidence and their
inner peace. 'The African', he sighs, 'has not yet endured that utter
alienation of himself from his people and his past.' Yet at the same
time he feels a sense of 'despair . . . and revulsion' and fear when he
thinks of them. By their presence, the Afro-American is, he believes,
sharply confronted with his own predicament and forced to ask himself
'how much he has gained and lost during his long sojourn in the
American republic'. Whatever the balance-sheet may show in this
respect, faced with Africans, Baldwin, the Afro-American, is overcome
by feelings of deep bitterness, as he begins to appreciate the high price
which he had to pay for his 'civilization'. But these are not the only
unpleasant feelings which Africans arouse in Baldwin. Back in the
United States, he had time and again experienced humiliation and
scorn because of his dark skin, ending in a hatred of himself. Yet 'the
Africans were much darker than I; I was a paleface among
them . . . And the disturbance thus created caused all my extreme
ambivalence about color to come floating to the surface of my mind.'
Although Africans did not, in Baldwin's view, know the self-hatred
from which so many Afro-Americans suffered, he nevertheless feared
'that they had good reason to despise me', just as he had been despised
by his 'African' father.

To be sure, it was not merely the colour question which alienated
Baldwin from the Africans. No less important for his attitude towards
Africa was his conviction, abandoned only in later years, that blacks
were without a culture. He began to despise blacks simply 'because they
failed to produce Rembrandt'. Even the most uneducated among the
whites, he maintains, is superior to the blacks since he 'is related, in a
way that I am not, to Dante, Shakespeare, Michelangelo, Aeschylus,
Da Vinci, Rembrandt, and Racine; the cathedral at Chartres says
something to them which it cannot say to me, as indeed would New
York's Empire State Building, should anyone here ever see it'. White
folk-tunes formed the basis of Bach's and Beethoven's music. His own
ancestors, on the other hand, had nothing of cultural relevance to show
for : 'Go back a few centuries and they are in their full glory – but I am
in Africa watching the conquerors arrive.' The modern world had been
created by whites alone who therefore took it to be theirs. All a black
man could do was 'to appropriate these white centuries'. And he adds :
'I would have to make them mine – I would have to accept my special

attitude, my special place in this scheme – otherwise I would have no place in *any* scheme.'[92]

Baldwin's attempt to turn the colour of the skin into the decisive criterion of cultural affiliation and even of access to culture is fraught with problems. Surely, the 'illiterate' Swiss peasant, whom Baldwin referred to, had as much or as little in common with Rembrandt or Chartres Cathedral as Baldwin. At least it is difficult to see why geographical distance should be more important than distance in time. On the contrary, as David Levin has argued, 'the way in which Baldwin is related to Shakespeare and Dante is more important than the way an illiterate European is related to either of them'.[93] In short, Baldwin oversimplifies historical and cultural connections. His strictly Manichaean world-view creates a cultural polarity between black and white which was just as non-existent in reality as the unity of 'white' culture which he posits. His attitude is apparently based on the assumption – as we have had occasion to observe at various times – that culture is, so to speak, fixed to the colour-gene. Only in this way can one explain Baldwin's conviction that all whites, i.e. all carriers of this gene, participate in some mysterious fashion in the cultural achievements of their 'race'. Non-whites, on the other hand, allegedly have to struggle very hard to gain access to these achievements.

Since black culture, according to Baldwin, had been destroyed by the whites, there was hence nothing of positive values that might bind Africa and Black America together. Although he admits that 'there was undoubtedly something African in all American Negroes', he immediately adds, 'the great question of what this was and how it had survived remained wide open'. At this early stage of his work as a writer, he discerns only one common bond between all blacks : 'Their precarious, their unutterably painful relation to the white world.' This applies to Afro-Americans as much as to Africans, 'for they were all, now, whether they liked it or not, related to Europe, stained by European visions and standards, and their relation to themselves, and to each other, and to their past had changed.'[94]

In view of the ubiquitous presence of the white world from which it was impossible to escape, especially in the 1940s and 1950s, Africa does not present an alternative to the United States. Baldwin cannot conceive of it as his physical or emotional 'home'. Rather he tries to define more precisely the position of the Afro-Americans within American society. The Afro-American, he postulates, 'is not a visitor to the West, but a citizen there, an American; as American as the Americans who despise him, the Americans who fear him, the Americans who love him'. 'Four hundred' years of alienation from Africa had turned the blacks into 'Americans and their destiny is the country's destiny. They have no other experience besides their experience on this continent and it is an experience which cannot be rejected, which yet remains to be embraced.' Of course, the 'Americanness' of the Afro-Americans was not yet something tangible but was reflected in their *search* for an identity. And 'in this need to establish himself in relation to his past he is most American, this depthless alienation from oneself and one's people is, in sum, the American experience'.[95] Baldwin, the writer, considers it his most important task to act as a guide on the black path towards this new identity. Again it is necessary to deal with his ideas on this particular subject in order to understand those aspects of Baldwin's image of Africa which remain to be discussed.

The first thing to remember here is that Baldwin developed his concept of the Black American largely in reaction to Wright, his 'spiritual father'. It has been mentioned above that he was very critical of Wright's idea of seeing the Afro-American predicament purely in terms of dehumanisation. This he rejected, by implication. It was tantamount to pushing the Afro-Americans into a total void and, unlike Wright, Baldwin finds this position intolerable. Basically all human beings, he writes, yearn to be accepted by the society in which they live. However, Baldwin is not an assimilationist. Total assimilation, he argues, would be based on the assumption 'that the black man, to become truly human and acceptable, must first become like us'. But this would amount to an 'obliteration of his own personality, the distortion and debasement of his own experience'. It implied a 'surrendering to those forces which reduce the person to anonymity'. It was only on his specific existence as a black in the United States that the black man's true self and his human dignity were based.[96] He would remain an outcast, a 'non-being', as long as he did not identify with his existence as an Afro-American and with his past. He would have to integrate his life as a member of American society into this self-image of his. In other words, what Baldwin tries to do is to generalise the very personal evolution of his own consciousness.

It reminds one of John's subjection to Noah's Curse when Baldwin explains :

> We cannot escape our origins, however hard we try, those origins which contain the key – could we but find it – to all that we later become . . . It is a sentimental error, therefore, to believe that the past is dead; it means nothing to say that it is all forgotten, that the Negro himself has forgotten it . . . The man does not remember the hand that struck him, the darkness that frightened him, as a child; nevertheless, the hand and the darkness remain with him.

However, it is not just a matter of making sense of the present by including the historical aspect. Conversely, the task is also to come to terms with the Afro-American past. For 'the past will remain horrible for exactly as long as we refuse to assess it honestly.' Baldwin can thus be placed in a tradition which started at the end of the nineteenth century and which flourished during the Harlem Renaissance, of identifying with one's past rather than repressing it in shame. But Baldwin carries this argument further than previous writers. He urges Afro-Americans to refrain from protest and to subscribe to the black experience and its consequences. The Negro, he says, should make his peace with 'darkness' and with the 'nigger in himself'. And he should do so without allowing himself, like Bigger, to be overwhelmed and dehumanised by it. Otherwise hatred and self-hatred would destroy him – just as Bigger was destroyed by it.[97]

Baldwin realises that adopting this position involves taking over the biblical notion of the blacks being the symbol of 'the evil, the sin and suffering'. Afro-Americans would have to 'accept the status which myth, if nothing else, gives [them] in the West before [they] can hope to change the myth'.[98] Death, violence and hate are the crosses which Afro-Americans have to bear, not merely for the sake of their own humanity, but also, and above all, to save white America. In fact, Baldwin interprets America's problems as deriving from the refusal of the whites to recognise the 'dark' and 'subterranean' spheres of life. They had created a world of illusions around them and refused to abandon them in favour of a more 'realistic' view of life. The role of the blacks in the United States is therefore to liberate the whites from their 'ignorance' and 'innocence'. They were messengers from 'that terrifying darkness from which we come', where they had experienced suffering, violence and hatred. It was their duty to testify to the existence of this world which the whites ignored. They were supposed to contribute this knowledge to the 'American experience' in order to generate a genuine sense of reality.[99] In other words, the blacks, purified by their suffering, are expected to provide a kind of 'moral rearmament' of white America.[100] In postulating this, Baldwin starts from the assumption that the whites did not know what they were doing when supporting racism. Through love and compassion, Afro-Americans should therefore make them aware of reality and carry some light into their 'spiritual darkness': 'If it is true, and I believe it is, that all men are brothers, then we have the duty to try to understand this wretched man; and while we probably cannot hope to liberate him, begin working toward the liberation of his children.'[101]

This appeal to 'love thine enemies' and to refrain from rebellion, reflects quite distinctly those Christian elements in Baldwin's thinking which his upbringing had instilled in him.[102] But it is also indicative of his belief in something like an '*Ur*-love' between whites and blacks which the Fall of Man – in this case his racial hatred – had destroyed.

The white father chased his black son (and thereby ultimately himself) from paradise – an argument which again is partly reminiscent of Noah's curse.[103] But man must find his way back to this '*Ur*-love'. Love – as Baldwin tries to show in his novels with their frequently racially mixed couples – is the only cure against the evils of this world.[104]

What, in view of the black 'group reality' of Baldwin's novels, raises considerable problems is that love and reconciliation are to be achieved through the suffering of the Afro-Americans who are supposed to accept their own 'darkness'. His own criticism of Wright that he disregarded the humanity of blacks could also be levelled against Baldwin. Accepting one's 'black' existence is, after all, most unlikely to have a humanising effect. On the contrary, it was bound to lead to a further isolation and alienation of the Afro-Americans. In the final analysis they would be driven into hatred and self-hatred just as Wright's characters had been. They are – like Baldwin himself – totally orientated towards the white man, whom they want to 'educate' and who, despite his 'one-dimensionality', time and again emerges from the narrative as a more convincing and 'fuller' character than his black counterparts.[105] The life of the Afro-Americans serves more as a fill-in and hardly possesses a dimension of its own.[106] In so far as a black 'group reality' is at all depicted, it tends to be oppressive rather than 'sustaining'. It is more destructive of self-respect and geared to an adaptation to white norms (above all, where the repression of sexuality is concerned) than orientated towards generating a new self-confidence.[107] *Another Country*, Baldwin's most important novel as far as his 'love theory' is concerned, offers a good example. In this novel it is Eric, a white man, who appears as the most humane, most intuitive character, as the person who is most capable of genuine love. Rufus, the Afro-American, on the other hand, destroys the life of his girl-friend as well as his own because he is so depressed by his inability to overcome his feelings of hatred and to love her.

Another paradox in Baldwin's thinking, but again characteristic of his approach, is how he associates the relatively intact self-confidence of some of his black characters with Africa and how he turns more and more towards Black Nationalism. One reason for this may be that his rejection of hatred and his exhortation to show compassion and even love for the whites might meet with the disapproval of militant blacks 'whom he both fears and respects'. And since 'he senses betrayal in his own attitudes he fears writing what may be interpreted as a betrayal of his own race'.[108] By blowing the nationalist trumpet, he tries to link up with separatism at a time when the intellectual and political climate in the United States underwent a marked shift away from earlier plans of integration and racial reconciliation. This conclusion emerges most clearly from a later novel, which will be analysed in greater detail in a moment. However, it must be added that a genuine interest in Africa and an appetite for 'revelations of superiority'[109] can be traced back to Baldwin's 'pre-nationalist' phase. Even *Go Tell It On The Mountain* contains a reference to this when Richard – John's real and Baldwin's 'ideal' father – visits the Metropolitan Museum of Art with his wife Elizabeth. But whereas his wife is not really attracted by the African department, Richard is fascinated :

She did not know why he so adored things that were so long dead; what sustenance they gave him, what secrets he hoped to wrest from them. But she understood, at least, that they *did* give him a kind of bitter nourishment, and that the secrets they held for him were a matter of his life and death. It frightened her because she felt that he was reaching for the moon and that he would, therefore, be dashed down against the rocks.[110]

In fact, Elizabeth's premonitions were to come true. Richard's self-confidence. bolstered by his acquaintance with Africa, gives him a new sense of human dignity. His pride is awakened in him. He is driven into rebellion against his predicament as a black. Unlike John he does not find a sense of purpose in suffering. Ultimately the tension between his will to assert himself and the frustration which he experiences becomes so intolerable that he commits suicide.

In *Another Country* it is 'black, filthy foolish' Rufus[111] who finds a life of humiliation in white society unbearable when he comes to realise that God is 'white' and that life 'belongs' to the whites. To Rufus, by contrast, 'belongs only the black, cold water. The water of life . . . has become a dark river of death for Rufus and his race.'[12] It is 'race-conscious' Ida, Rufus's sister, who proves to be stronger and thus survives; for Ida is endowed with a 'profound' and 'powerful' self-confidence. To give an impression of her personality Baldwin resorts to a nationalist rhetoric which he seems to have borrowed from the Harlem Movement. Ida, at any rate, was 'very, very dark, she was beautiful'. Baldwin stresses repeatedly that her beauty stems from her African origin :

Ages and ages ago, Ida had not been merely the descendant of slaves. Watching her dark face in the sunlight, softened and shadowed by the glorious shawl, it could be seen that she had once been a monarch. Then he looked out of the window, at the air shaft, and thought of the whores of Seventh Avenue. He thought of the white policemen and the money they had made on black flesh, the money the whole world made.[113]

An interest in Africa as a potential source of a positive self-image which, accompanied by a reluctant protest against the hard, white God, had been more overt in *Go Tell It On The Mountain*, becomes even more noticeable in Baldwin's writings from about 1959 onwards. Thus he wrote in a report on the Pan-African Cultural Congress at Paris, published in 1960, that Afro-Americans and Africans are joined together by the need 'to remake the world in their own image, to impose this image on the world, and no longer be controlled by the vision of the world, and of themselves, held by other people. What, in sum, black men held in common was their ache to come into the world as men.' And only a year later he asserts that 'the American Negro can no longer, nor will ever again, be controlled by white America's image of him'.[114]

The causes of this change are seen by Baldwin to lie above all in the growing importance of the new post-colonial African states. He considers the rise of Africa most important. It puts the Afro-American in the position of identifying with Africa at last and even 'to think of himself as an African [which] is a necessary step in the creation of his morale'.[115] This is particularly true of Baldwin himself, who now moves more in the direction of a close (positive) identification with Africa. The emergence of independent states, he maintains, shows that Africa is not 'uncivilized'. Hence Afro-Americans would no longer have to be ashamed of that continent. The younger generation of Afro-Americans lived in very different circumstances :

By the time they were able to react to the world, Africa was on the stage of history. This could not but have an extraordinary effect on their own morale, for it meant that they were not merely the descendants of slaves in a white, Protestant, and puritan country : they were also related to kings and princes in an ancestral homeland, far away. And this has proved to be a great antidote to the poison of self-hatred.[116]

But this self-confidence is not yet so strong that he does not have to resort to over-compensation. An 'ordinary' African is apparently not capable of satisfying the demand for 'civilized' behaviour. As in the above quotation (and in *Another Country* or other works) 'kings and princes' have to bear witness to this capability.[117]

Finally, in the first half of the 1960s Baldwin decides to visit Africa. He offers the following explanation for his decision :

I think there is a great deal I can discover about myself there. There is something beautiful about it. I want to find out. It is at the gateway of the modern world, and I could help to be a guide . . . I might also find that part of me I had to bury when I grew up, the capacity for joy, of the sense, and something almost dead, real good-naturedness I think they still believe in miracles there and I want to see it.[118]

Somewhat more subdued are the words which he wrote to his publisher in 1961 :

My bones know, somehow, something of what waits for me in Africa. That is one of the reasons I have dawdled so long – I'm afraid. And, of course, I am playing it my own way, edging myself into it : it would be nice to be able to dream about Africa, but once I have been there, I will not be able to dream any more . . . One flinches from the responsibility which we all now face, of judging black people solely as people.

This means that, deep down in his heart, Baldwin still feared that the traditional arguments about the African's lack of civilisation, which he had learned to believe in, might be confirmed and thus increase his inferiority complex. But in the course of the journey which he finally made to Africa he found that his fears were without foundation : 'It was *marvellous*. Something in me recognized it. Recognised it all, I was never uneasy in myself – in view of, you know, *them*.' Though exhilarated by the success of his African encounter, Baldwin does not conceive of it as a 'homeland'. He continues to uphold his concept of the 'American-ness' of Afro-Americans and of the specific role which blacks had to fulfil *vis-à-vis* the whites. What he did feel, however, was a sense of responsibility for Africa, 'because . . . whatever is going to happen in Africa, I was in one way or another involved. Or *affected* by it, certainly. But . . . I didn't feel it could happen on the basis of *colour* . . . I loved Africa. I want to go back.'[119]

There is behind these simple words the attempt to perform a difficult balancing act. On the one hand, Baldwin joins the chorus of Black Nationalists. He promotes the idea of 'Black is beautiful'; he develops a keen interest in Africa and advocates the formation of a united front with Africans. The newly-won independence of the African states offers, he believes, at last an opportunity of liberating the blacks from the spiritual domination of the whites. On the other hand, he argues that colour is unimportant. In fact, as before, he explicitly includes the whites in his notion of universal love. Obviously it was bound to be most difficult to avoid a collision between these two approaches to the problem. Thus one finds on one and the same page : 'The value placed on the colour of the skin is always and everywhere and forever a delusion'; and 'black people, though I am aware that some of us, black and white, do not know it yet, are very beautiful.' Nor is it particularly logical for instance – at least not from a nationalist point of view – that it is the main task of 'race-conscious' Ida to rescue the white Liberals, represented here by Vivaldo, from their 'innocence'.[120]

This ambivalence which is typical of Baldwin is also the keynote of his novel, *Tell Me How Long The Train's Been Gone*.[121] Once again this novel contains a strong autobiographical element. His rhetoric is evidently influenced by the Black Power Movement and reflects his attempt to adapt to the changing consciousness of the 1960s and to establish contact with the much-vaunted 'soul' community of all blacks. But he is never quite successful. We have seen repeatedly how Afro-American writers were often strongly influenced by experiences earlier on in their life. Baldwin is yet another example. He is too deeply rooted in the ideas of the 1940s and 1950s to participate in the 'revolution in black consciousness'[122] with ease. Thus one reviewer, admittedly not particularly well-disposed towards Baldwin, certainly had a point when he wrote about *Tell Me* : 'The most important thematic progression to be noted in this work is that for the first time in a Baldwin novel, black man gets black boy.'[123] Again the basic themes of this particular novel are the depressing boyhood of the main character, Leo Proud-hammer, in Harlem; heterosexual as well as homosexual relations; the isolation of Proudhammer, most of whose friends are whites, from other blacks; self-hatred and group-hatred among Afro-Americans. His denial notwithstanding, there is finally even an attempt to bring the whites to their senses, i.e. to make them see their prejudices and to persuade them to recognise their past 'sins'.

Leo is completely orientated towards the whites. Descriptions of an organic and positive Afro-American group life are missing, and black characters in *Tell Me*, like those of *Another Country*, often lack vitality and conviction. This is what separates him not only from other writers of the 1960s towards whom he is trying to move, but also from Wright and Ellison who draw a much more vivid picture of Afro-American life than Baldwin. One possible explanation of this might be, as Eckman has pointed out, that he had more friends among whites than among Afro-Americans since early childhood.[124] Accordingly he tends to look upon other blacks more through the eyes of a white man than through those of someone who is directly affected. Thus, probably in order to avoid giving the (white) reader an unfavourable impression of the Afro-American world, Baldwin feels obliged to explain the behaviour of blacks as follows :

I saw, with a peculiar shock, the root of the despicable and tenacious American folk-lore concerning the happy, prancing niggers. Some of these people were moving, indeed, and the jukebox was loud; their movements followed the music which their movements had produced; but prancing scarcely fairly described their uses of their vigor. Only someone who no longer had any sense of what constituted happiness could ever have confounded happiness with this rage . . . It was my own uneasiness as we entered which afforded me my key to the domestic fantasy . . .

No less characteristic of his relationship with Afro-Americans and whites alike is his endeavour to weave references to black culture into his narrative. Thus Leo has little contact with Afro-Americans and it is somewhat difficult for Baldwin to integrate black culture into his plot. Accordingly, black folklore appears in places where it is really somewhat misplaced. For example, Leo goes to a party given by famous and wealthy whites at which he is the only black person. And suddenly he feels the urge to play and sing a blues to a (white) girl whom he has met at this party. To do so, he says somewhat clumsily, 'helps – to – keep me in touch with myself'. Then, much to the delight of his (white) audience, he begins to sing : 'Blues, you're driving me crazy, what am I to do? . . . I ain't got nobody to tell my troubles to.' Baldwin does not seem to be aware of the irony in this scene.[125]

Striking passages influenced by Black Nationalism, such as this one, are added to Baldwin's traditional repertoire, evidently in an attempt to narrow the gap between himself and other blacks. Whereas Rufus – shortly before his death – quarrels with his fate as a black and levels accusations against the white world, Leo, suffering a heart attack (at the beginning of the novel), is reminded of the myth that the soul of dead Afro-Americans returns to Africa.[126] Moreover, it is remarkable how often Baldwin uses the word 'black', mainly in description of persons : 'Black Christopher : because he was black in so many ways – black in color, black in pride, black in rage . . . Christopher looked like a black sun . . . , opened his big black face and clapped his big black hands.' The fact that the main character of the novel calls himself an 'Ethiopian' and that the father-figure is depicted as a militant nationalist and former Garveyite is also new.[127] Certainly, James Baldwin never mentions anywhere in his earlier writings that David Baldwin held such sympathies.[128] Just as David Baldwin maintained that he was a descendant of African kings, so Leo's father tells his children that

he came from a race which had been flourishing at the very dawn of the world – a race greater and nobler than Rome or Judea, mightier than Egypt – he came from a race of kings, kings who had never been taken in battle, kings who had never been slaves. He spoke to us of tribes and empires, battles, victories, and monarchs of whom we had never heard – they were not mentioned in our schoolbooks.

G

Yet these words made little impact. The contrast between these dreams of a glorious and proud past and the misery of the present was too stark :

> If our father was of royal blood and we were royal children, our father was certainly the only person in the world who knew it . . . It was scarcely worthwhile being the descendant of kings if the kings were black and no one had ever heard of them, and especially, furthermore, if royal status could not fill the empty stomach.[129]

In these circumstances Africa did not have much attraction. As before, Baldwin is not prepared to emigrate from the United States. There has been little change in his ambiguous position *vis-à-vis* America as his 'strange home'.[130]

If these lines may be taken to imply a mild criticism of the cultural nationalism of the 1960s, Baldwin nevertheless came to show great sympathy for a militant kind of nationalism and is even prepared to accept the need for armed resistance against white domination. This is clearly a surprising metamorphosis in Baldwin's thinking after his earlier preference for moral appeals over political action or even politically motivated analyses of the black predicament. In *The Fire Next Time* he still spoke up against violence by blacks. He was convinced of a vengeance 'that cannot be prevented by any police force or army : historical vengeance, a cosmic vengeance, based on the law that we recognize when we say "Whatever goes up must come down" '.[131] Since then Baldwin has come to believe that the younger generation of Afro-Americans (represented by 'black Christopher' in *Tell Me*) had a right to search for alternative solutions. He even admits ashamedly that earlier generations have been unable to effect a basic change of conditions by peaceful means. Hence his conclusion : 'I had to agree because I loved him and valued him. I had to agree because it is criminal to counsel despair. I had to agree because it is always possible that, if one man can be saved, a multitude can be saved . . . Perhaps God would join us later, when He was convinced that we were on the winning side.'

The sarcasm of the final sentence demonstrates that Baldwin's increasingly militant nationalism is accompanied by a rebellion against his Christian God. It was barely noticeable in his earlier writings, but now it is unrestrained :

> A faint breeze struck, but it did not cool my Ethiopian brow. Ethiopian hands : to what God indeed, out of this despairing place, was I to stretch these hands? . . . I had had quite enough of God — more than enough, more than enough, the horror filled my nostril,

I gagged on the blood-drenched name; and yet was forced to see that this horror, precisely, accomplished His reality and undid my unbelief.

Although he does not abandon his faith in God, he is very outspoken in his criticism of Christianity as an institution and against those 'god-dam missionaries' who had destroyed the Africans and hence also himself. The task of today, he writes, is 'to prevent these Christians from once again destroying this pagan', i.e. Christopher who embodies the 'proud' and 'beautiful' black – a new 'New Negro', as one might also call him, who represents a world different from that in which Baldwin had grown up.[132] The close association of this 'New Negro' with 'Black Christ' throws an interesting light on Baldwin's frame of reference within which his 'New World' is supposed to emerge. It does not seem to be mere coincidence that the name 'Christopher' appears most of the time in connection with the adjective 'black'.

What Baldwin's 'new' values were supposed to be can be looked up in the more important writings which he has published since *Tell Me*. What immediately strikes the eye in them is that his criticism has become even more radical. It is partly directed against Christianity which he accuses of having betrayed all its ideals : 'The Christian church has betrayed and dishonoured and blasphemed that Saviour in whose name they have slaughtered millions and millions and millions of people.' The Christian world is thus 'nothing but a tissue of lies, nothing but an excuse for power, as being as removed as anything can possibly be from any sense of worship, still more, from any sense of love'. But then Baldwin moves beyond Christianity and finds harsh words for Western civilisation as a whole. His position is now the exact opposite of what it was before, as can be seen from the literal repetition of certain of his key notions, except that they have been 'transvalued' completely. For example, Baldwin had written in his first volume of essays that, because the blacks lacked a culture of their own, they had no choice but to adopt Western values. Now he maintains that the history of the West is

nothing but an intolerable yoke, a stinking prison, a shrieking grave . . . And whatever this history may have given to the subjugated is of absolutely no value, since they have never been free to reject it; they will never be able even to assess it until they are free to take from it what they need, and to add to history the monumental fact of their presence. The South African coal miner, or the African digging for roots in the bush, or the Algerian mason working in Paris, not only have no reason not to bow down before Shakespeare, or Descartes, or Westminster Abbey, or the cathedral at Chartres : they have, once these monuments intrude on their attention, no honourable access to them. Their apprehension of this history cannot fail to reveal to them that they have been robbed, maligned, and rejected : to bow down before that history is to accept that history's arrogant and unjust judgment.

And the West's claim to cultural superiority, he continues, is nothing but 'a mask of power'. Liberating the blacks (and in this case, the African) from economic exploitation would lead to their liberation from Western cultural domination. 'Later, of course, one may welcome [Western cultural traditions] back, but on one's own terms, and absolutely on one's own land.' In other words, Baldwin had moved to the other extreme. But at the same time he had left open his retreat.

Nor does he have the slightest doubt that the blacks will achieve self-determination. White corruption and demoralisation spelt disaster for the West. The future belongs to the blacks. In fact they had already begun 'to forge a new morality, to create the principles on which a new world will be built'.[133] But as Margaret Mead rightly asked Baldwin : 'Where do you get your conception of morality?' Apparently this question had not occurred to him before, as can be seen from the following dialogue : 'B. : "I get my conception of morality from – from the way I watched . . . I get it partly from . . . where indeed do I get it?" M. : "Where do you get it?" B. : "That is a good question." ' At first he refuses to believe that his conception of morality is based on the same Christian ethic which he condemns for its 'inhumanity'. In the end, however, he cannot but agree with Margaret Mead when she tells him that 'the good that we have, the good things you are insisting on – that people should love each other and recognise each other as brothers – is a Christian idea'.[134]

Unlike many other Black Nationalists of the 1960s and 1970s, Baldwin did *not* base the 'new morality' of his black counter-world on a system of values which is in some way derived from African norms. Basically he does no more than call for a revival of Christian ideals, or, as he puts it a year later, 'to make the kingdom new, to make it honourable and worthy of life'. His candid criticism of the West notwithstanding, his attitude towards Africa likewise continues to be contradictory. Thus he now proclaims those same representatives of Africa who once raised his spirits to be nothing but puppets of the former colonial powers. A politician from Dakar, he argues, is 'not necessarily a man from Senegal. He is much more likely to be a spiritual citizen of France, in which event he cannot possibly convey the actual needs of this part of Africa, or of Africa.' To this day Africa is chained to Europe 'and as long as this is so, it is hard to speak of Africa except as a cradle and a potential'. Only when the Africans have assumed complete control of their country and their resources 'will the African personality flower or genuinely African institutions flourish and reveal Africa as she is'. In short, in Baldwin's view Africa is not yet in a position to offer an alternative. But in contrast with his earlier ideas, he now thinks a spiritual and hence cultural rebirth of Africa to be possible. His notion of what is 'civilised' or 'uncivilised', which had worried him so much in earlier years, has now become very much more balanced : 'One realizes that what is called civilization lives first of all in the mind, has the mind above all as its province, and that the civilization, or its rudiments, can continue to live long after its externals have vanished – they can never entirely vanish from the mind.'[135]

In revising his early image of Africa, Baldwin joins the ranks of a younger generation of writers who ushered in a new era of Afro-American literature. However, the above analysis has shown he can be called a representative of this era only to a limited extent. Especially the striking contradictions in his attitude towards Africa make him a typical representative of a phase of transition. It was a phase in which feelings of shame about one's African descent, acquired at a time of detachment from and rejection of Africa, went side-by-side with a strong support for that continent, stimulated by the subsequent period of a lively interest in things African. It was rather a confused mixture with the component parts unevenly distributed.

Although Baldwin has resorted to a militant rhetoric in recent years, he did not take the decisive step in this direction. By criticising the West he hopes that this will remind the whites of the basic ideals of their culture and bring about their renewal. He is too deeply influenced by the West and above all by Christianity to cast it off completely. But unlike Wright he does not fail to recognise just how much he is influenced by Western culture. This enables him to 'transcend' his Western value system, as *No Name In The Street* testifies.

## V SUMMARY

In spite of Baldwin's turn to nationalism his relations with the younger generation of Afro-Americans are nevertheless looser than those which connect him with the generation of Wright and Ellison. All three writers considered it their most important task to reflect upon the position of the Afro-Americans within American society as a whole. Their African origins play a subordinate role in this, though by no means an unimportant one. As we have seen, Africa presents a challenge to the post-Renaissance writers which forces them into dealing with it in one way or another. Occasionally, the image of Africa as the 'homeland' lingers on, in an idealised version not dissimilar to that of the primitivists of the 1920s. But most importantly the post-Renaissance period to the 1960s is characterised by a sense of alienation. In the case of Ellison this feeling leads to a complete lack of interest in Africa. Wright, on the other hand, tried to establish a link with Africa and to overcome his detachment. But it was, paradoxically, due to his unconsciously shared Western system of values, which he otherwise sharply rejected, that the significance of Africa eluded him. Baldwin was much more successful than Wright in surmounting much of his alienation which he, too, felt quite strongly. However, this was a recent development in his writings, and he benefited from a change in the general intellectual climate. In marked contrast with Wright, Baldwin's affiliation with the Western cultural sphere and his preparedness to open himself to other cultures are not mutually exclusive.

All three authors reacted differently to the 'African challenge'. They thus testify to the great variety of attitudes towards Africa reflected in Afro-American literature. To trace changes and continuities in this sphere was the objective of this study and we have now reached a point where we may venture a conclusion.

# Conclusion

We have been trying to trace the attitudes of Afro-American writers towards Africa over a longer time-span. Looking back on the literature which has been examined it seems justified to uphold our introductory statement that Africa, negatively or positively, never ceased to occupy a tangible place in Afro-American life and in particular in the writings of Afro-American intellectuals. But we have also seen that two aspects must be kept apart. The first is that Africa possesses a considerable weight as a cultural element within Afro-American culture, even if few Afro-Americans are themselves conscious of this. The other and probably more important aspect touched upon the subjective dimension of the black image of Africa. We analysed what sort of ideas Afro-American writers developed about Africa and how they interpreted their own relationship with the continent. These ideas were, of necessity, very personal impressions and hence would not have provided a reliable yardstick for assessing the actual quality of a particular – and changing – image of Africa. We had to rely, therefore, on the knowledge which has been acquired about African societies through modern anthropology. Only in this way was it possible to obtain a matrix against which the subjective attitudes of Afro-Americans towards Africa could be reflected.

It was against this background that it became clear how black ideas about Africa can only be seen in the light of the negative Western image of the continent. The 'white' image had been strongly influenced by the theory of evolution and provided the basis of racism in its modern and scientifically discredited shape and form. For it was this image according to which blacks belonged to the 'inferior races' which confined the Afro-Americans to the status of an underprivileged minority with all the political, social and economic discriminations and their psychic repercussions that accompany such a status. Among the damages done must be counted above all the loss of self-respect and the identification with the values of the dominant culture. Inevitably, identification with this culture implied the acceptance of its notions about Africa and black men in general.

This image, i.e. the idea of an 'uncivilised' pagan and wild continent, inhabited by people who were allegedly morally and intellectually inferior, can be traced through the whole of black literature. On it were based the poems of the eighteenth century which approved of slavery as a salvation from pagan barbarity. It also provides an explanation of why in the nineteenth century so many emancipated Afro-Americans rejected a return to Africa. In the twentieth century, then, the 'white' image reappears, in particular in the works of Wright and the early writings of Baldwin.

The deep impact of this image on Afro-Americans also emerges from an examination of the writings of black nationalists. Although they regard themselves as Africans and consider Africa their homeland, they did not challenge the nineteenth and early twentieth-century notion of the superiority of Western civilisation and of the 'primitive-ness' of African societies. This belief goes so deep that not only the technological but also the moral standards of the West are held up as an example to Africa, regardless of the system of slavery and of racism which, of course, the nationalists condemned. Their image of Africa, therefore, does not differ appreciably from that of white racists. However, they did develop a more positive idea of the Africans. They did not regard them as condemned to perennial 'inferiority'. On the contrary, they were considered capable of reaching the same level of development as the whites. Proof of this was seen in the former existence of highly developed African or partially African civilisations. Nevertheless, towards the end of the nineteenth century black nationalists definitely began to dissociate themselves from the Western world. As the example of DuBois, one of the sharpest Afro-American critics of the West, shows, this does not imply that they also succeeded in casting off the West's system of values. DuBois may not have been conscious of it, but the traditional 'white' image of Africa was just as much alive in him. Certainly, he found it most difficult to accept African life for what it is. Rather he felt obliged to create an idealised picture of Africa within the framework of a purified and puritanical Western culture. He appears to have found it impossible to identify with Africa otherwise.

The writers of the Harlem Renaissance made a more thorough-going attempt to cut themselves loose from occidental values. They identified with Africa without reservation and portrayed it in their poetry as a country in which the black man can live free from repression. They thus revived an image of Africa which can be traced back to the beginnings of Afro-American literary activity and which emerged in the slave songs in particular. This revival is frequently accompanied by a tendency to idealise Africa as a Garden of Eden in which blacks will be able to live a life free from conflict and worry about the future. Allegedly it is their 'natural' way of life which has saved them from the psychic mutilations which afflict industrial man. It was one of the main characteristics of the Harlem Renaissance that it concentrated on bringing out this polarity. Unlike earlier black nationalists, the writers of the Harlem Renaissance did not talk about the need to educate the Africans, that is to 'civilise' them. On the contrary, they considered African societies superior to Western ones, as emerges particularly clearly from the writings of Toomer and McKay. They condemned the Western system of values with its emphasis on success and material gain as having a dehumanising effect on the individual.

If we look back now to our starting-point it is possible to say that it is the Harlem Renaissance which provides the closest link between the cultural movement of the 1960s and 1970s and the past. Many of the themes of the 1920s have reappeared, such as the association of Africa with freedom from oppression, the harsh criticism of Western civilisation, the emphasis on racial pride and the celebration of the 'beautiful black'. But the militancy and the radicalism of the younger movement by far exceeded that of the Harlem Renaissance, as regards both the aims and the modes of expression. Certainly no previous generation has dared to voice its feelings as openly as that of the 1960s. It is easy to condemn this radical 'anti-whitism', and moderates were quick to denounce the nationalists as 'racists'. Indeed, one may point out – and quite a few Afro-Americans, with Baldwin as their most articulate spokesman, were quite aware of it – that if the blacks let themselves be dragged down to the low level of white racism, they are clearly in danger of becoming as morally corrupt as their enemies and of losing the integrity they often claimed to possess. If one tries, however, to discover something positive in black 'counter-racism' – and this applies to earlier periods as well – it is perhaps to be found in its therapeutic function. For if one remembers the crippling effects of the *repression* of feelings of hatred and self-hatred, which have been mentioned in the first chapter and which could be observed in several of the authors we have dealt with, the killing of whites, as advocated in a number of poems and plays in the sixties, can also be seen as an indication of a slow healing process.

The same argument could be applied to the search for and celebration of the 'African identity'. After an analysis of the manifold relationships between Afro-Americans and Africa one cannot dismiss these efforts any more as fanciful of illusory. The veneration of Africa and of 'blackness' as it appeared in the writings of some earlier authors and particularly in the most recent literature, represents, it seems, a necessary intermediate step in the painful and tortuous process of finding a 'positive' black identity. For, as Kathryn Johnson argues : 'People who have not yet seen the glory of their blackness need propaganda as much as they need food.' And even Leroi Jones confesses in the end that a subsequent generation will, perhaps, be in a position to leave the realm of pure negation and a simplistic view of the world behind it and to make a positive contribution to the emancipation of the blacks : 'We live in a world now, where the real work cannot be spoken of clearly. We believe our children will get to the real work. We will make the real work possible. Before the real work can be done, the disease, the power of evil, must be cleared away. The bringer of positive change must have places prepared for them to work.'

# Notes

INTRODUCTION

1  See also Francis L. Broderick and August Meier, *Negro Protest in the Twentieth Century*, Indianapolis 1965, 318.

2  In Clarence Reed, *Not Forever Tears*, Newark, N.J. 1967.

3  In Jon Eckel, *Home Is Where The Soul Is*, Detroit 1969.

4  'The Black Writer and his Role', in Addison Gayle (ed.), *Black Expression. Essays by and about Black Americans in the Creative Arts*, New York 1969, 349, 353, 352.

5  Askia M. Touré, in Woodie King (ed.), *Black Spirits. A Festival of New Black Poets in America*, New York 1972, 221.

6  Leroi Jones, *Raise Race Rays Raze. Essays Since 1965*, New York 1972, 147.

7  See e.g. Stokely Carmichael, 'Toward Black Liberation' in Jules Chametzky and Sidney Kaplan (eds), *Black & White in American Culture. An Anthology from 'The Massachusetts Review'*, Amherst, Mass. 1969, 76–87; Leroi Jones, *Home. Social Essays*, New York 1966.

8  'A Different Image', in Dudley Randall (ed.), *The Black Poets. A New Anthology*, New York 1971, 142.

9  Don L. Lee, 'Words in Early Time', in King (ed.), *Black Spirits*, XVII; Eugene Perkins, *An Apology To My African Brother*, Chicago 1965.

10  Gerald Simmons, Jr., 'Take Tools Our Strength . . .', in Clarence Major (ed.), *The New Black Poetry*, New York 1969.


CHAPTER 1

1  See also August Meier and Elliot M. Rudwick, *From Plantation to Ghetto*, New York 1966, 2f.; Harold Isaacs, *The New World of Negro Americans*, New York 1968, 105; Franklin E. Frazier, 'What Can the American Negro Contribute to the Social Development of Africa?', in John A. Davis (ed.), *Africa Seen by American Negroes*, Paris 1958, 271; Rupert Emerson and Martin Kilson, 'The American Dilemma in a Changing World: The Rise of Africa and the Negro American', in *Daedalus*, 94 (autumn 1965), 1067.

2  St. Clair Drake, 'Negro Americans and the African Interest', in John P. Davis (ed.), *The American Negro Reference Book*, Englewood Cliffs, N.J., 1969, 663; Emerson and Kilson, 'The American Dilemma', 1067.

3  Winthrop D. Jordan, *White over Black. American Attitudes toward the*

*Negro, 1550–1812*, Baltimore 1971; David Brion Davis, *The Problem of Slavery in Western Culture*, New York 1970; George M. Fredrickson, *The Black Image in the White Mind: The Debate on Afro-American Character and Destiny, 1817–1914*, New York, 1971; Bruce Clayton, *The Savage Ideal: Intolerance and Leadership in the South, 1890–1914*, Baltimore 1972; Claude H. Nolen, *The Negro's Image in the South. The Anatomy of White Supremacy*, Lexington 1967; I. A. Newby, *Jim Crow's Defense. Anti-Negro Thought in America, 1900–1930*, Baton Rouge, La., 1965; Stanley M. Elkins, *Slavery–A Problem in American Institutional and Intellectual Life*, Chicago 1968; Thomas F. Gossett, *Race. The History of an Idea in America*, New York 1969; Carl Degler, 'Slavery and the Genesis of American Race Prejudice', in *Comparative Studies in Society and History*, II (October 1959) 49–66; William Stanton, *The Leopard's Spots: Scientific Attitudes Toward Race in America, 1815–1859*, Chicago 1965; see also Philip D. Curtin, *The Image of Africa. British Ideas and Action, 1780–1850*, London 1965; Martin Steins, *Das Bild des Schwarzen in der europäischen Kolonialliteratur 1870–1918*, Frankfurt/M. 1972

4   See e.g. Eric Williams, *Capitalism and Slavery*, London 1964; see also Robert Starobin, 'The Negro: A Central Theme in American History', in *Journal of Contemporary History*, vol. 3, no. 2 (1968) 45; Pierre L. Van den Berghe, *Race and Racism. A Comparative Perspective*, New York 1967, 17.

5   For a very general definition of the term 'racism' see Ruth Benedict: 'Racism is an unproved assumption of the biological and perpetual superiority of one human group over another', in *Race and Racism*, London 1951, VII. See also Gossett, *Race*, 3; other authors prefer to differentiate between a widespread ethnocentrism or racial prejudice in the broadest sense on the one hand, and actual racism as a 'rationalized ideology grounded in what were thought to be the facts of nature' on the other. This type of racism, they argue, represents a typically Western phenomenon: 'Racism, understood as a developed theoretical justification for a system of discrimination and ethnic exploitation, is a distinctly European contribution to world civilization'. Fredrickson, *The Black Image*, 2; Eugene D. Genovese, *In Red and Black*, New York 1971, 56; see also Erik H. Erikson, 'The Concept of Identity in Race Relations', in Peter J. Rose (ed.), *Americans from Africa*, vol. II: *Old Memories, New Moods*, New York 1970, 330f.

6   Jordan, *White over Black*, 4; Eugene D. Genovese, *The World the Slaveholders Made*, New York 1970; Harold Isaacs, 'Group Identity and Political Change', in *Daedalus*, 96 (spring 1967) no. 2, 364; Degler, 'Slavery and Prejudice', 94f.; Elkins, *Slavery*, 37–52; on the extent of the slave trade across the Atlantic see Philip D. Curtin, *The Atlantic Slave Trade: A Census*, Madison, Wisc., 1969, and Basil Davidson, *Black Mother*, London 1961.

7   See esp. Davis, *Slavery*, part I; Elkins, *Slavery*, 37.

8   Jordan, *White over Black*, 56; see also Karl R. Popper, *The Open Society and Its Enemies*, vol. I: *The Spell of Plato*, London 1966, *passim*.

9   Jordan, *White over Black*, 77.

10  Quoted in Elkins, *Slavery*, 40; see also Oscar and Mary F. Handlin, 'Origins of the Southern System', in *William and Mary Quarterly*, 3rd series, VII (April 1950) 199–222; Jordan, *White over Black*, 66–98.

11  Of fundamental importance in this context are the studies by Jordan and Davis which have been mentioned repeatedly. See also George P. Rawick, *The American Slave: A Composite Autobiography*, vol. I, Westport, Conn., 1972, 127–49.

12  Christopher Hill, *Society and Puritanism in Pre-Revolutionary England*, New York 1964; Roger Lockyer, *Tudor and Stuart Britain, 1471–1714*, New York 1964; Barrington Moore Jr., *Social Origins of Dictatorship and Democracy: Lord and Peasant in the Making of the Modern World*, London 1967; see also Davis, *Slavery*, 501; Jordan, *White over Black*, 24f.

13  See Harry Levin, *The Power of Blackness*, London 1958; Harold Isaacs, *The New World*, 72–96; id., 'Blackness and Whiteness', in *Encounter*, XXI (August 1963) 8–21; Kovel, *White Racism*, 62ff., 232ff., 237ff.; Franz Fanon, *Peau Noire–Masques Blancs*, Paris 1965, *passim*; Caroline Spurgeon, *Shakespeare's Imagery and What It Tells Us*, Boston 1958; Roger Bastide, 'Color, Racism and Christianity', in *Daedalus*, 96 (spring 1967) no. 2, 312, 327; C. Eric Lincoln, 'Color and Group Identity in the United States', ibid., 527–41; Mercer Cook and Stephen E. Henderson, *The Militant Black Writer in Africa and the United States*, Madison, Wisc., 1969; 86–92.

14  Kenneth Gergen, 'The Significance of Skin Color in Human Relations', in *Daedalus*, 96 (spring 1967) no. 2, 398; Isaacs, *The New World*, 73; Bernard Lewis, 'Race and Colour in Islam', in *Encounter*, XXXV (August 1970) 18–36. Victor Turner, *The Forest of Symbols, Aspects of Ndembu Ritual*, Ithaca and London 1967.

15  Bastide, 'Color, Racism and Christianity', 313; see also Jordan, *White over Black*, 597; Isaacs, *The New World*, 74f.

16  Jordan, *White over Black*, 20–24; Isaacs, *The New World*, 75.

17  Charles Feidelson, *Symbolism and American Literature*, Chicago 1966, 77.

18  Levin, *Blackness*, 15.

19  Ibid., 35; see also Ralph Ellison, *Shadow and Act*, New York 1966, 63; Perry Miller, *The New England Mind*, New York 1939.

20  Bastide, 'Color, Racism and Christianity', 321; see also Levin, *Blackness*, 24; Gossett, *Race*, 17ff.; Arnold Toynbee, *A Study of History*, New York 1948, vol. I, 211; Feidelson, *Symbolism*, 80.

21  See esp. Levin, *Blackness*, *passim*; Feidelson, *Symbolism*, *passim*; Leslie Fiedler, *Love and Death in the American Novel*, Aylesbury 1966, 363–97 (on Poe's 'racial phobia'); Kovel, *White Racism*, 232ff.; Richard Harter Fogle, *Melville's Shorter Tales*, Norman 1960, 121ff.; Perry Miller, *The Raven and the Whale*, New York 1956; F. O. Mathiessen, *American Renaissance*, London 1962; Eleanor E. Simpson, 'Melville and the Negro: From "Typee" to "Benito Cereno"', in *American Literature*, March 1969, 19–38, 133, May 1969, 255; Sidney Kaplan,

'Herman Melville and the American Sin', in Seymour L. Gross and John E. Hardy, *Images of the Negro in American Literature*, Chicago 1966, 148ff.

22　Moses 1, Verse 25ff.; see also Silberman, *Crisis in Black and White*, 173f.; Jordan, *White over Black*, 17ff.; Davis, *Slavery*, 79f., 485; Gossett, *Race*, 5; Kovel, *White Racism*, 63f.

23　Jordan, *White over Black*, 19.

24　Montaigne, *Essais*, vol. i, Paris 1962, 235; on primitivism in general see Arthur O. Lovejoy and George Boas, *Primitivism and Related Ideas in Antiquity*, New York 1935; Hoxie N. Fairchild, *The Noble Savage: A Study in Romantic Naturalism*, New York 1928; John R. Cooley, *Modes of Primitivism: Black Portraits by White Writers in Twentieth Century American Literature*, unpubl. PhD thesis, Univ. of Mass., 1st chapter; Davis, *Slavery*, 405, 413f., 479; Gossett, *Race*, 24f., 391; Curtin, *Image of Africa*, 48ff.

25　Detailed discussion of *Oroonoko* in Davis, *Slavery*, 507–16; see also Fairchild, *Noble Savage*, 34ff.

26　See below p. 13.

27　Jordan, *White over Black*, 30f.; Davis, *Slavery*, 488; Gossett, *Race*, 15.

28　Gossett, *Race*, 4, 12; John Higham, *Strangers in the Land: Patterns of American Nativism, 1860–1925*, New Brunswick 1955; see also ibid., the cartoon pp. 212–13.

29　Jordan, *White over Black*, 28ff.; Davis, *Slavery*, 486; both studies contain a more detailed analysis of further associations.

30　Gossett, *Race*, 153; Gordon Allport, *The Nature of Prejudice*, Garden City 1958, 349–55; Oscar Handlin, *Race and Nationality in American Life*, New York 1957, 124; John Dollard, *Caste and Class in a Southern Town*, New York 1937, 160–3; Fredrickson, *Black Image*, 253f., 273–87f;. Newby, *Jim Crow's Defense*, 122f., 137–9; Fanon, *Peau Noire–Masques Blancs*, 153ff.; Calvin Hernton, *Sex and Racism in America*, New York 1968; Roger Bastide, 'Dusky Venus, Black Apollo', in Paul Baxter and Basil Sansom (eds), *Race and Social Difference*, Harmondsworth 1972, 187–98; Jordan, *White over Black*, 30, 32–40; Genovese, *Roll, Jordan, Roll. The World the Slaves Made*, London 1974, 458–75.

31　Contemporaries were already aware of this. See Davis, *Slavery*, 487.

32　Arthur O. Lovejoy, *The Great Chain of Being: A Study of the History of an Idea*, Cambridge, Mass., 1936; Jordan, *White over Black*, 216–68; Davis, *Slavery*, 486ff.; Gossett, *Race*, 32–83; Henri V. Vallois, 'Race', in Sol Tax (ed.), *Anthropology Today: Selections*, Chicago 1962, 46–64; Margaret Mead *et al.*, *Science and the Concept of Race*, New York 1968; Marvin Harris, *Patterns of Race in the Americas*, New York 1964; M. F. Ashley Montagu, *Man's Most Dangerous Myth: The Fallacy of Race*, New York 1946; Creighton Gabel, 'Prehistoric Populations of Africa', in Jeffry Butler (ed.), *Boston University Papers on Africa*, ii, Boston 1966, 3–15.

33　See esp. the authors mentioned in n. 3 to this chapter. For the following see also Louis L. Snyder, *The Idea of Racialism. Its Meaning and History*, Princeton, N.J., etc, 1962; Richard Hofstadter, *Social Dar-*

*winism in American Thought*, Boston 1955; Van den Berghe, *Race and Racism*.

34 Gunnar Myrdal, *An American Dilemma: The Negro Problem and Modern Democracy*, New York 1944, 99.

35 Edmund Leach, 'Ourselves and the Others', in *Times Literary Supplement*, 6 July 1973, 771; see also George W. Stocking, *Race, Culture, and Evolution: Essays in the History of Anthropology*, New York 1968, 119; *International Encyclopedia of the Social Sciences*, New York 1968, vol. 5, 200ff.

36 John Beattie, *Other Cultures. Aims, Methods and Achievements in Social Anthropology*, London 1966, 6; Marvin Harris, *Culture, Man and Nature. An Introduction to General Anthropology*, New York 1971, 447; Fredrickson, *Black Image*, 245–52, 322, 324.

37 Myrdal, *American Dilemma*, 930; James M. McPherson, *The Struggle for Equality: Abolitionists and the Negro in the Civil War and Reconstruction*, Princeton 1964, 137; Fredrickson, *Black Image*, 253f., Newby, *Jim Crow's Defense*, 42.

38 See esp. Marvin Harris, *The Rise of Anthropological Theory: A History of Theories of Culture*, London 1968; Beattie, *Other Cultures*; E. E. Evans-Pritchard, *Social Anthropology*, London 1951.

39 Beattie, *Other Cultures*, 5, 9.

40 Davidson, *Black Mother*; Worsley, *Third World*, 26; for other similarities see Curtin, *African History*, New York 1964, 32f.: 'African society was also accustomed to trade, and African merchants merely had to adapt themselves to the new economic demand . . . In a very real sense, it was African commercial organization, not the alleged primitiveness of African society, that made the slave trade possible. A genuine primitive society could not possibly have reorganized itself to supply up to 100,000 captives a year.'

41 See also Lucy Mair, *An Introduction to Social Anthropology*, London 1972, 21–5; *International Encyclopedia*, vol. 5, 222ff.; among the most influential anthropologists adhering to the idea of evolution were J. F. McLennan, *Primitive Marriage*, London 1865; Lewis H. Morgan, *Ancient Society*, London 1877; Sir James Frazer, *The Golden Bough*, London 1911.

42 Claude Lévi-Strauss, *Race et Histoire*, Paris 1961, 42; author's italics.

43 Ibid.; Curtin, *African History*, 18f.; See also chapter 'Psychological Theories' in Evans-Pritchard, *Primitive Religion*, 20ff.

44 Leo Frobenius, *Monumenta Africana. Der Geist eines Erdteils*, Weimar 1939, 47.

45 Mair, *Primitive Government*, Harmondsworth 1970, 8; Evans-Pritchard, *Primitive Religion*, 31, 107f.

46 Benedict, *Race and Racism*, 79; Hofstadter, Social Darwinism, 175; Evans-Pritchard, *Primitive Religion*, 107; O. A. Ladimeji, 'Language, Society and Literature', in *The Conch*, vol. IV, no. 1, March 1972, 48ff.

47 Nolen, *Negro's Image*, XI–XIX; Handlin, *Race and Nationality*, 30ff.; Elkins, *Slavery*, 34ff., 140; Curtin, *Image of Africa*, 364.

48 Joseph Boskin, 'Sambo: The National Jester in the Popular Culture', in Baxter and Sansom, *Race and Social Difference*, 152–64; Sterling Brown *et al* (eds), *The Negro Caravan*, New York 1969, 495; Genovese, *Red and Black*, 75–8.

49 Racialism was by no means confined to the slave states. Garrison, one of the most famous abolitionists of the nineteenth century, came close to being lynched at a meeting in Boston in 1835. See Elkins, *Slavery*, 186; Leon Litwack, *North of Slavery: The Negro in the Free States, 1780–1860*, Chicago 1961; Lewis M. Killian, *The Impossible Revolution? Black Power and the American Dream*, New York 1968, 29.

50 Almost all blacks in Melville's works are stereotyped in this way. The folklore and plantation literature is full of 'Sambos'. Similarly many blacks of Faulkner's novels and short stories fall into this category. See Jean Wagner, *Les Poètes Nègres des Etats-Unis. Le sentiment racial et religieux dans la poésie de P. L. Dunbar à L. Hughes (1890–1940)*, Paris 1963, 50ff. (now available in Engl. translation); Boskin, 'Sambo'; Nancy M. Tischler, *Black Masks. Negro Characters in Modern Southern Fiction*, London 1969; Sterling A. Brown, 'Negro Characters as Seen by White Authors', in *Journal of Negro Education*, 2 (January 1933), 180–201.

51 Elkins, *Slavery*, 82; similarly Robert Penn Warren, *Who Speaks for the Negro?*, New York 1965, 52; Elkins's study, called by Genovese (*Red and Black*, 73) 'one of the most influential historical essays of our generation', has led to a revival of the earlier discussion on the true character of 'Sambo'. As a result there have been heated controversies over whether 'Sambo' is a mere stereotype based on a real type created by slavery or nothing but an invention by the whites in justification of slavery. See *The Newberry Library Bulletin*, 'The Question of "Sambo" – A Report of the Ninth Newberry Library Conference on American Studies', (December 1958) 14–40; Ann J. Lane (ed.), *The Debate over Slavery, Stanley Elkins and his Critics*, Urbana, Ill. 1972; Mina D. Caulfield, 'Slavery and the Origins of Black Culture: Elkins Revisited', in Rose, *Americans from Africa*, vol. I, 171–93; Genovese, *Red and Black*, 73–101; Arnold A. Sio, 'Interpretations of Slavery: The Slave Status in the Americas', in *Comparative Studies in Society and History*, VII (April 1965) 289–308; Sidney Mintz, Review in *American Anthropologist*, LXII (June 1961) 579–87.

52 Handlin, *Race and Nationality*, 31ff.; Fredrickson, *Black Image*, 47; Elkins, *Slavery*, 190; Gossett, *Race*, 63, 231; Manning Nash, 'Race and the Ideology of Race', in Baxter and Sansom, *Race and Social Difference*, 111–22; William W. Freehling, *Prelude to Civil War: The Nullifications Controversy in South Carolina, 1816–1836*, 301; Davis, *Slavery*, 198, 224f., 247, 427.

53 Quoted in Fredrickson, *Black Image*, 51.

54 Ibid., 103.

55 See McPherson, *Struggle for Equality*, 144; Fredrickson, *Black Image*, 103–29, 163; Elkins, *Slavery*, 164ff.; William H. Pease and Jane H. Pease, 'Antislavery Ambivalence: Immediatism, Expediency, Race', in August

Meier and Elliott Rudwick (eds), *The Making of Black America*, New York 1969, vol. I, 302–14; Benjamin Quarles, *Black Abolitionists*, New York 1969, 47ff.

56 Vann C. Woodward, *Origins of the New South, 1877–1913*, Baton Rouge 1951; id., *The Strange Career of Jim Crow*, New York 1966; Rayford Logan, *The Betrayal of the Negro. From Rutherford B. Hayes to Woodrow Wilson*, New York and London 1968; Cash, *The Mind of the South;* Fredrickson, *Black Image*, 284ff.; Pease and Pease, 'Antislavery Ambivalence', 307; Brawley, *Black Abolitionists*, 46ff.; Benjamin G. Brawley, *The Negro Genius*, New York 1937.

57 See above p. 7.

58 Boskin, 'Sambo', 153.

59 Quoted in Fredrickson, *Black Image*, 54; on 'The Brute' see ibid., 52ff.; Nolen, *Negro's Image, passim*; Cantor, 'Negro in Colonial Literature', 33ff.

60 Cash, *The Mind of the South*, 103.

61 Genovese, *Red and Black*, 56.

62 Quoted in Gossett, *Race*, 271.

63 See Logan, *Betrayal of the Negro*, 242–75 on the image of blacks in literary magazines; Fredrickson, *Black Image*, 256–82 on racist literature.

64 On the psychology of racism see e.g. Leonard Bloom, *The Social Psychology of Race Relations*, London 1971; Abram Kardiner and Lionel Ovesey, *The Mark of Oppression. Explorations in the Personality of the American Negro*, Cleveland and New York 1968, 13ff.; Dollard, *Caste and Class, passim*; O. C. Cox, *Caste, Class and Race: A Study in Social Dynamics*, New York 1959; Allport, *Nature of Prejudice, passim*; Erikson, 'Identity in Race Relations'; Louis L. Snyder, *The Idea of Racialism. Its Meaning and History*, Princeton 1962, esp. 68ff.

65 Leach, 'Ourselves and the Others', 771.

66 Phillip V. Tobias, 'The Meaning of Race', in Baxter and Sansom, *Race and Social Difference*, 30; see also Snyder, *Idea of Racialism*, 29; Ken Richardson and Davis Spears (eds), *Race, Culture and Intelligence*, Harmondsworth 1972.

67 *International Encyclopedia*, vol. 3, 527.

68 Clyde Kluckhohn, 'Universal Categories of Culture' in Tax (ed.), *Anthropology Today*, 317; F. S. C. Northrop, 'Cultural Values', ibid., 422ff.; Roger M. and Felix M. Keesing, *New Perspectives in Cultural Anthropology*, New York, 1971, 144; *International Encyclopedia*, vol. 3, Cultural Relativism'; vol. 1, 'Anthropology'.

69 Keesing, *Cultural Anthropology*, 120f.

70 *International Encyclopedia*, vol. 5, 232; see also Harris, *Culture, Man and Nature*, 14, 447f.; Leach, 'Ourselves and the Others', 771.

71 Wolfgang Rudolph, *Der Kulturelle Relativismus*, Berlin 1968, 90f.; Lévi-Strauss, *Race et Histoire*, 38f.

72 Beattie, Other Cultures, 4f.; Mair, *Primitive Government*, 7ff.; Lloyd A. Fallers, 'Equality and Inequality in Human Societies', in Sol Tax (ed.), *Horizons of Anthropology*, London 1964, 237ff.

73 Benjamin Lee Whorf, *Language, Thought and Reality*, Cambridge,

Mass., 1956; preceding Whorf, Sapir had been arguing 'that variability and complexity of grammar and syntax are totally unrelated to degree of technological or sociopolitical organization' quoted in *International Encyclopedia*, vol. 13, 266.

74   Lévi-Strauss, *Strukturale Anthropologie*, Frankfurt/M 1971, 253f.; see also id., *The Savage Mind*, London 1966; P. Radin, *Primitive Man as Philosopher*, New York 1957; Evans-Pritchard, *Primitive Religion*, 29, 80, 91.

75   *International Encyclopedia*, vol. 3, 545.

76   Beattie, *Other Cultures*, 274, see also Keesing, *Cultural Anthropology*, 145

77   *International Encyclopedia*, vol. 5, 232.

78   Keesing, *Cultural Anthropology*, 120f.

79   Leach, 'Ourselves and the Others', 772.

80   Kardiner and Ovesey, *Mark of Oppression*, 49.

81   Adelaide Cromwell Hill, 'What is Africa to Us?', in Floyd B. Barbour (ed.), *The Black Power Revolt. A Collection of Essays*, Boston 1968, 151; see also Isaacs, *The New World*, 263; Walter L. Williams, 'Black American Attitudes Towards Africa, 1877–1900', in *Pan-African Journal*, vol. IV, no. 2 (spring 1971) 185.

82   Isaacs, *The New World*, 159.

83   See esp. Isaacs, *The New World*, 105–94; see also St. Clair Drake, 'Negro Americans and the African Interest', in Davis (ed.), *American Negro Reference Book*, 663; Alvin F. Poussaint, 'The Negro American: His Self-Image and Integration', in Barbour (ed.), *Black Power Revolt*, 108.

84   W. E. B. DuBois, *Dusk of Dawn. An Essay toward an Autobiography of a Race Concept*, New York 1969 (1st ed. 1940), 174; *The Souls of Black Folk*, New York 1969 (1st ed. 1903) 122.

85   See also Kardiner and Ovesey, *Mark of Oppression*, 77ff.; Bertram P. Karon, *The Negro Personality. A Rigorous Investigation of the Effects of Culture*, New York 1958; W. H. Grier and P. M. Cobbs, *Black Rage*, New York 1970; Nathan Hare, *The Black Anglo-Saxons*, London 1970; Poussaint, 'The Negro American', in Barbour (ed.), *Black Power Revolt*, 106–16; Hill, 'What is Africa to Us?', ibid., 150ff.; Mary E. Goodman, *Race Awareness in Young Children*, New York 1964.

86   Isaacs, *The New World*, 170, 171; author's italics.

87   Poussaint, 'The Negro American', 109f.; see also Goodman, *Race Awareness in Young Children*, 105, 124, 128ff.

88   Isaacs, *The New World*, 92.

89   Lincoln, 'Color and Group Identity', 529, 527.

90   See for a more detailed account Saunders Redding, *On Being a Negro in America*, Indianapolis 1951, *passim*.

91   Frazier, *Black Bourgeoisie*, 130ff.; see also Hare, *Black Anglo-Saxons*; Lee Rainwater, 'Crucible of Identity: The Negro Lower-Class Family', in Meier and Rudwick, *Making of Black America*, vol. II, 458, see also below p. 27f.

92  See esp. Isaac's Interviews with the 'Inquirers' and 'Affirmers', *The New World*, 182–94.

93  DuBois, *Dusk*, 179.

94  Quoted in Isaacs, *The New World*, 100.

95  Harold Cruse, *The Crisis of the Negro Intellectual*, New York 1967, 12f.; on Cruse's study see Genovese, *Red and Black*, 188–99; Christopher Lasch, 'The Trouble with Black Power', in *The New York Review of Books*, 29 February 1968, 4–13.

96  On the problematical relationship between 'ethnic identity' and 'ethnocentricism' see Erikson, 'Concept of Identity in Race Relations', 330f.

97  Lasch, 'Black Power', publ. in Rose, *Americans from Africa*, vol. ii, 276.

98  Nathan Glazer and Daniel P. Moynihan, *Beyond the Melting Pot*, Cambridge, Mass. 1968, 13; see also ibid., 288; Myrdal, *American Dilemma*, 54; Golo Mann, *Vom Geiste Amerikas*, Stuttgart 1954, 44; Milton M. Gordon, *Assimilation in American Life. The Role of Race, Religion, and National Origins*, New York 1964, 129; Nathan Glazer, *American Judaism*, Chicago 1957; Stuart E. Rosenberg, *The Search for Jewish Identity in America*, Garden City, N.Y. 1965; *Daedalus*, 'Ethnic Groups in American Life' no. 2, (spring 1961); Robert P. Swierenga, 'Ethnocultural Political Analysis: A New Approach to American Studies', in *Journal of American Studies*, vol. 5, no. 1 (April 1971) 77; Malcolm Cross, 'On Conflict, Race Relations, and the Theory of the Plural Society', in *Race*, vol. xii (April 1971) no. 4, 477–94.

99  See esp. Jordan, *White over Black*, 335ff.; see also Gordon, *Assimilation*, 127ff.; Glazer and Moynihan, *Beyond the Melting Pot*, 15.

100  Crèvecoeur, *Letters from an American Farmer*: 'Here individuals of all nations are melted into a new race of men', quoted in Gordon, *Assimilation*, 116; see also Jordan, *White over Black*, 336f., 340f.; Israel Zangwill's very successful play *The Melting Pot* was first shown in New York in 1909; see for a more detailed discussion Glazer and Moynihan, *Beyond the Melting Pot*, 289f.

101  See below p. 39ff.

102  Glazer and Moynihan, *Beyond the Melting Pot*, 289; see also Higham, *American Nativism*, *passim*; Gossett, *Race*, Chapters v, vii, and xii.

103  James P. Comer, 'The Social Power of the Negro', in Robert L. Scott and Wayne Brockriede (eds), *The Rhetoric of Black Power*, New York 1969, 11; see also Swierenga, 'Ethnocultural Political Analysis', *passim*.

104  Meier and Rudwick, *From Plantation to Ghetto*, 1.

105  Myrdal, *American Dilemma*, 54; Karl E. Taueber, 'Is the Negro an Immigrant Group', in *Integrated Education*, i (June 1963) 25–8; Silberman, *Crisis in Black and White*, 40ff.; Robert Johnson, 'Negro Reactions to Minority Group Status', in Milton L. Barron (ed.), *American Minorities*, New York 1957, 192–212.

106  Myrdal, *American Dilemma*, 54; Rosenberg, *Jewish Identity*, 27ff.

107  Charles I. Glicksberg, 'Negro Americans and the African Dream', *Phylon*, 4th quarter 1947, 324.

108  Cruse, *Crisis, passim*; Genovese, *Red and Black*, 195.

109 Three leading experts in the field, Bracey, Meier and Rudwick, define black nationalism as 'a body of social thought, attitudes, and actions ranging from the simplest expressions of ethnocentrism and racial solidarity to the comprehensive and sophisticated ideologies of Pan-Negroism or Pan-Africanism. Between these extremes lie many varieties of black nationalism, of varying degrees of intensity'. See John H. Bracey, Jr., August Meier and Elliott Rudwick, *Black Nationalism in America*, Indianapolis 1970, xxvi; see also Louis L. Snyder, *The Meaning of Nationalism*, Greenwood 1954, 196f.; 'Nationalism is a psychological fact. It is that socially approved symbol used by modern society in its search for security.' Territorial self-determination is frequently seen as one element of nationalism and occasionally it is even made the decisive criterion. Thus e.g. Theodore Draper, *The Rediscovery of Black Nationalism*, New York 1970, *passim*; E. U. Essien-Udom, *Black Nationalism: The Rise of the Black Muslims in the U.S.A.*, Harmondsworth 1966, 21f.; Popper, *Open Society*, 49ff.; considering that such a condition could hardly be fulfilled by black nationalists in the United States, a statement by Hans Kohn, one of the foremost writers in the field of nationalism, is of interest here: 'The condition of statehood need not be present when a nationality originates; but in such a case ... it is always the memory of a past state and the aspiration toward statehood that characterizes nationalities in the period of nationalism ... At one time in history the French or the German nation was also nothing more than a distant idea.' – *The Idea of Nationalism: A Study of its Origin and Background*, New York 1944, 15, 17ff.

110 Bracey *et al.*, *Black Nationalism*, xxxii.

111 For further names see Williams, 'Black American Attitudes Toward Africa', 185; Adelaide Cromwell Hill and Martin Kilson (eds), *Apropos of Africa: Sentiments of Negro American Leaders on Africa from the 1800s to the1950s*, London 1969, 76; Richard B. Moore, 'Africa-conscious Harlem', in John H. Clarke (ed.), *Harlem. A Community in Transition*, New York 1969, 80; E. U. Essien-Udom, 'The Nationalist Movement of Harlem', ibid., 97f.

112 Bracey *et al.*, *Black Nationalism*, xxvi; xxxff.

113 Robert Blauner, 'Black Culture: Myth or Reality?', in Norman E. Whitten, Jr., and John F. Szwed (eds), *Afro-American Anthropology*, New York 1970, 361; Genovese, *Red and Black*, 249.

114 Blauner, 'Black Culture', 357.

115 Ellison, *Shadow and Act*, 301f.; author's italics.

116 The exception, of course, was Melville Herskovits with his *The Myth of the Negro Past*, publ. 1941 for the first time.

117 See esp. Charles A. Valentine, *Culture and Poverty: Critique and Counter Proposals*, Chicago 1968, and John Herzog's criticism in *Harvard Educational Review*, vol. 41, no. 3 (August 1971) 375–85.

118 Barbara Lerner, *Therapy in the Ghetto: Political Impotence and Personal Disintegration*, Baltimore 1972; Joanna Ryan, 'IQ – The Illusion of Objectivity', in Richardson and Spears, *Race, Culture and Intelligence*, 36–55; Peter Watson, 'Can Racial Discrimination Affect IQ?', ibid.,

56–67; Charles Keil, *Urban Blues*, Chicago 1970, 'Introduction'; Erikson, 'Concept of Identity in Race Relations', 332ff.; Albert Murray, *The Omni Americans. New Perspectives on Black Experience and American Culture*, New York 1970, 5ff.; Herskovits, *Myth of the Negro Past*, chap.1.

119 Whitten and Szwed, *Afro-American Anthropology*, 41; on the problem of 'normality' see Erikson, 'Concept of Identity in Race Relations', 333f.; 332; author's italics.

120 Ellison, *Shadow and Act*, 301; Keil, Urban Blues, 5, n. 4.

121 Whitten and Szwed, *Afro-American Anthropology*; Watson, 'Can Racial Discrimination Affect IQ?'; Herskovits, *Myth of the Negro Past*, 151f., 275ff.; Weston la Barre 'Die kulturelle Grundlage von Emotionen und Gesten', in Mühlmann and Müller (eds), *Kulturanthropologie*, Köln 1966, 264–85; 'Exploring the Racial Gap', in *Time Magazine*, 9 May 1969, 53f.

122 U. G. Weatherly, 'The West Indies as a Sociological Laboratory', in *American Journal of Sociology*, 29, 1923, 292, quoted in Herskovits, *Myth of the Negro Past*, 13.

123 Among them Elkins, Frazier, Myrdal. See also Roger Bastide, *Les Amériques Noires. Les Civilisations Africaines dans le Nouveau Monde*, Paris 1967.

124 Herskovits, *Myth of the Negro Past*, 2.

125 Curtin, *The Atlantic Slave Trade*, *passim*.

126 Herskovits, *Myth of the Negro Past*, 38f.; Rawick, *American Slave*, 6. Rosenberg's statement on the Jewish immigrants is of interest here. Although the conditions are similar, Rosenberg draws opposite conclusions: 'The American environment, however, has erased the lines of regional or national demarcation among Jews – lines of divisiveness caused by their Europeanization . . . At the side of the melting pot which was supposed to make the various immigrant groups into good Americans, there was another melting pot in the Jewish community – one which made the Jews who came here from a host of different European countries and regions into that new phenomenon, 'The American Jew'. Nowhere else and in no other time in their history (save perhaps the very current and sociologically similar process taking place in the State of Israel) had so many Jews, from so many parts of the world, come together to form a single community' (Rosenberg, *Jewish Identity, 46*).

127 Blauner, 'Black Culture', 350.

128 Rawick, *American Slave*, 6; Sidney W. Mintz, 'Foreword' Whitten and Szwed, *Afro-American Anthropology*, 8f.

129 Frazier, *The Negro Church in America*, Liverpool 1964, 6ff.; John W. Blassingame, *The Slave Community: Plantation Life in the Antebellum South*, New York 1972, 21ff.

130 Richard Thurnwald, 'Beiträge zur Analyse des Kulturmechanismus', in Mühlmann and Müller, *Kulturanthropologie*, 362.

131 Rawick, *American Slave*, 11f. See also Genovese, *Roll, Jordan, Roll, passim*.

132 Keil, *Urban Blues*, 16ff.; Herskovits, *Myth of the Negro Past, passim*; Angelina Pollak-Eltz, 'Kulturwandel bei Negern der Neuen Welt', in *Die Umschau in Wissenschaft und Technik*, Heft 19, 1967, 623–6; Lorenzo D. Turner, 'African Survivals in the New World with special Emphasis on the Arts', in David (ed.), *Africa Seen by American Negroes*, 101–16; Arthur Ramos, *Die Negerkulturen in der Neuen Welt*, Erlenbach-Zürich s.d.; Lewis NKosi, *Home and Exile*, London 1965, 74ff.; James A. Porter, 'The Trans-cultural Affinities of African Art', in Davis (ed.), *Africa Seen by American Negroes*, 119–30; Beatrice Landeck, *Echoes of Africa in Folk Songs of the Americans*, New York 1961; Alan Lomax, *Folk Songs of North America*, New York 1960; Whitten and Szwed, *Afro-American Anthropology, passim*; Genovese, *Roll, Jordan, Roll*, 432ff.

133 Blauner, 'Black Culture', 351ff.

134 Sterling Stuckey, 'Through the Prism of Folklore. The Black Ethos in Slavery', in Jules Chametzky and Sidney Kaplan (eds), *Black & White in American Culture. An Anthology From 'The Massachusetts Review'*, Amherst, Mass. 1969, 172–91; Ulf Hannerz, *Soulside: Inquiries into Ghetto Culture and Community*, New York 1969; Rainwater, 'Crucible of Identity', in *Daedalus*; Murray, *The Omni Americans*; Keil, *Urban Blues*, 164ff.; Whitten and Szwed, *Afro-American Anthropology*, Part III; Genovese, *Red and Black*, Part II; id., *Roll, Jordan, Roll, passim*.

CHAPTER 2

1 On Hammon see Sterling Brown, Arthur P. Davis, Ulysses Lee (eds), *The Negro Caravan*, New York 1969 (1st ed. 1941), 274; Wagner, *Les Poètes Nègres*, 16f.

2 Benjamin Brawley, *Early American Writers*, Chapel Hill, N.C. 1935, 26ff.; Wagner, *Les Poètes Nègres*, 17.

3 Jupiter Hammon, 'An Address to the Negroes of the State of New York' (1787), printed in Carter G. Woodson, *The Mind of the Negro as Reflected in Letters Written during the Crisis, 1800–1860*, Washington 1926, XII, IX.

4 J. Saunders Redding, *To Make a Poet Black*, Chapel Hill 1939, 5.

5 Ibid., 6.

6 Vernon Loggins, *The Negro Author: His Development in America to 1900*, Port Washington, N.Y. 1964, 17ff.; Wagner, *Les Poètes Nègres*, 47; Brown *et al.*, *Negro Caravan*, 283.

7 Herman Dreer (ed.), *American Literature by Negro Authors*, New York 1950.

8 Wagner, *Les Poètes Nègres*, 18.

9 From 'On Being Brought . . .', in Dreer, *American Literature*.

10 From 'On the Death of the Rev. Mr. George Whitefield', in Brawley, *Early Negro Writers*, 37f.; and 'To the Right Honourable William, Earl of Dartmouth, His Majesty's Secretary of State for North America', ibid., 39.

11 Redding, *To Make a Poet Black*, 10f.; see also M. J. C. Echeruo, 'American Negro Poetry', *Phylon*, 24 (spring 1963) 65; Wagner, *Les Poètes Nègres*, 20.

12 Redding, *To Make a Poet Black*, 11; Cook and Henderson, *Militant Black Writer*, 84.

13 Sterling Brown, *Negro Poetry and Drama*, New York 1969, 6.

14 Brown *et al.*, *Negro Caravan*, 275, 287f.

15 From 'On Liberty and Slavery', in Brown *et al.*, *Negro Caravan*, 288f.

16 Ibid., 287f.; Loggins, *Negro Author*, 109f.; Brawley, *Early Negro Writers*, 111ff.; Redding, *To Make a Poet Black*, 14.

17 On the emigration movement in general see: P. J. Staudenraus, *The African Colonization Movement 1816–1865*, New York 1961; Imanuel Geiss, *Panafrikanismus. Zur Geschichte der Dekolonisation*, Frankfurt 1968; Edwin S. Redkey, *Black Exodus: Black Nationalist and Back-to-Africa Movements*, *1890–1910*, New Haven, Conn. 1969; Penelope Campbell, *Maryland in Africa: The Maryland State Colonization Society, 1831–1857*, Urbana 1971; Howard H. Bell, 'Negro Nationalism: A Factor in Emigration Projects 1858–1861', in *Journal of Negro History*, XLVII (January 1962) no. 1, 45–53; id., *A Survey of the Negro Convention Movement, 1830–1861*, unpubl. PhD thesis, Northwestern Univ. 1953; Hollis R. Lynch, 'Pan-Negro Nationalism in the New World, Before 1862', in Jeffry Butler (ed.), *Boston University Papers on Africa*, II, Boston 1966, 149–79; August Meier, *Negro Thought in America 1880–1915*, Ann Arbor 1963, 59–68; Drake, 'Negro Americans and the African Interest', in Davis (ed.), *American Negro Reference Book*, 662–701; Richard West, *Back to Africa. A History of Sierra Leone and Liberia, and of the Black Repatriation Movement*, London 1970; Draper, *Rediscovery of Black Nationalism*.

18 Herbert Aptheker (ed.), *A Documentary History of the Negro People in the United States*, New York 1969, vol.I, 7ff.

19 Geiss, *Panafrikanismus*, 73.

20 Bracey *et al.*, *Black Nationalism*, XXXI.

21 Lynch, 'Pan-Negro Nationalism', 152; Redkey, *Black Exodus*, 237; Frazier, *Black Bourgeoisie*, 12, 14, id., *The Negro in the United States*, New York 1965, 44ff.

22 Frederick Douglass, *Life and Times of Frederick Douglass. Written by Himself*, With a New Introduction by Rayford Logan, repr. from the rev. ed. of 1892, New York 1962, 59.

23 Frazier, *Black Bourgeoisie*, 14f., 71; E. Ophelia Settle, 'Social Attitudes during the Slave Regime: Household Servants versus Field Hands', in Meier and Rudwick, *Making of Black America*, 148–52; Genovese, *Red and Black*, 122ff.; Bernhard W. Hoeter, *Die amerikanische Negerpresse: 1827–1950*, unpubl. diss., München 1952, III; D. W. Cohen and Jack P. Greene, *Neither Slave Nor Free. The Freedmen of African Descent in the Slave Societies of the New World*, Baltimore 1972; Benjamin Quarles, *Black Abolitionists*, New York 1969, 4ff. In his latest book, however, Genovese suggests that the gap between house and field slaves

was not as marked as has been hitherto assumed; see his *Roll, Jordan, Roll*, 327ff.

24   Woodson, *Mind of the Negro*, 244, 243, 245.

25   Bradford Chambers (ed.), *Chronicles of Black Protest*, New York 1968, 52.

26   Philip S. Foner (ed.), *The Life and Writings of Frederick Douglass*, New York 1950, vol. I, 351; see also Williams, 'Black American Attitudes Toward Africa', 176f.; nor did Booker T. Washington's image of Africa differ from the common stereotypes; see Louis R. Harlan, 'Booker T. Washington and the White Man's Burden', in *American Historical Review*, LXXI, no. 2 (January 1966) 441–67.

27   John Hope Franklin, *From Slavery to Freedom. A History of American Negroes*, New York 1964, 235; Isaacs, *The New World*, 114.

28   Woodson, *Mind of the Negro*, 5, 6.

29   Chambers, *Black Protest*, 52; see also William Lloyd Garrison, *Thoughts on African Colonization*, New York 1968 (1st ed. 1832), 74ff.; James Forten's Letter to Cuffe, in Bracey *et al.*, *Black Nationalism*, 46; Frazier, *The Free Negro Family*, New York 1968, 5.

30   Foner, *Life and Writings of Frederick Douglass*, vol. II, 251ff., 387, 441ff.

31   Douglass with reference to the African Civilization Society in Hill and Kilson, *Apropos of Africa*, 164.

32   Williams, 'Black American Attitudes Toward Africa', 177; see also Richard Wright's attitude, p. 164 below.

33   Woodson, *Mind of the Negro*, 137.

34   Forten's letter in Bracey *et al.*, *Black Nationalism*, 46; ibid., 86; on the importance of Liberia see n.17 to this chapter.

35   Delany, *The Condition, Elevation, Emigration, and Destiny of the Colored People of the United States*, New York 1968 (1st ed. 1855) 205.

36   Lynch, 'Pan-Negro Nationalism', 166f.; Geiss, *Panafrikanismus*, 76f.

37   Quoted in Essien-Udom, *Black Nationalism*, 34.

38   Geiss, *Panafrikanismus*, 76; see also John H. Clarke, 'Two Roads to Freedom: The Africans' and the Afroamericans' long Fight', in *Présence Africaine*, no. 66, 1968, 160.

39   Delany, *Official Report of the Niger Valley Exploring Party*, New York 1861, 55, 61; id., *The Condition, Elevation*, 200, 53ff. 63, 64; Woodson, *Mind of the Negro*, 293.

40   Drake, 'Negro Americans and the African Interest', 669.

41   Quoted in Drake, 'Negro Americans and the African Interest', 674; Redkey, *Black Exodus*, Chapter 2, 8, provides a detailed examination of Turner's thought: he was one of the leading nationalists around the turn of the century and stands out as a highly articulate protagonist of the emigration movement in his time.

42   Meier, *Negro Thought*, 67, 42.

43   See the interviews in Isaacs, *The New World*, 155ff.; on the role of the Black Churches see Carter G. Woodson, *The History of the Negro Church*, Washington 1921; Frazier, *The Negro Church in America*, Liverpool 1964; Williams. 'Black American Attitudes', 181.

44   Woodson, *Mind of the Negro*, 129, 142, 51, 141.

45   Quoted in Lynch, 'Pan-Negro Nationalism', 158f.

46   Woodson, *Mind of the Negro*, 6.

47   Lynch, 'Pan-Negro Nationalism', 161.

48   Woodson, *Mind of the Negro*, 7.

49   Bracey *et al.*, *Black Nationalism*, 171; see also George Schuyler, *Slaves Today: A Story of Liberia*, New York 1931.

50   Meier, *Negro Thought*, 42f.

51   Robert July, *The Origins of Modern African Thought*, London 1968, 104.

52   His mother was a freed slave and his father an African immigrant to the United States.

53   July, *Modern African Thought*, 104; see also DuBois, 'Of Alexander Crummell', in *The Souls of Black Folk*, 233–44; Meier, *Negro Thought*, 42; Loggins, *Negro Author*, 199–209.

54   July, *Modern African Thought*, 108; Crummell, 'Our National Mistakes and the Remedy for them', from *Africa and America* (1891), printed in Henry S. Wilson (ed.), *West African Nationalism*, London 1969, 107, 108f.

55   Bracey *et al.*, *Black Nationalism* 128f.

56   Crummell in Wilson, *West African Nationalism*, 110; see also ibid., 'What prevents our government organizing an armed police, and a line of forts to the interior, whose presence and power could be felt up to the border line of our territory?'

57   Crummell, 'Description of Africa and its people', 'Sermon on civilization in Africa', quoted in July, *Modern African Thought*, 106.

58   Wilson, *West African Nationalism*, 117; July, *Modern African Thought*, 108.

59   Bracey *et al.*, *Black Nationalism*, 129ff.; see also Meier, *Negro Thought*, 43.

60   July, *Modern African Thought*, 108, 109.

61   See esp. Lilyan Kesteloot, *Les Ecrivains Noirs de Langue Française: Naissance d'une Littérature*, Brussels 1963.

62   Hollis R. Lynch, *Edward Wilmot Blyden. Pan-Negro Patriot, 1832–1912*, London 1967, 248, n.1.

63   July calls him 'the first African Personality', *Modern African Thought*, 208ff.; on the notion of 'African Personality' see also Ezekie Mphahlele, *The African Image*, London 1962, 19ff.

64   July, *Modern African Thought*, 210, 212.

65   Ibid., 213.

66   Edward W. Blyden, 'Study and Race', from *Sierra Leone Times*, 3 June 1893, printed in Wilson, *West African Nationalism*, 253.

67   Wilson, *West African Nationalism*, 251, 250, 36, 253. There is a remarkable congruity between Blyden's words and an editorial which appeared in the *A.M.E. Church Review* in 1886: 'We must learn to love ourselves. We must learn to respect ourselves. Until this is done, we cannot expect them [the whites] to love that that we ourselves despise, or respect that that we condemn. Race Pride has need to be cultivated among us.' (in Bracey *et al.*, *Black Nationalism*, 127).

68  Blyden, 'Africa's Service to the World', from *Christianity, Islam and the Negro Race* (1887), in Wilson, *West African Nationalism*, 246; id., 'Africa for the Africans', from *African Repository*, XLVIII (1872), 14–20, in Wilson, *West African Nationalism*, 238.

69  Blyden, *African Life and Customs* (1908), in Wilson, *West African Nationalism*, 255, 245, 37.

70  Wilson, *West African Nationalism*, 245, 247, 235.

71  Apparently Blyden does not appreciate that this kind of selection principle would have been most difficult to implement and would have excluded the majority of Afro-Americans from emigrating to Africa; see also Lynch, *Blyden*, 120; ibid., 106, 59.

72  Wilson, *West African Nationalism*, 255, 259.

73  Lynch, *Blyden*, 62.

74  Wilson, *West African Nationalism*, 242, 246.

75  July, *Modern African Thought*, 226f.

76  July, *Modern African Thought*, 229.

77  Separatism was by no means always linked with emigration. There are quite a number of blacks who tried to establish independent settlements in North and Central America; William H. and Jane H. Pease, *Black Utopia: Negro Communal Experiments in America*, Madison 1963; Meier, *Negro Thought*, 59ff.

78  Franklin, *From Slavery to Freedom*, 377ff.

79  See esp. Aptheker, *Slave Revolts*.

80  Patterson, 'Rethinking Black History', 312.

81  James M. McKim, quoted in Bernard Katz (ed.), *The Social Implications of Early Negro Music in the United States*, New York 1969, 2; see also Newman I. White, *American Negro Folk-Songs*, Hatboro, Pa., 1965 (1st ed. 1928) 29, who describes them as 'greatest single outlet for the expression of the Negro folk-mind'; see also Lawrence W. Levine, 'Slave Songs and Slave Consciousness: An Exploration in Neglected Sources', in Tamara K. Hareven (ed.), *Anonymous Americans. Explorations in Nineteenth-century Social History*, Engelwood Cliffs, N.J. 1971, 99ff.

82  Johnson, *Negro Spirituals*, 20; David McD. Simms, 'The Negro Spiritual: Origin and Themes', in *Journal of Negro Education*, XXXV (winter 1966) 35–41; see also John Lovell, 'The Social Implications of the Negro Spiritual', in Katz, *Early Negro Music*, 133; Levine, 'Slave Songs', 111; Wagner, *Les Poètes Nègres*, 26.

83  Johnson, *Negro Spirituals*, 41; Brown, *Negro Poetry and Drama*, 21f.; id., 'Negro Folk Expression: Spirituals, Seculars, Ballads and Work Songs', in Meier and Rudwick, *Making of Black America*, 215f.

84  Levine, 'Slave Songs', 99f.; Miles Mark Fisher, *Negro Slave Songs in the United States*, Ithaca, N.Y., 1953, 14; Katz, *Early Negro Music*, XI.

85  Genovese, *Roll, Jordan, Roll*, 161–284.

86  Levine, 'Slave Songs', 122, 123, 121; see also Rawick, *American Slaves*, 32f.; Brown et al., *Negro Caravan*, 419.

87  Brown et al., *Negro Caravan*, 419; Wagner, *Les Poètes Nègres*, 28; Lovell, 'Social Implications', 133; Gary T. Marx, 'Religion: Opiate or Inspiration of Civil Rights Militancy among Negroes?', in Meier and Rudwick,

*Making of Black America*, 364; Harding, 'Religion and Resistance', ibid., *passim*.

88   Levine, 'Slave Songs', 108f.; on function of African songs and dances as a 'psychological release', see ibid.

89   Booker T. Washington, *Up from Slavery. An American Autobiography*, New York 1956 (1st ed. 1900), 13.

90   Quoted in Katz; *Early Negro Music*, xvi.

91   As Douglass writes, 'Canaan' symbolised for him and other slaves the Northern states; see Levine, 'Slave Songs', 121f.

92   Meier and Rudwick, *From Plantation to Ghetto*, 3.

93   See above p. 39.

94   Meier, *Negro Thought*, 4; in view of the fact that Garvey succeeded in mobilising several millions of followers from the lower classes for his 'Back-to-Africa' movement within a very short time, there is some reason to believe that the desire to emigrate was even stronger under the conditions of slavery.

95   See esp. the correspondence with the ACS in Woodson, *Mind of the Negro*, 15ff., 46, 48.

96   Blassingame, *Slave Community*, 25; Rawick, *American Slaves*, 33ff.; Freeling, *Prelude to Civil War*, 11.

97   Jacob Stroyer, *My Life in the South*, Salem, Mass., 1898, 45.

98   Quoted in Levine, 'Slave Songs', 105; see also Blassingame, *Slave Community*, 27f.

99   Ibid., 70, 72.

100  Quoted in Freeling, *Prelude to Civil War*, 301f.

101  Woodson, *Mind of the Negro*, 93; see also ibid., 88.

102  Redkey, *Black Exodus*, 16.

103  The following spirituals are taken from: Fisher, *Slave Songs*; Johnson, *Negro Spirituals*; Levine, 'Slave Songs'.

104  Woodson, *Mind of the Negro*, 112, 87.

105  Blassingame, *Slave Community*, 25, 37.

106  Woodson, *Mind of the Negro*, 85; see also Bracey *et al.*, *Black Nationalism*, 170.

107  Woodson, *Mind of the Negro*, 65; see also ibid., 15.

108  Quoted in Redkey, *Black Exodus*, 313.

109  Rawick, *American Slaves*, 33f.

110  Redkey, *Black Exodus*, 236f.

111  Levine, 'Slave Songs', 115

112  Levine, 'Slave Songs', 116, 120.

113  Woodson, *Mind of the Negro*, 77–80; see also Bracey *et al.*, *Black Nationalism*, 36, 66f.

114  Ibid., 75, 106.

115  Meier, *Negro Thought*, 64, 66; see also Redkey, *Black Exodus*, *passim*; Bracey *et al.*, *Black Nationalism*, xl.

116  Drake, 'Negro Americans and the African Interest', 677.

117  Geiss, *Panafrikanismus*, 85ff.; Williams, 'Black American Attitudes', 177ff.

118   Hill and Kilson, *Apropos of Africa*, 387f.; Frazier, *The Negro*, 462ff.
119   Ulysses Lee, 'The ASNLH, *The Journal of Negro History*, and American Scholarly Interest in Africa', in Davis (ed.), *Africa Seen by American Negroes*, 409.
120   See Crummell's address on the occasion of the founding of the Academy, printed in Bracey *et al.*, *Black Nationalism*, 139–43.
121   Meier, *Negro Thought*, 266.
122   See esp. Cruse, *Black & White: Outlines of the Next Stage*, printed in *Black World* (March 1971) vol. xx, no. 5, 20ff.; Frazier, *The Negro*, 520ff.; Franklin, *From Slavery to Freedom*, 377–405, 426–84; Shepperson, 'Negro American Influences on African Nationalism', 503ff.; Gilbert Osofsky, *Harlem: The Making of a Ghetto*, New York 1966, 17–24; Meier, *Negro Thought, passim*.
123   Ibid., 277.

CHAPTER 3

1   See also Rayford W. Logon (ed.), *W. E. B. DuBois. A Profile*, New York 1971, viiiff.; the most important assessments are: Elliott M. Rudwick, *W. E. B. DuBois: A Study in Minority Group Leadership*, diss., University of Pennsylvania 1956; August Meier, *Negro Thought in America 1880–1915*, Ann Arbor 1963; August Meier and Elliott M. Rudwick, 'Radicals Conservatives: Black Protest in Twentieth-Century America', in Peter Rose (ed.), *Americans from Africa: Old Memories, New Moods* (vol. II), New York 1970, 119–48; Francis L. Broderick, *W. E. B. DuBois: Negro Leader in a Time of Crisis*, Stanford, Ca. 1959; August Meier, 'From "Conservative" to "Radical": The Ideological Development of W. E. B. DuBois, 1885–1905' in *The Crisis* (November 1959) 527–36; Vincent Harding, 'W. E. B. DuBois and the Black Messianic Tradition', in *Freedomways* (winter 1969) 44–58; Immanuel Geiss, *The Pan-African Movement*, London 1974, part II; for a purely personal view see Shirley Graham DuBois, *His Day is Marching On: A Memoir of W. E. B. DuBois*, New York 1972.
2   Cruse, *The Crisis*, 41, quoting Philip Randolph's *Messenger*.
3   Meier, *Negro Thought*, 190ff.
4   Isaacs, *The New World*, 200.
5   Ibid., 196; also Broderick. *W. E. B. DuBois*, 231.
6   The best examples are to be found in the editorials of *The Crisis*, the journal of the NAACP which he edited. Very eloquent are also *The Gift of Black Folk: Negroes in the Making of America*, Boston 1924; *Black Folk, Then and Now: An Essay in the History and Sociology of the Negro Race*, New York 1939; *The World and Africa: An Inquiry into the Part which Africa has played in World History*, New York 1947; *An ABC of Color: Selections from over a Half Century of the Writings of W. E. B. DuBois*, Berlin 1963.
7   Alvin F. Poussaint in his introduction to DuBois, *The Souls of Black Folk*, New York 1969, XLII; and recently Léopold Sédar Senghor, 'The

Problematics of Negritude', in *Black World* (August 1971) xx, no. 10, 11.

8 Broderick, *W. E. B. DuBois*, 128.
9 DuBois, *The Souls of Black Folk*, New York 1969, (1st ed. 1903) 267f.; *Dusk of Dawn*, New York 1969 (1st ed. 1940), 114; *The Autobiography of W. E. B. DuBois: A Soliloquay on Viewing My Life from the Last Decade of Its First Century*, n.d., repr. 1969, 62.
10 *Dusk*, 116.
11 *Darkwater. Voices from Within the Veil*, New York 1969 (1st ed. 1920), 22.
12 *Autobiography*, 93. The autobiographical data of the following section are taken from DuBois *Autobiography*, *Dusk of Dawn* and *Darkwater*.
13 Isaacs, *The New World*, 201.
14 Ibid., 229.
15 See Harold Cruse, *Rebellion or Revolution?*, New York 1969.
16 See particularly: Frazier, *Black Bourgeoisie*.
17 'Of Mr. Booker T. Washington and Others', in *Souls*, 79ff.; Booker T. Washington and W. E. B. DuBois, *The Negro Problem*, New York 1903; see also Frazier, *The Negro*, 556.
18 Hans-Ulrich Wehler, *Bismarck und der Imperialismus*, Cologne 1969, 458.
19 Fritz Stern, 'Die politischen Folgen des unpolitischen Deutschen', in Michael Stürmer (ed.), *Das kaiserliche Deutschland, Politik und Gesellschaft 1870–1918*, Düsseldorf 1970, 169f.
20 Wehler, *Bismarck*, 484.
21 Stern, 'Die politischen Folgen . . .', 176, 179.
22 Wehler, *Bismarck*, 484; see also Walter Mogk, *Paul Rohrbach und das 'größere Deutschland', Ethischer Imperialismus im Wilhelminischen Zeitalter*, Munich 1972.
23 Stern, 'Die politischen Folgen . . .', 177; see also C. E. McClellan, *The German Historians and England*, Cambridge 1971.
24 See Mildred S. Wertheimer, *The Pan-German League*, New York 1924, particularly 90ff.
25 Cruse, *Rebellion*, 156.
26 *Dusk*, 47.
27 *Autobiography*, 157, 160.
28 Ibid., 177.
29 Ibid., 171, 170.
30 William T. Fontaine, 'Vers une philosophie de la littérature noire américaine', in *Présence Africaine*, no. 24–5 (Feb–May 1959) Número spécial, vol. I, 157; Frazier, *The Negro*, 506.
31 *Autobiography*, 171.
32 Printed in Bracey *et al.*, *Black Nationalism*, 250–62.
33 Ibid., 251, 252, 253, 254, 255.
34 *Dusk*, 130.
35 Ibid., 102.
36 Conservation, 257f., 256.
37 Ibid., 258, 256.

38 Conservation, 258.
39 Shirley Graham-DuBois, *Selected Poems,* Accra, n.d.; also printed in A. Chapman (ed.), *Black Voices. An Anthology of Afro-American Literature,* New York/London 1968, 359.
40 Broderick, *W. E. B. DuBois,* 135.
41 Edward Margolies, *Native Sons,* Philadelphia 1969, 21.
42 *The Souls,* 117, 118.
43 See his autobiography: *Up from Slavery, passim.*
44 *The Souls,* 87, 188, 139.
45 Ibid., 45, 46, 52, 135.
46 Ibid., 116, 126, 222; *Autobiography,* 404.
47 A statement by Baldwin reads like a commentary on DuBois's words: 'America proves, certainly, if any nation ever has, that man cannot live by bread alone; on the other hand, men can scarcely begin to react to this principle until they – and, still more, their children – have enough bread to eat. Hunger has no principles, it simply makes men, at worst, wretched, and, at best, dangerous.' (*No Name in the Street,* London 1972, 80f.); see also Woodson's statement: 'Regardless of his lack of vision as to the situation of his people and how to deal with it, his works [*The Souls of Black Folk, Darkwater*] must be regarded as a significant contribution to American literature.' (*The African Background Outlined,* Washington 1936, 421).
48 For the following see *The Souls,* chapters VI, VIII.
49 Ibid., 46, 275, 212, 218. DuBois judges more soberly in *The Negro Church,* Atlanta 1903, partly printed in Julius Lester, *The Seventh Son,* New York 1971, vol. I, 252ff.
50 *The Souls,* 50, 46.
51 'A Day In Africa', in *Horizon,* 1908, no. 1.
52 *Autobiography,* 343. As an article written in 1902 for *Atlanta Studies* shows, DuBois had acquired considerable knowledge of African civilisation for some time before 1906; see 'The Negro Artisan', printed in Lester, *The Seventh Son,* 334ff.; Boas is already mentioned there: ibid., 337.
53 DuBois was fully aware of his unsociable nature, see *Autobiography* particularly the chapter on 'My Character', 277ff.
54 Broderick, *W. E. B. DuBois,* 128; Isaacs, *The New World,* 207.
55 'The Negro Mind Reaches Out', in Alain Locke (ed.), *The New Negro,* New York 1969 (1st ed. 1925), 413.
56 *Dusk,* 117, 123.
57 The American Senate had refused to vote for important funds for Liberia and merely sent DuBois as a 'gesture of courtesy', ibid., 122.
58 Isaacs, *The New World,* 210.
59 *Dusk,* 125.
60 Isaacs, *The New World,* 214f.; Broderick, *W. E. B. DuBois,* 134f.
61 'The Negro Mind', 409.
62 *The Souls,* 132; *Dusk,* 128.
63 'The Negro Mind', 413, 409.

64 *Dusk*, 125, 126.
65 'The Negro Mind', 410.
66 *Dusk*, 126ff.
67 Isaacs, *The New World*, 210f.
68 *Dusk*, 128f., 129.
69 'The Negro Mind', 413, 411.
70 Bone, *The Negro Novel*, 43 (faulty pagination); see also Nathan Irvin Huggins, *Harlem Renaissance*, New York 1971, 145.
71 Broderick, *W. E. B. DuBois*, 153f.; Redding, *To Make a Poet Black*, 81; Brown, *Negro Poetry and Drama and the Negro in American Fiction*, 103.
72 Broderick, *W. E. B. DuBois*, 153. DuBois himself is not aware of this broader implication of his novel and calls it 'an economic study of some merit', *Dusk*, 269.
73 *The Souls*, 132.
74 *The Quest*, 96.
75 Clotel, for instance, the heroine of the first Afro-American novel (William Wells Brown, *Clotel, or the President's Daughter*, London 1853, 98), is almost white. The same is true of the characters in Dunbar's and Chesnutt's novels.
76 DuBois, editorial in *The Crisis*, Oct 1920; printed in Bracey *et al.*, *Black Nationalism*, 276f.
77 *The Quest*, 14f., 44.
78 *The Gift of Black Folk*, Boston 1924; repr. New York/London 1968, 287, 320.
79 See *The Quest*, 70ff.; *Dusk*, 126, 'The Princess of the Hither Isles', in *Darkwater*, 76.
80 *The Quest*, 75.
81 'Of the Quest of the Golden Fleece', in *The Souls*, 162ff.; *The Quest*, 35.
82 Ibid., 31, 125, 54f.
83 *The Quest*, 110, 115, 123, 232, 242, 247, 255, 256, 299.
84 Bone, *Negro Novel*, 45.
85 *Dark Princess*, 7, 236, 273, 244, 8, 17, 19, 20, 21.
86 See Broderick, *W. E. B. DuBois*, 126ff.; Geiss, *Panafrikanismus*, 202f.
87 *Dark Princess*, 20ff., 256, 272.
88 *Autobiography*, 29ff.
89 *Dark Princess*, 285.
90 See Broderick, *W. E. B. DuBois*, chapter v; see also below.
91 *Dark Princess*, 283ff., 25, 261f. It is interesting that DuBois should use arguments which had already been used by the classical Arabian writer Jahiz of Basra (*c.* A.D. 776–869), a mulatto to defend the blacks against the prejudices of the Arabs. Janiz similarly saw South-East Asia and China as parts of the black world and emphasised the numerical inferiority of the whites; see Lewis, 'Race and Colour in Islam', 23.
92 *Dark Princess*, 247, 227, 228, 220, 268, 221.
93 Ibid., 282, 245, 257, 279, 285, 286.

94   Isaacs, *The New World*, 221; *Dusk*, 277 (as a reproach against Garvey's plans for colonisation).
95   *Autobiography*, 405.
96   A talk with Isaacs (*The New World*, 227f.) shows him deeply disillusioned with the 'moral' development of the Afro-Americans.
97   See document 74 in Eшcey *et al.*, *Black Nationalism*; Brother Imari Abubakari Obadele I, 'The Republic of New Africa – An independent Black Nation', in *Black World* (May 1971) xx, no. 7, 81ff.; it is somewhat ironic that white racists planned as early as 1860 to transform the deep South into a kind of reservation for the 'black race' as it was supposedly most suitable for the 'nature' of the blacks. But the main aim was 'to check the extension of Africa in our country', to be better able to control 'this mass of barbarism' and to keep the rest of the U.S.A. 'pure'; see Frederickson, *Black Image*, 143.
98   *Dark Princess*, 279, 277f.
99   Isaacs, *The New World*, 219.
100  *Dark Princess*, 309, 311, 307.
101  *Autobiography*, 393, 392.
102  See his talk to Isaacs, *New World*, 227.
103  *Autobiography*, 401.
104  'There are those illusions which men must retain in order to hold on to their sanity', is the resigned comment in the autobiography of another Afro-American, for, he continues, 'Black people . . . are a people alone; we have no allies and no friends. We face the darkness alone.' (Addison Gayle, *The Black Situation*, New York 1970, 158).
105  *Autobiography*, chapter xxiii.
106  Ibid., 408, 405, 401, 402, 404.
107  'Live simply. Refuse to buy big capital from nations that cheat and overcharge. Buy of the Soviet Union and China as they grow able to sell at low prices. Save thus your own capital and drive the imperialists into bankruptcy or into Socialism.' ('Message for Africa sent from Tashkent', *Autobiography*, 402).
108  Ibid., 403.
109  *Dark Princess*, 279.
110  *Autobiography*, 406, 407, 401, 400.
111  July, *Modern African Thought*; Geiss, *Panafrikanismus*; Wilson, *West African Nationalism*; Michael Crowder (ed.), *West African Resistance. The Military Response to Colonial Occupation*, London 1971; Robert J. Rotberg, *The Rise of Nationalism in Central Africa. The Making of Malawi and Zambia 1873–1964*, Cambridge, Mass., 1966.
112  See also Howard Brotz, (ed.), *Negro Social and Political Thought, 1850–1920. Representative Texts*, New York/London 1966, 21.

CHAPTER 4

1   Robert Hayden in preface to Alain Locke (ed.), *The New Negro*, New York 1969, x.
2   On Garvey see esp. Edmund David Cronon, *Black Moses: The Story*

of *Marcus Garvey and the Universal Negro Improvement Association*, Madison 1962; Amy Jacques-Garvey, *Garvey and Garveyism*, New York 1970; id. (ed.), *Philosophy and Opinions of Marcus Garvey*, New York 1969; Harold Cruse, *The Crisis of the Negro Intellectual*, New York 1967, 115–46.

3  Locke, *New Negro*, 4ff., 49, 14f.

4  Ibid., 7.

5  See also Nathan Irvin Huggins, *Harlem Renaissance*, New York 1971, 56.

6  John A. Williams, 'The Harlem Renaissance: Its Artists, Its Impact, Its Meaning', in *Black World*, November 1970, vol. xx, no. 1, 18.

7  Wagner, *Les Poètes Nègres*, 172, 173 (161 in Engl. edition).

8  See also Richard Long, 'Alain Locke: Cultural and Social Mentor', in *Black World*, November 1970, vol. xx, no. 1, 87–90.

9  Arthur A. Schomburg, 'The Negro Digs Up His Past', in *New Negro*, 231.

10  See Locke, 'The Legacy of the Ancestral Arts', in *New Negro*, 231; Wagner, *Les Poètes Nègres*, 174f.; Frederick J. Hoffman, *The Twenties*, New York/London 1965, 307ff.

11  Locke, 'Ancestral Arts', 254ff.

12  Typical example: Huggins, *Harlem Renaissance*, 79.

13  See also Samuel W. Allen, 'La Négritude et ses rapports avec le Noir américain', in *Présence Africaine*, no. 27–8 (Aug–Nov 1959) vol. ii, 24.

14  Locke, *New Negro*, 53.

15  Redding, *To Make a Poet Black*, 106; Addison Gayle, Jr., 'The Harlem Renaissance. Towards a Black Aesthetic', in *Midcontinent American Studies Journal*, vol. xi, no. 2 (autumn 1970) 84.

16  Locke, *New Negro*, 52.

17  Langston Hughes, *The Big Sea*, New York 1963 (1st ed. 1940); Arna Bontemps, *Personals*, London 1963.

18  Thus Harold Cruse's reproach in *The Crisis*, esp. Parts i and ii. Claude McKay has made a cautious attempt to formulate such a philosophy; see below.

19  Huggins, *Harlem Renaissance*, 22; Johnson, *Black Manhattan*, New York 1968; Hughes, *Big Sea*; Cruse, *The Crisis*; Richard B. Moore, 'Africa-Conscious Harlem'; Holmes, 'Locke', in Clarke, *HARLEM, U.S.A.*, 20f.

20  Hughes, *Big Sea*, 228.

21  However, it is unfair to say that much of the Renaissance literature was mediocre. After all, this is true of most art at any time. See Huggins, *Harlem Renaissance*, 129; Edward Margolies, *Native Sons*, Philadelphia New York 1969, 30.

22  Hughes, *Big Sea*, 228.

23  Thus Huggins, *Harlem Renaissance*, 128f.

24  This was, above all, the role of Van Vechten. Similarly O'Neill deserves mention in this context: it was thanks to him that black actors were given an opportunity to appear in serious roles and with established

companies. See George Schuyler 'Phylon Profile XXII: Carl Van Vech-
ten', in *Phylon*, XI, 4th quarter 1950, 362–8; Edward Lueders, *Carl Van
Vechten and the Twenties*, Albuquerque 1955; Van Wyck Brooks, *The
Confident Years*, New York 1952, 544. But see below n. 40.

25    Hughes, *Big Sea*, 226f.

26    Ibid., 272, 218, 325; see also Bone, *Negro Novel*, 61. The competition
organised by *Opportunity* in the mid-1920s had made an important
contribution to the discovery of young talented writers. See Huggins,
*Harlem Renaissance*, 29; see also Donald C. Dickinson, *A Bio-Biblio-
graphy of Langston Hughes, 1902–1967*, s.l. 1967, 23, 49.

27    Blanche E. Ferguson, *Countee Cullen and the Negro Renaissance*, New
York 1966.

28    Cooley, *Modes of Primitivism*, 76.

29    Gertrude Stein, *Three Lives*, New York 1936, 195, 86.

30    Sherwood Anderson, *Dark Laughter*, 16, 17, 51, 62, 73ff., 106, 248; see
also Irving Howe, *Sherwood Anderson*, London 1951; Cooley, *Modes of
Primitivism*, 72ff.

31    Waldo Frank, *Holiday*, New York 1923; see also Cooley, *Modes of
Primitivism*, 185ff.; Irving Howe, *William Faulkner: A critical Study*,
New York 1952; Charles Nilon, *Faulkner and the Negro*, New York
1965.

32    Carl Van Vechten, *Nigger Heaven*, New York 8th ed. 1928 (1st ed.
1926), 82, 224f., 246; there is a good analysis of this novel in Huggins,
*Harlem Renaissance*, 107–12.

33    Vachel Lindsay, *Collected Poems*, New York 1923; Eugene O'Neill,
*Nine Plays*, New York (Modern Library); see esp. Arthur and Barbara
Gelb, *O'Neill*, New York 1962.

34    Thus the title of Part II of 'Congo'.

35    Lindsay, 'The Congo', Part III: 'The Hope of Their Religion', 183,
184.

36    Cooley, *Modes of Primitivism*, 63f.

37    Franz H. Link, *Eugene O'Neill und die Wiedergeburt der Tragödie
aus dem Unbewußten*, Frankfurt/Bonn 1967, 19.

38    Cooley, *Modes of Primitivism*, 55.

39    Steven Marcus, 'The American Negro in Search of Identity', in
*Commentary*, 16 (November 1953) 456.

40    Cooley, *Modes of Primitivism*, 73. Lack of understanding and disrespect
*vis-à-vis* blacks was not confined to literature but extended to the private
sphere as well. See e.g. Mabel Dodge Luhan, *Intimate Memories*, New
York 1971 (repr.), vol. III, 801; O'Neill to Gilpin, who was playing the
leading part in *Emperor Jones*: 'If I ever catch you rewriting my lines
again, you black bastard, I'm going to beat you up!' (Gelb, *O'Neill*, 237,
238). Gertrude Stein was no less brutal when she concluded 'that negroes
were not suffering from persecution, they were suffering from nothingness . . . [She] did not like hearing [Paul Robeson] sing spirituals. They
do not belong to you any more than anything else, why claim them,
she said. He did not answer.' (Gertrude Stein, *The Autobiography of
Alice B. Toklas*, New York 1933, 254).

41 'Cudjoe Fresh from De Lecture', in Wagner, *Les Poètes Nègres*, 260.
42 Claude McKay, *A Long Way from Home*, New York 1937, 110: '[The Souls of Black Folk] shook me like an earth quake. Dr. DuBois stands on a pedestal illuminated in my mind'; Wagner, *Les Poètes Nègres*, 215.
43 *Harlem Shadows*, New York 1922.
44 See Johnson, *Black Manhattan*, 246.
45 'Exhortation: Summer 1919', in *Harlem Shadows*.
46 'Outcast', in *Selected Poems*, New York, 1953.
47 'Tiger' and 'Enslaved', in *Selected Poems*. For a detailed analysis of McKay's protest poetry, see Wagner, *Les Poètes Nègres*, 240ff.
48 Interestingly enough in 1917 DuBois refused to publish an early militant poem 'The White Fiends' in *Crisis*, and McKay had to turn to a 'white' journal; see McKay, *A Long Way from Home*, 26.
49 Waring Cuney, 'No Images', in Arna Bontemps, *American Negro Poetry*, New York 1963, 98. This poem was awarded the first prize in the competition organised by *Opportunity*; Franklin, *From Slavery to Freedom*, 502.
50 In *Harlem Shadows*. Wagner's view that Africa has got a negative connotation here, is unconvincing. See *Les Poètes Nègres*, 261.
51 'Afro-American Fragment', in *Selected Poems*.
52 See above p. 128; only Redding mentions the pessimism of the Afro-Americans in the 1920s: *They Came in Chains*, 264f.
53 In *The Weary Blues*, New York 1947; see also Bontemps 'The Return', in *Personals*, 82f.
54 Countee Cullen, 'Heritage', in Bontemps, *American Negro Poetry*; author's italics.
55 'The Negro in American Culture', in Chapman (ed.), *Black Voices*, 536.
56 Ferguson, *Countee Cullen*.
57 Cullen seems to have suffered from emotional and sexual disturbances; see Wagner, *Les Poètes Nègres*, 319ff.
58 Quoted in Locke, 'The American Negro in American Culture', 536.
59 Wagner, *Les Poètes Nègres*, 362; see also Lloyd W. Brown, 'The Expatriate Consciousness in Black American Literature', in *Studies in Black Literature*, vol. 3, no. 2 (summer 1972) 11.
60 Claude McKay, *Home to Harlem*, New York 1928, 157f.
61 Cullen, 'Brown Boy to Brown Girl', in *Color*, New York, 1925.
62 In *The Weary Blues*.
63 See n. 60; *Banjo*, New York 1929.
64 Van Vechten took the title of his novel from this.
65 *A Long Way from Home*, 145f.
66 In *Color*, 26–33f.
67 Cullen, 'Atlantic City Waiter', in *Color*; see also ibid., 'A Song of Praise': 'Her walk is like the replica / Of some barbaric dance / Wherein the soul of Africa / Is winged with arrogance'.
68 'To the White Fiends', in *Selected Poems*. Wagner (*Les Poètes Nègres*, 262) interprets this poem as showing McKay's ignorance of and lack of respect for Africa. This view is not particularly convincing, however.

McKay would hardly have included it in the anthology which he prepared for publication shortly before his death, if he had really meant it to be taken literally. His novels demonstrate that he knew Africa well and held the continent in great admiration. Nor is Wagner's interpretation supported by any other poem which McKay published after 1912.

69   See e.g. Hughes, 'Lament for Dark Peoples', in *The Weary Blues.*

70   Jean Toomer, *Cane,* New York 1969 (1st ed. 1923) 1.

71   In *The Weary Blues;* see also 'Black Beloved', ibid.; Cullen, 'Black Majesty', 'Song of Praise', in *Black Christ,* New York 1929.

72   Thus Wagner, *Les Poètes Nègres,* 438.

73   See e.g. Hughes, 'Dream Variation', in Bontemps, *American Negro Poetry,* 66.

74   Id., 'Winter Moon', in *The Weary Blues.*

75   Hughes, 'Me and My Song', in *Jim Crow's Last Stand,* New York 1943; see also Wagner, *Les Poètes Nègres,* 451.

76   McKay, 'Heritage', in *Harlem Shadows.*

77   Cullen, 'The Shroud of Color', 34.

78   See above. p. 83.

79   Hughes, 'The Negro Speaks of Rivers', in *The Weary Blues.*

80   See Bontemps's introduction to the Perennial Classic edition, 1969.

81   Quoted in Bernard W. Bell, *The Afroamerican Novel and its Tradition,* unpubl. thesis, Univ. of Massachusetts 1970, 43.

82   Toomer, *Cane,* 21.

83   Bell, *Afroamerican Novel,* 38.

84   See Bontemps in *Cane,* viiff. There is a remarkable similarity between Toomer's life and that of the hero in Johnson's novel *The Autobiography of an Ex-Coloured Man,* New York 1912.

85   Toomer, *Cane,* 175, 161f., 191.

86   Huggins, *Harlem Renaissance,* 186.

87   Toomer, *Cane,* 212ff., 232ff.

88   Bell, *Afroamerican Novel,* 44.

89   This demoralisation was partly caused by rum, which the plantation owners distributed liberally among the slaves on holidays. According to Frederick Douglass the idea was to keep them from thinking of escape or rebellion in their spare time. Toomer may have had this in mind when he wrote 'Conversion'. In this poem, enslavement is seen as a betrayal of the African gods: these gods in a state of drunkenness have allowed themselves to be overwhelmed by the white God and have abandoned their people to him: 'African Guardian of Souls, / Drunk with rum, / Feasting on a strange cassava, / Yielding to new words and a weak palabra / Of a white-faced sardonic god— / Grins, cries / Amen, / Shouts hosanna. / ' (*Cane,* 49).

90   Toomer, *Cane,* 22f., 229.

91   Huggins, *Harlem Renaissance,* 185, 183.

92   Toomer, *Cane,* 38, 39.

93   Quoted in Bell, *Afroamerican Novel,* 44.

94   Huggins, *Harlem Renaissance,* 186.

95   Toomer, *Cane,* 105f.

96  Huggins, *Harlem Renaissance*, 184.
97  Toomer, *Cane*, 104, 111ff., 118ff.
98  McKay, *Banjo*, New York 1929, 323; *Home to Harlem*.
99  Id., *Home to Harlem*, 337, 266, 338, 108, 196f., 263, 265f., 274.
100  McKay, *Banjo*, 319.
101  New York 1933, 129f.
102  McKay, *Banjo*, 252, 253, 201f., 320.
103  Huggins, *Harlem Renaissance*, 126.
104  McKay, *Banjo*, 200f., 314, 320ff. In 1922, McKay spent some time in Russia, where he met Lenin and Trotsky; see *A Long Way from Home*, 154ff.
105  McKay, *Banjo*, 323ff.
106  See above n. 101.
107  See also Kenneth Ramchaud, 'Claude McKay and *Banana Bottom*', in *Southern Review*, vol. IV, no. 1, 58.
108  Johnson, *Fifty Years and Other Poems*, Boston 1917; Wagner, *Les Poètes Nègres*, 397f.

CHAPTER 5

1  Bone, *Negro Novel*, 107; see also Margolies, Native Sons, 45; Huggins, *Harlem Renaissance*, 302ff., 190.
2  Huggins, *Harlem Renaissance*, 48, 303.
3  Franklin, *From Slavery to Freedom*, 511; Wagner, *Les Poètes Nègres*, 161; Margolies, *Native Sons*, 192.
4  Franklin, *From Slavery to Freedom*, 504.
5  Term by Dudley Randall, *The Black Poets. A New Anthology*, New York 1971, 103.
6  Bone, *Negro Novel*, 107; Margolies, *Native Sons*, 46.
7  Huggins, *Harlem Renaissance*, 190; Myrdal, *American Dilemma*, 750.
8  Bone, *Negro Novel*, 118.
9  Ibid., 112.
10  See e.g. Melvin B. Tolson, *Harlem Gallery*, New York 1965; Robert Hayden, 'O Daedalus Fly Away Home', in Hughes and Bontemps (eds), *The Poetry of the Negro, 1746–1949*, New York 1951; Margaret Walker, *For My People*, New York 1942.
11  Bone, *Negro Novel*, 151.
12  Russell C. Brignano, *Richard Wright. An Introduction to the Man and His Works*, Pittsburgh 1971, chap. 2; see also Richard Crossman (ed.), *The God That Failed*, New York 1949, 115–62.
13  Richard Wright, *Black Power*, London 1954, 9, 35, 39. George Padmore became particularly well-known through his book *Pan-Africanism or Communism? The Coming Struggle for Africa*, London 1956.
14  It is important to emphasise that Wright identified himself very directly with his protagonists. See Wright, 'How Bigger was born', in Chapman, *Black Voices*, 538–63.
15  New York 1958, 29ff.
16  Ibid., 62.

17  Wright, *Black Boy*, New York 1966.
18  Id., *Long Dream*, 62.
19  See Wright's introduction for St. Clair Drake and Horace R. Cayton, *Black Metropolis*, London 1946 (New York 1945), xviii.
20  Wright, 'How Bigger was born', 549.
21  In *The New Challenge*, II (autumn 1937), printed in *Amistad* 2 (February 1971) 3–20.
22  Wright 'How Bigger was born', 549.
23  See Constance Webb, *Richard Wright. A Biography*, New York 1968, 117ff.; Cruse, *The Crisis*, 181ff.; Dan McCall, *The Example of Richard Wright*, New York 1969, 45ff.
24  Wright, 'Blueprint', 12, 9.
25  New York 1938.
26  See esp. ibid., 'Fire and Cloud' and 'Bright and Morning Star'.
27  See also Wright's article 'I tried to be a Communist', in *Atlantic Monthly*, 184 (August 1944), 61–70; ibid. (Sept 1944) 48–56; printed in Crossman, *The God That Failed*.
28  Wright, 'Blueprint', 10.
29  Id., *Long Dream*, 326.
30  New York 1965. Here Wright combined his own 'personalism', which he developed quite early on, with existentialism, which he adopted after his emigration to France and which he considered to be identical with his 'personalism' (Webb, *Biography*, 138).
31  Wright, quoted in Cruse, *The Crisis*, 185.
32  Wright, *Outsider*, 120, 129.
33  See also Margolies, *The Art of Wright*, 136; Ellison, *Shadow and Act*, 250.
34  See also Brignano, *Wright*, 97, 108.
35  Wright, *Long Dream*, 178.
36  Fish and Wright emigrated; Bigger and Cross get killed.
37  Wright, *Long Dream*, 144.
38  Baldwin, *Notes of a Native Son*, London 1965, 26.
39  See e.g. Wright, *Long Dream*, 189.
40  Wright, *Native Son*, Signet Book ed. 1964 (1st ed. 1940) 275, 289.
41  Baldwin, *Notes*, 30.
42  Wright, *Native Son*, 307, 255.
43  Id., *Black Boy*, 112.
44  Id., *Native Son*, 260. While writing *Native Son*, a black youth committed a murder in Chicago. His case is strikingly similar to that of Bigger. Apparently Wright used certain press reports some of which are quoted in McCall, *The Example of Richard Wright*, 4.
45  His early short stories are set in the South and do not use this symbolism yet. It was only through his later experience in the ghetto of Chicago that Wright became alienated from his group and, like Bigger, an uprooted man.
46  Wright, *Long Dream*, 62; id., *Lawd Today*, New York 1963 (1st ed. 1937), 135; id., *Savage Holiday*, 36.

47 Id., *Native Son*, 8ff., 19ff., 226ff., 248.
48 Id., 'Hokku Poems', in Bontemps, *American Negro Poetry*, 105.
49 Id., 'How Bigger was born', 554.
50 James Baldwin, 'Many Thousands Gone', in *Notes*, 28.
51 Drake/Cayton, *Black Metropolis*, 752. The occupation of Ethiopia by Italy in 1935–6 gave a fresh stimulus to the 'Africa-consciousness' of the blacks. See Moore, 'Africa-Conscious Harlem', 50f.; Myrdal, *American Dilemma*, 813.
52 Webb, *Biography*, 115.
53 Wright, *Lawd Today*, 112, 110, 148.
54 Id., 'How Bigger was born', 549.
55 Id., *Long Dream*, 329.
56 Id., *Lawd Today*, 99ff.
57 Id., *Black Power*, 10, 11, 35.
58 D. Padmore, 'A Letter', in *Studies in Black Literature*, vol. 1, no. 3 (autumn 1970) 5–9. Dorothy Padmore, who spent a longer period in Ghana herself, reports that Africans did not trust Wright and treated him with reserve. See also Ernest Dunbar, *The Black Expatriate*, London 1968, 109.
59 Wright, *Black Power*, 110.
60 Id., *White Man, Listen!*, New York 1957, 47; see also Saunders Redding, 'The Alien Land of Richard Wright', in Gibson, *'Five Black Writers*, 3 : 'No modern writer of comparable gifts and reputation has been so mistaken in his judgment of himself, nor understood and valued the sources of his spirit less.'
61 Wright, *Black Power*, 10, 107, 110, 127, 289ff.; see also Mphalele, *The African Image*, 47.
62 Id., *White Man, Listen!*, 49, 50.
63 See also *The Outsider*, 135f.
64 As Wright repeatedly shows in *Black Boy*, his only acquaintance with religion was in the form of sadism combined with ignorance and injustice. He became the victim of his bigoted and cold-hearted family which treated him with extreme cruelty and rejected him. These childhood memories no doubt provide another important key for an understanding of Wright's concept of the 'outsider'.
65 Wright, *Black Power*, 57.
66 Id., *White Man, Listen!*, 59f.; Baldwin, Notes, 46, quoting Wright, *White Man, Listen!*, 63.
67 Wright, *White Man, Listen!*, 62, 59, 34, 62f.
68 Isaacs, *The New World*, 250f.
69 Baldwin, *Nobody Knows my Name*, New York 1961, 185, 184.
70 Wright, *Black Power*, 341f.
71 Baldwin, *Nobody*, 215.
72 Isaacs, *The New World*, 261, 264, 267.
73 Ellison, *Shadow and Act*, New York 1966, 302. See also Warren, *Who Speaks for the Negro?*, 329, 347.
74 Isaacs, *The New World*, 266f.

75    Ellison, *Invisible Man*, Harmondsworth 1965 (1st ed. 1952), 148.
76    Barbara Christian, 'Ralph Ellison: A Critical Study', in Addison Gayle (ed.), *Black Expression*, New York 1969, 360.
77    Ellison, *Invisible Man*, 215.
78    See also Christian, 'Ralph Ellison', 357; Ester M. Jackson, 'The American Negro and the Image of the Absurd', in John M. Reilly (ed.), *Twentieth Century Interpretations of Invisible Man. A Collection of Critical Essays*, Englewood Cliffs, N.J., 1970, 71; Margolies, *Native Sons*, 141.
79    Gene Bluestein, 'The Blues as Literary Theme', in *The Massachusetts Review*, vol. VIII, no. 4 (autumn 1967) 254. See also Richard Kostelanetz, 'The Politics of Ellison's Booker: *Invisible Man* as Symbolic History', in *Chicago Review*, vol. XIX, no. 2 (1967) 5–26.
80    Ellison, *Invisible Man*, 299, 300, 301, 302.
81    Christian, 'Ralph Ellison', 362, 363.
82    Ellison, *Invisible Man*, 454, 447ff.
83    London 1964 (1st ed. 1954), 30, 222, 100ff., 230, 232, 224ff., 237.
84    Isaacs, *The New World*, 275.
85    Baldwin, *Nobody*, 79f.; see also Baldwin, in Isaacs, *The New World*, 275; Fern M. Eckman, *The Furious Passage of James Baldwin*, New York 1966, 79.
86    Baldwin, *Notes*, 72.
87    Id., in Isaacs, *The New World*, 275. See also *Go tell It*, 16f.
88    Id., in Eckman, *James Baldwin*, 79, 80.
89    Steven Marcus, 'The American Negro in Search of Identity', in *Commentary*, 16 (November 1953) 456–63.
90    Baldwin, *Nobody*, 215.
91    Id., *Go Tell It*, 45.
92    Id., *Nobody*, 204, 214, 203; Notes, 103, 4, 140.
93    David Levin, 'Baldwin's Autobiographical Essays: The Problem of Identity', in *Massachusetts Review*, 5 (winter 1964) 247.
94    Baldwin, *Nobody*, 31f., 29, 36.
95    Id., *Notes*, 147, 33, 104.
96    Id., *Nobody*, 201; *Notes*, 16, 36.
97    Id., *Notes*, 20, 22, 4, 30, 33.
98    Ibid., 34, 148.
99    Id., *The Fire Next Time*, Harmondsworth 1965, 79.
100   Calvin C. Hernton, 'Blood of the Lamb', in *Amistad* 1 (February 1970) 183–225, 198.
101   Baldwin, *Blues for Mister Charlie*, 6; id., *The Fire Next Time*, 78f., 17.
102   Hernton, 'Blood of the Lamb', 198; Hortense Powdermaker, 'The Channeling of Negro Aggression by the Cultural Process', in *American Journal of Sociology*, vol. XLVIII (May 1943) 94–105.
103   Baldwin, *Blues for Mister Charlie*, 7.
104   See also George Kent, 'Baldwin and the Problem of Being', in Gibson (ed.), *Five Black Writers*, 151; Walter Meserve, 'James Baldwin's Agony Way', in Bigsby (ed.), *The Black American Writer*, vol. I, 174.

105 Thus Eric and Vivaldo in *Another Country* and Barbara in *Tell Me* are livelier characters than Rufus and Ida or Christopher respectively.

106 See Rufus in particular, whose main role in *Another Country* is to bring about the 'conversion' of the whites towards a sober relationship with reality. See also Mike Thelwell, '*Another Country*: Baldwin's New York Novel', in Bigsby, *Black American Writer*, vol. I, 193; Howard M. Harper, Jr., *Desperate Faith*, Chapel Hill, N.C. 1969, 153.

107 Thus in Baldwin, *Go Tell It*, and *Amen Corner*, London 1969; see also Bell, *Afroamerican Novel*, 133f.

108 Meserve, 'James Baldwin's "Agony Way" ', 175.

109 Eckman, *James Baldwin*, 121, 100.

110 Baldwin, *Go Tell It*, 191. As Baldwin indicated to Isaacs he too had an interest in African sculpture when he was a boy. In this way he hoped to establish contact with his 'homeland' (Isaacs, *The New World*, 276).

111 Baldwin, *Another Country*, 61.

112 Harper, *Desperate Faith*, 153; see also Baldwin, *Another Country*, 69.

113 Ibid., 5; see ibid., 195: '. . . she still smiling, wearing all her beauty as a great queen wears her robes . . .', and 197, 112f.

114 Baldwin, *Nobody*, 29, 79. See also *Présence Africaine* (June–November 1956) on the 'Premier Congrès international des écrivains et artistes noirs'.

115 Baldwin, in Warren, *Who Speaks for the Negro?*, 283; see also id. 'The Fire This Time', interview in *Student*, vol. 1, no. 3, (autumn 1968) 16.

116 Baldwin, *Nobody*, 79f., 81.

117 Thus in *Blues for Mister Charlie*, 82; *The Fire Next Time*, 68.

118 Baldwin in Isaacs, *The New World*, 276f.

119 Id., in Eckman, *James Baldwin*, 168 (author's italics), 169.

120 Id., *The Fire Next Time*, 88; *Another Country*, 335.

121 New York 1968.

122 Thus Baldwin in an Open Letter to Angela Davis; 'Dear Sister', in the *Guardian*, 16 Dec 1972.

123 'Milk Run' (review) in *Time Magazine*, 7 June 1968.

124 Eckman, *James Baldwin*, 79.

125 Baldwin, *Tell Me*, 145, 76, 79, 89.

126 Ibid., 10.

127 Ibid., 56, 87, 75.

128 Baldwin; in Isaacs, *The New World*, 275f. This appears to be the root of Baldwin's frequent mention of 'African kings and princes'.

129 Baldwin, *Tell Me*, 11ff.

130 Id., *Blues for Mister Charlie*, 104f.; see also *Tell Me*, 254f.

131 Baldwin, *The Fire Next Time*, 89.

132 Id., *Tell Me*, 255; see also 369f., 75f., 245, 359.

133 Baldwin, *No Name in the Street*, London 1972, 49f., 95, 48, 83; see also ibid., 166.

134 James Baldwin/Margaret Mead, *A Rap on Race*, London 1972, 96, 97, 98.

135 Baldwin, *No Name*, 166, 48f., 164f.

# Select list of secondary sources

Allport, Gordon, *The Nature of Prejudice* (Garden City, N.J.: 1958)
Aptheker, Herbert, *American Negro Slave Revolts* (New York: 1943)
——, *A Documentary History of the Negro People in the United States* (New York: 1969)

Barbour, Floyd (ed.), *The Black Power Revolt* (Boston: 1968)
Barron, Milton L. (ed.), *American Minorities* (New York: 1957)
Bastide, Roger, *Les Amériques Noires* (Paris: 1967)
Baumbach, Jonathan, *The Landscape of Nightmare* (New York: 1965)
Baxter, Paul and Sansom, Basil, *Race and Social Difference* (Harmondsworth: 1972)
Beattie, John, *Other Cultures* (London: 1966)
Bell, Bernard W., *The Afroamerican Novel and its Tradition* (Diss., Univ. of Mass.: 1970)
Bell, Howard, *A Survey of the Negro Convention Movement. 1830–1861* (Diss., Northwestern Univ.: 1953)
Benedict, Ruth, *Race and Racism* (London: 1951)
Bennett, Lerone, *The Negro Mood* (New York: 1965)
——, *Before the Mayflower. A History of Black America* (Chicago: 1969)
Bigsby, Christopher (ed.), *The Black American Writer* (2 vols) (Deland, Fla.: 1969)
Blassingame, John W., *The Slave Community: Plantation Life in the Antebellum South* (New York: 1972)
Bone, Robert A., *The Negro Novel in America* (New Haven, Conn.: 1958)
Bontemps, Arna (ed.), *American Negro Poetry* (New York: 1963)
——, *Personals* (London: 1963)
Bracey, John *et al.* (eds), *Black Nationalism in America* (Indianapolis: 1970)
Brawley, Benjamin, *Early Negro American Writers* (Chapel Hill, N.C.: 1935)
Broderick, Francis and Meier, August, *Negro Protest Thought in the Twentieth Century* (Indianapolis: 1965)
Bronz, Stephen, *Roots of Negro Racial Consciousness* (New York: 1964)
Brotz, Howard (ed.), *Negro Social and Political Thought, 1850–1920* (New York: 1966)
Brown, Sterling *et al.* (eds), *The Negro Caravan* (New York: 1969)

Cayton, H. R., and Drake, St. Clair, *Black Metropolis* (London: 1946)
Chambers, Bradford (ed.), *Chronicles of Black Protest* (New York: 1968)
Chametzky, Jules, and Kaplan, Sidney (eds), *Black & White in American Culture* (Amherst, Mass.: 1969)
Chapman, Abraham, (ed.), *Black Voices* (New York: 1968)

——, *New Black Voices* (New York: 1972)

Clarke, John Henrik (ed.), *Harlem, U.S.A.* (New York: 1971)

——, *Harlem: A Community in Transition* (New York: 1969)

Cook, Mercer, and Henderson, Stephen, *The Militant Black Writer in Africa and the United States* (Madison: 1969)

Crowder, Michael (ed.), *West African Resistance, The Military Response to Colonial Occupation* (London: 1971)

Cruse, Harold, *The Crisis of the Negro Intellectual* (New York: 1968)

Curtin, Philip, *The Image of Africa, British Ideas and Action, 1780–1850* (Madison: 1964)

——, *The Atlantic Slave Trade. A Census* (Madison: 1969)

Davidson, Basil, *The Africans. An Entry to Cultural History* (London: 1969)

Davis, David B., *The Problem of Slavery in Western Culture* (New York: 1970)

Davis, John A. (ed.), *Africa Seen By American Negroes* (Paris: 1958)

—— (ed.), *The American Negro Writer and His Roots* (New York: 1960)

—— (ed.), *American Negro Reference Book* (Englewood Cliffs, N.J.: 1969)

*Daedalus*, 90 (Spring 1961), 'Ethnic Groups in American Life'

*Daedalus*, 96 (Spring 1967), 'Colour and Race'

Degler, Carl, *Out of Our Past* (New York: 1962)

Drimmer, Melvin (ed.), *Black History. A Reappraisal* (Garden City, N.J.: 1968)

Elkins, Stanley, M., *Slavery* (Chicago: 1968)

Essien-Udom, E. U., *Black Nationalism. The Rise of the Black Muslims in the U.S.A.* (Harmondsworth: 1966)

Evans-Pritchard, E. E., *Social Anthropology* (London: 1951)

Fairchild, Hoxie N., *The Noble Savage* (New York: 1928)

Fanon, Frantz, *Peau Noire – Masques Blancs* (Paris: 1965)

*Five Slave Narratives. A Compendium* (New York: 1968)

Franklin, John Hope, *From Slavery to Freedom* (New York: 1964)

Frazier, E. Franklin, *The Negro in the United States* (New York: 1949)

——, *Black Bourgeoisie* (New York: 1965)

Fredrickson, George M., *The Black Image in the White Mind* (New York: 1971)

Frucht, R. (ed.), *Black Society in the New World* (New York: 1971)

Gayle, Addison (ed.), *Black Expression* (New York: 1969)

—— (ed.), *The Black Aesthetic* (New York: 1972)

Genovese, Eugene D., *In Red and Black. Marxian Explorations in Southern and Afro-American History* (New York: 1971)

Gibson, Donald B. (ed.), *Five Black Writers. Essays on Wright, Ellison, Baldwin, Hughes and Leroi Jones* (New York: 1970)

Glazer, Nathan, and Moynihan, D. P., *Beyond the Melting Pot* (Cambridge, Mass.: 1968)

Gloster, Hugh M., *Negro Voices in American Fiction* (Chapel Hill, N.C.: 1965)

Goodman, Mary E., *Race Awareness in Young Children* (New York: 1964)

Gordon, Milton M., *Assimilation in American Life* (New York: 1964)

Gossett, Thomas F., *Race. The History of an Idea in America* (New York: 1969)

Grier, W. H., and Cobbs, P. M., *Black Rage* (New York: 1970)

Gross, Seymour, and Hardy, J. E., *Images of the Negro in American Literature* (Chicago: 1966)

Handlin, Oscar, *Race and Nationality in American Life* (New York: 1957)

Hannerz, Ulf, *Soulside. Inquiries into Ghetto Culture and Community* (New York: 1969)

Hareven, Tamara K. (ed.), *Anonymous Americans. Explorations in Nineteenth-Century Social History* (Englewood Cliffs, N.J.: 1971)

Harris, Marvin, *Patterns of Race in the Americas* (New York: 1964)

Herskovits, Melville J., *The Myth of the Negro Past* (New York: 1958)

Hill, Adelaide Cromwell, and Kilson, Martin (eds), *Apropos of Africa* (London: 1969)

Huggins, Nathan Irvin, *Harlem Renaissance* (New York: 1971)

Hughes, Langston, *The Big Sea* (New York: 1963)

Hughes, Langston, and Bontemps, A. (eds), *The Poetry of the Negro* (New York: 1951)

Isaacs, Harold R., *The New World of Negro Americans* (New York: 1968)

Jackson, Kathryn, 'Leroi Jones & the Black Writers of the Sixties', in *Freedomways*, vol. iii, no. 9 (Summer 1969), 232–47

Johnson, James W., *Black Manhattan* (New York: 1968)

——, (ed.), *The Book of American Negro Spirituals* (London: 1926)

Jones, Leroi, *Raise Race Rays Raze* (New York: 1972)

Jones, Leroi, and Neal, Larry (eds), *Black Fire, An Anthology of Black American Writing* (New York: 1968)

Jordan, Winthrop D., *White over Black. American Attitudes Towards the Negro, 1550–1812* (Baltimore: 1971)

July, Robert W., *The Origins of Modern African Thought* (London: 1968)

Kardiner, Abram, and Ovesey, Lionel, *The Mark of Oppression* (Cleveland: 1968)

Katz, Bernard (ed.), *The Social Implications of Early Negro Music in the United States* (New York: 1969)

Keesing, Roger, *New Perspectives in Cultural Anthropology* (New York: 1971)

Keil, Charles, *Urban Blues* (Chicago: 1970)

Kent, George, *Blackness and the Adventure of Western Culture* (Chicago: 1972)

Ladimeji, O. A., 'Language, Society and Literature', in *The Conch*, iv (March 1972)

Landeck, Beatrice, *Echoes of Africa in Folk Songs of the Americas* (New York: 1961)

Lee, Don L., *Dynamite Voices, Black Poets of the 1960s* (Detroit: 1971)

Lerner, Barbara, *Therapy in the Ghetto* (Baltimore: 1972)

Lévi-Strauss, Claude, *Race et Historie* (Paris: 1961)

Levin, Harry, *The Power of Blackness* (London: 1958)

Lewis, Bernard, 'Race & Colour in Islam', in *Encounter*, 35 (August 1970), 99–130

Litwack, Leon, *North of Slavery. The Negro in the Free States, 1790–1860* (Chicago: 1961)

Logan, Rayford, *The Betrayal of the Negro* (New York: 1968)

Loggins, Vernon, *The Negro Author: His Development in America to 1900* (Port Washington, N.Y.: 1964)

Lomax, Alan, *Folk Songs of North America* (New York: 1960)

Lynch, Hollis, *Edward Wilmot Blyden, Pan-Negro Patriot, 1832–1912* (London: 1967)

Mair, Lucy, *An Introduction to Social Anthropology* (London: 1972)

Margolies, Edward, *Native Sons* (Philadelphia: 1969)

McPherson, James M., *The Struggle for Equality* (Princeton: 1964)

Mead, Margaret *et al.*, *Science and the Concept of Race* (New York: 1968)

Meier, August, *Negro Thought in America, 1880–1915* (Ann Arbor: 1963)

Meier, August and Rudwick, E. (eds), *The Making of Black America* (New York: 1969)

—— (eds), *From Plantation to Ghetto* (New York: 1966)

Montagu, M. F. Ashley, *Man's Most Dangerous Myth: The Fallacy of Race* (New York: 1946)

Mphalele, Ezekiel, *The African Image* (London: 1962)

Murray, Albert, *The Omni Americans. New Perspectives on Black Experience and American Culture* (New York: 1970)

Muse, Benjamin, *The American Negro Revolution* (Bloomington: 1969)

Myrdal, Gunnar, *An American Dilemma* (New York: 1944)

Nolen, Claude H., *The Negro's Image in the South* (Lexington: 1967)

Osofsky, Gilbert, *Harlem: The Making of a Ghetto* (New York: 1966)

Ottley, Roi, *New World A-Coming* (New York: 1968)

Parrinder, Geoffrey, *Religion in Africa* (Harmondsworth: 1969)

Patterson, Orlando, 'Rethinking Black History', in *Harvard Educational Review*, 41 (August 1971), 297–315

Randall, Dudley (ed.), *The Black Poets. A New Anthology* (New York: 1971)

Rawick, George P., *The American Slave. A Composite Autobiography* (Westport, Conn.: 1972)

Redding, Jay Saunders, *To Make A Poet Black* (Chapel Hill, N.C.: 1939)

——, *On Being a Negro in America* (Indianapolis: 1951)

Redkey, Edwin S., *Black Exodus. Black Nationalist and Back-to-Africa Movements 1890–1910* (New Haven, Conn.: 1969)

Richardson, Ken and Spears, David (eds), *Race, Culture and Intelligence* (Harmondsworth: 1972)

Rose, Peter I, (ed.), *Americans from Africa* (2 vols) (New York: 1970)
Rotberg, Robert J. and Mazrui, A. (eds), *Protest and Power in Black Africa* (New York: 1870)

Schuyler, George, *Slaves Today. A Story of Liberia* (New York: 1931)
Scott, Robert L., and Brockriede, W. (eds), *The Rhetoric of Black Power* (New York: 1969)
Silberman, Charles E., *Crisis in Black and White* (London: 1965)
Snyder, Louis L., *The Meaning of Nationalism* (Greenwood: 1954)
——, *The Idea of Racialism* (Princeton, N.J.: 1962)
Staudenraus, P. J., *The African Colonization Movement, 1816–1865* (New York: 1961)
Stocking, George W., *Race, Culture and Evolution* (New York: 1968)
Stroyer, Jacob, *My Life in the South* (Salem, Mass.: 1898)

Tax, Sol (ed.), *Anthropology Today* (Chicago: 1962)
—— (ed.), *Horizons of Anthropology* (London: 1964)
Thompson, Edgar T. (ed), *Race Relations and the Race Problem* (Durham, N.C.: 1939)
Tischler, Nancy M., *Black Masks. Negro Characters in Modern Southern Fiction* (Pittsburgh: 1969)
Tolson, Melvin B., *Harlem Gallery* (New York: 1965)
Toomer, Jean, 'Chapters from Earth-Being. An Unpublished Autobiography', in *The Black Scholar*, 2 (January 1971), 3–14

Valentine, Charles A., *Culture and Poverty. Critique and Counter-Proposals* (Chicago: 1968)
Van den Berghe, Pierre L., *Race and Racism* (New York: 1967)

Wagner, Jean, *Black Poets of the United States* (Urbana: 1973)
Walker, Margaret, *For My People* (New York: 1942)
Washington, Booker T., *Up From Slavery* (New York: 1956)
West, Richard, *Back to Africa. A History of Sierra Leone and Liberia and of the Black Repatriation Movement* (London: 1970)
White, Newman J., *American Negro Folk Songs* (Hatboro, Pa.: 1965)
Whitten, Norman E., and Szwed, John F. (eds), *Afro-American Anthropology* (New York: 1970)
Williams, Eric, *Capitalism and Slavery* (London: 1944)
Wilson, Henry S., *Origins of West African Nationalism* (London: 1969)
Woodson, Carter G., *The Mind of the Negro as Reflected in the Letters Written during the Crisis, 1800–1860* (Washington: 1926)
——, *The African Background Outlined* (Washington: 1936)
——, *The Negro in Our History* (Washington: 1947)
Wright, Nathan, *Black Power and Urban Unrest* (New York: 1967)

Young, Richard P. (ed.), *Roots of Rebellion* (New York: 1970)

# Index